Chris —

Keep up one
great
work!

ESSAYS

ON

GOVERNANCE

ANDREW J. SHERMAN

ESSAYS
ON
GOVERNANCE

36 Critical Essays
To Drive Shareholder Value and
Business Growth

Published by Advantage, Charleston, South Carolina.
Member of Advantage Media Group.

ADVANTAGE is a registered trademark and the Advantage colophon is a trademark of Advantage Media Group, Inc.

Printed in the United States of America.

ISBN: 978-159932-333-6
LCCN: 2012940085

This publication is designed to provide accurate and authoritative information in regard to the subject matter covered. It is sold with the understanding that the publisher is not engaged in rendering legal, accounting, or other professional services. If legal advice or other expert assistance is required, the services of a competent professional person should be sought.

Advantage Media Group is proud to be a part of the Tree Neutral® program. Tree Neutral offsets the number of trees consumed in the production and printing of this book by taking proactive steps such as planting trees in direct proportion to the number of trees used to print books. To learn more about Tree Neutral, please visit www.treeneutral.com. To learn more about Advantage's commitment to being a responsible steward of the environment, please visit www.advantagefamily.com/green

Advantage Media Group is a leading publisher of business, motivation, and self-help authors. Do you have a manuscript or book idea that you would like to have considered for publication? Please visit www.advantagefamily.com or call 1.866.775.1696

❖

Dedicated to the loving memory of my great-grandfather, Samuel Goldman, whose candor, leadership, street smarts, and work ethic should be a model of governance and leadership for us all. He strongly embraced principles of stewardship and was a true patriarch and visionary.

Acknowledgements

I want to thank all of the leaders who have had the responsibility of governing me and thank all of those whom I have had the honor of governing.

There are a few people whose conduct and commitment to adopt and follow model governance practices stand out in my mind as genuine leaders: Ronald Reagan, Winston Churchill, Sam Walton, A.G. Lafley, Lou Gerstner, Mario Morino, Steve Brogan, Rudy Lamone, Tom Donohue, Steve Jobs, Colin Powell, Captain Richard Phillips, and Chip "Sully" Sullenburger. I also want to acknowledge some of the greatest thinkers and innovators, people who have influenced the minds of those who govern effectively: Peter Drucker, Ram Charan, Ayn Rand, Ralph Waldo Emerson, Jim Collins, Tom Peters and Jack Stack. Finally, I want to acknowledge and honor our day-to-day leaders—the people in our military, members of police and fire departments, and emergency medical and homeland security personnel—whose daily heroic acts keep us safe and secure.

I also want to thank all of my guest essayists for their excellent guidance and meaningful contributions. I owe special thanks to my assistant, Jo Lynch, who often serves as my right arm, for her organizational skills, patience and persistence.

In addition, I want to acknowledge the excellent editing support of the team at Advantage Media Group. I am also very grateful for the research and input of Georgetown University Law Center students R. Christian Walker and Andrea Gonzalez; I am confident both of them have very bright futures ahead.

Last, but certainly not least, I am grateful to my wife, Judy, and to my children, Matthew and Jennifer, who sacrificed time with me so that I could complete this manuscript. My prayer is that my children, and all of the members of their generation, will be guided by this book's governance and leadership principles.

Preface

By Ely Razin

Managing Director, Business Law and Governance Division, Thomson Reuters

Corporate governance has burst to the forefront of corporate consciousness: it is delivered to us daily in disturbing sound bites and media headlines, which scream of governance gone awry. This new attention may appear inevitable, though things were not always so. Our era of shareholder activism, investor caution, heightened media scrutiny, and increased regulation has brought this on. Now that governance and transparency are under such a focus, though, it is hard to argue against steps forward, as investment decisions, regulatory approval and risk management all benefit.

At each corporation, the board of directors primarily drives corporate governance. This group has the obligation to shape a company's strategy and establish its direction while representing the interests of its shareholders and—in some circumstances—its stakeholders, too. This is a tall order, since board members must often balance tough business decisions against nuanced legal obligations and growing sets of regulatory responsibilities. The latter, true for companies across many industries, is particularly true for those that are in certain highly regulated sectors or publicly traded.

Board members' jobs are not easy ones; both the rules of their game and their playbook are largely unpublished. As a result, people place great reliance on their "business judgment." In fact, many jurisdictions hold the general legal presumption that these directors have exercised sound business judgment, which they believe to be in the company's best interests.

This attitude may be justified, as many directors undoubtedly bring a wealth of experience and insight to their positions. However, in many cases, they scarcely have enough of a chance to weigh in. Busy—and, at times, sprawling—companies must be rapidly diagnosed and intelligently advised; often, these decisions can only be made on a quarterly basis. To make matters worse, this advice is often doled out during meetings of incredibly tight duration: given this time limit, it's difficult to cover all of the company's strategic ground, to say nothing of operational details associated with such decisions.

Making things even more complicated are new regulatory efforts, which come along at intervals. These are intended to boost governance across publicly listed companies, certain sectors, or both. However, when a board and its executives focus on regulators' directives, they run the risk of diverting attention from other shareholder interests. Once again, skilled governance and directorial prudence is called for.

To be clear, new regulation is not necessarily a bad thing. In fact, as each piece of new regulation comes into play, it drives governance into new corners that may need attention: it affects everything from environmental systems to executive compensation. These regulatory changes not only lend their names to an era (think of Dodd-Frank or Sarbanes Oxley in the United States), but they also force newly attentive boards to consider even broader ranges of issues. In addition to these new rules, other factors motivating such renewed attention are the newly attentive regulators and enforcement agencies that often accompany these changes (to return to the above-mentioned examples, in those cases that would be the Securities and Exchange Commission, among others).

What is the net result? Governance becomes a concern for shareholders, regulators, and the public alike. Until quite recently, this dry-sounding area resided in a quiet corner, smelling of mustiness and polished wood, which was populated primarily by lawyers and specialist consultants. That is no longer true, though; ultimately, the drivers of this new governance are financial, reputational, and . . . quite personal. To explain, in each case, financial considerations are paramount: good governance translates to transparency. It provides visibility and comfort to institutional investors, thereby enhancing liquidity in markets. Just look at today's news; you will see both the importance of good governance and, in contrast, the impact of bad governance, which may negatively affect companies, their reputations, their stock prices, and their directors personally.

We must weigh in on legal matters, too, as courtrooms and regulators alike are reconsidering their expectations of board members. Further complicating this legal picture is business' increasingly cross-border nature, a factor that subjects the global director to multi-jurisdictional considerations regarding both business and governance.

Board members' personal issues must be taken into consideration, too. While they may pay particular attention to their overall reputation, each board member's own financial issues are also important. Even unjustified claims by shareholders or regulators can divert valuable time and resources; in fact, these could even lead to disputes over insurance or indemnities that had been relied upon as the directors' backstop.

So, what is the remedy? We can start with rules, guidance, and best practices. As former Federal Reserve Chairman Alan Greenspan said in the years following Enron's collapse, it may be that "rules cannot substitute for character"—but I'd add that rules don't necessarily hurt. The context for that comment is telling: Enron, an energy trading company, provided its era with emblematic episodes of poor corporate governance.

In fact, both rules and sound judgment can help—as can advice from experienced auditors, counselors, and consultants. Advice need not come only from expensive outsider help. Books like this one, from recognized experts like Andrew J. Sherman at Jones Day, play an important role in this process. These books not only help educate—though they certainly accomplish that—but they also help advance public conversation about good corporate governance. This book provides a potent analysis of corporate governance principles; moreover, it does so in an accessible manner, making it valuable reading for business leaders who wish to ensure their own best practices regarding corporate governance.

Ultimately, it is up to executives and board members to lead corporations into the future. Let's hope they will be guided by these sorts of sound governance principles, in the quest to ensure the best possible results for their shareholders, other stakeholders, and our economy overall.

New York City
Spring 2012

Foreword

Never before in the history of our great nation has there been such a real, perceived, deep, and wide gap between those who govern and those who are governed. This gap separates those who lead and those who follow, those who decide and those who are affected by such decisions, and those who allocate resources and those who depend on those resources.

This most recent wave of crisis in leadership began with Watergate; it increased during the failures of Enron and WorldCom, growing larger a few years later with the similar failures of Lehman Brothers and AIG; it widened further during the investigations of Bernard Madoff and Alan Stanford; and it finally crescendoed in summer 2011 when the public's confidence in Congress fell to historical lows of less than 9 percent. During that same period, the President's approval rating dropped to 30 percent, while confidence in our nation's business leaders and financial markets fell to 13 percent. We are living through a volatile period: political leaders must resign in disgrace; high profile entertainers and athletes can't restrain their temptations; corporate CEOs are on hot seats, with disturbingly high and disruptive turnover rates; leaders are hiding in the shadows at times of crisis and national disaster; and wild reputational swings, driven by the power of social media, occur frequently.

During the past decade, our society has placed corporate governance under the microscope, which has resulted in regulators, shareholders, and market representatives asking how we can get boards of directors refocused and better prepared for their critical tasks and responsibilities. Several times over the last decade, many believed our financial markets were on the brink of complete collapse. While calmer and more patient heads prevailed, and we experienced remarkable resiliency, this resilience did not come without significant govern-ment intervention (in the form of bailout packages; QE1 and QE2; and extensive legislative reform at the SEC, NYSE, FINRA, NASAA, and PCAOB levels). Dodd-Frank legislation brought us both greater oversight of the financial services industries and greater incentives for whistle-blowers to come forward to report governance or leader-ship breakdowns. This legislation also mandated that publicly traded companies include on their ballots advisory resolution for approving executive compensation, which opened up a new, much more trans-parent "say-on-pay" participation paradigm for ordinary sharehold-ers, their activist compatriots, and their proxy advisory firms.

As for our political governance, it seems as if we can't have a healthy democratic debate over the role of government, the appropri-ate federal level of debt, or tax policy without the threat of defama-tion, deadlock, default or downgrade. In 2011, citizens lost faith in their governments; stakeholders lost confidence in their corporate leaders. Social networks toppled governments in Egypt and Tunisia in what is now referred to as the "Arab Spring," while public protests over government mismanagement and debt crowded streets in Greece, Italy, Spain, Ireland, Portugal, and even France. Remember, this took place well before the Occupy Movement decided to blame everything on Wall Street. When creating the euro in 1999, European leaders supported the adoption of this new currency as a means of ensuring their continent would continue to have economic influence in a changing world. A short eleven years later, many people are calling it the primary reason for Europe's economic downfall. Even in India and China's rapidly growing economies, governments are struggling to keep up with demands for energy and infrastruc-ture; they are shifting to greater reliance on domestic demand for consumer goods and services, moving away from exports and foreign investment. As an example, the Indian government repealed a long-standing law prohibiting foreign ownership in multi-unit retailing in November 2011: after a series of violent acts and protests, the government repealed the repeal just ten days later, modifying it yet again another two weeks later.

Leadership and governance issues are at the forefront of our daily headlines. Want proof? Over just a four-day period (from February 12, 2012, to February 15, 2012), I monitored the Business section of the *New York Times* and the Marketplace section of *The Wall Street Journal*. The headlines included:

- "The Deal Is Done, but Hold the Applause" (*NYT*, February 12, 2012): People spent millions of dollars and thousands of hours arriving at a settlement with bank representatives over mortgage practices and foreclosure abuses, but the settlement provided little actual relief for victims and stakeholders.
- "A Newspaper and a Legacy, Reordered" (*NYT*, February 12, 2012): This article discussed the strategic overhaul of *The Washington Post's* business model by its board in the face of the rapid growth of digital news media.
- "Yahoo Faces Stalled Deal and Fight Over Board" (*NYT*, February 12, 2012): Yahoo's board and CEO faced pressure from shareholders and the market to provide a clear vision for its business model and path for growth; the article observes Yahoo® had been directionless for many years as competitors Google® and Facebook® continue to grow.
- "Private Equity Industry Attracts S.E.C. Scrutiny" (*NYT*, February 13, 2012): This article makes allegations

regarding possible reporting, management, insider trading, and accounting problems widespread in the industry.

- "Senior Goldman Sachs Executive Set to Retire" (*NYT*, February 13, 2012): This article reports on a long list of recent executive departures in the wake of the once highly prominent investment bank's governance challenges.

- "Rescue of Europe's Banks May Hold Long-Term Perils" (*NYT*, February 13, 2012): This piece implies that our job of cleaning up the financial system meltdown in 2008-2009 is far from finished.

- "Arrests at News Corp Continue for Sun-Tabloid Abuses" (*WSJ*, February 13, 2012): Five high-ranking journalists are arrested for violations of privacy laws and illegal investigations.

- "Where's the Boss? Trapped In a Meeting" (*WSJ*, February 14, 2012): This piece observes that most CEOs of Fortune 500 companies have little time to actually think or innovate in their jam-packed days. An article two weeks later observed that the National Association of Corporate Directors (NACD) estimates that the average directorship reported a commitment of 228 hours per annum, up sharply from under 200 in 2006, calling into question if the average U.S. director is simply spread too thin to properly govern.

- "SEC Opens an Inquiry of Wynn Resorts" (*WSJ*, February 14, 2012): This piece alleges mismanagement of corporate investments and potential FCPA violations.

- "Sprint Adjusts Its Bonus Plan" (*WSJ*, February 14, 2012): As this piece reports, Sprint executives will still get hefty bonuses, notwithstanding effects on shareholder value due to questionable transactions with Apple and a problematic relationship with LightSquared.

- "America's Latest Export to Canada: Shareholder Activism" (*NYT*, February 15, 2012): This article observes that the push to hold boards accountable through shareholder activism has become a truly global phenomenon.
- "F.C.C. Bars LightSquared From the Use of Its Airwaves" (*NYT*, February 15, 2012): Philip Falcone and his board struggle to redefine their company in light of this technological breakdown, hiring lawyers and investment bankers to explore options.

Other articles published during this four-day span included reporting on the following topics:

- Conflicts of interest between drug companies and our nation's medical research universities;
- Ethical issues and allegations of deception by several candidates running for public office;
- Scandals involving drug, alcohol, or sexual abuse by athletes, coaches, and celebrities;
- Bribery and corruption of government leaders;
- Ethical and privacy issues due to unauthorized data mining by some of the world's leading social media networks;
- Multiple apologies and resignations by news media and corporate leaders over inappropriate, discriminatory, or defamatory blogs, tweets, and posts;
- Actions of shareholder activists, like Carl Icahn, who were pressuring the board of oil refiner CVR to sell certain key assets;

- Actions by the Public Company Accounting Oversight Board (PCAOB), which had settled forty-two cases since 2005 (nine of which resulted in monetary fines of nearly $5 million total);

- Urgent needs for boards and leaders of several household-name companies to retool their business models and redefine their boards;

- Questions over the integrity and the ethics of former government officials profiting in the private sector by tapping their old contacts;

- How one CEO's ego and stubbornness finally brought a publicly held snack food company to the brink of failure, kicking off an S.E.C. investigation of illegal vendor payments and accounting irregularities;

- Legal and ethical consequences and damages caused by digital piracy; and, finally,

- Heavy unexpected quarterly losses at social media darlings Zynga® and Groupon®.

How could our ability to govern have failed so hard and so fast over such a short period of time? How could the 535 men and women sent to Washington, D.C., as elected representatives of 300 million people, be entrusted with our nation's future only to fail so miserably? Can you imagine being in a workplace where less than one person in ten thinks you are doing a good job? How long would you last? What would be your chances of career advancement?

To answer these questions, *Essays on Governance* brings us back to our constitutional and organizational roots. At the heart of this book are basic principles reminding us that we live in a democracy: people elect each other to serve each other, while shareholders elect boards of directors and executives to protect the shareholders' best interests. When did our leaders lose sight of these basic principles? How could those who govern lose so much of their credibility in such a short period of time? Moreover, can they keep pace as the dynamics of the global economy and shareholders' expectations both rapidly evolve? When did the strategic and moral essence of the meaning of words such as "steward," "guardian," "fiduciary," and "trustee" get tossed aside in favor of "partisanship," "self-dealing," "insider trading," "conflicts of interest," "red-tape," "turfmanship," and "tunnel vision"? What can be done to restore honor, integrity, valor, objectivity, empathy, and selflessness back into the boardrooms, classrooms, and legislative offices both in our nation and around the globe? Finally, how can we use the collaboration and communication tools created by Web 2.0 and social media platforms to bring more transparency, accountability, participation, innovation, and clarity into the governance process?

First and foremost, leadership is protecting others' interests ahead of your own. Leadership is dedicating yourself to an institution or organization's legacy and treating that legacy as more important than any individual's legacies or relationships. Leadership is liberating yourself from conflicts of interests or hidden agendas and personal interests, and instead accepting responsibility for the consequences of decisions, actions, and inactions. Leadership is setting aside your own personal beliefs in favor of an alignment with the organization's mission and values. Leadership requires those who govern to be able to embody traits of integrity, modesty, transparency, flexibility, emotional intelligence, empathy, confidence, decisiveness, account-ability, and patience—and to balance all these with a sense of urgency.

Leaders must provide a sense of calm in times of crisis; they must inspire and motivate teams to accomplish organizational objectives, and they must be clear and concise communicators. As Colin Powell once said, "Great leaders are almost always great simplifiers who can cut through argument, debate, [and] doubt (whining, rhetoric, and turfmanship) to offer a solution everyone can understand."

Too many trends are converging which will force directors and leaders to be accountable to the stakeholders that they govern, no matter their positions in relation to good governance principles. Several driving forces will ultimately lead to transparent governance: social media's transparence and interconnectivity, rapid growth of shareholder activism and lawsuits, new whistleblowing rules (developed under Dodd-Frank), and significant expansion of staffs and budgets (at both federal and state regulatory and enforcement agencies). Finally, the legal and regulatory attempts to combat fraud and distrust will result in the development of an era of genuine compliance.

Overall, passages of new laws, significant upticks in shareholder activism, and government regulators' robust activity require a new era of transparency and effective governance. Board members must be selected to provide companies with the right mixture of skills, industry experience, market knowledge, diversity, and battle scars. The members must be thick-skinned enough to withstand criticism and scrutiny, while their processes, deliberations, and decision-making must be transparent enough to withstand periodic evaluation and healthy debate. This is a delicate balance and its key element is alignment. Board members must align their skills with strategic plans; the composition of the board must align with market demographics and consumer patterns; their interests must align with stakeholder values; and their board commitments must align with fulfilling fiduciary duties. Sharing visions, values, goals, and rewards is the best way to close the gap between leaders and the led.

The essays in the chapters that follow remind all who lead—and all who govern—of what people expect of them; these expectations are based on responsibilities created by the law, by ethics and morality, and by market conditions and circumstances. *Essays on Governance* is written for anyone who governs in any capacity. In short, this book is for anybody who has someone relying on him or her to do the right things, make the right decisions, or manage assets in the right way (that is, leading to enterprise protection and growth).

The various essays in this book are philosophical, legal, financial, and strategic, but each of their authors defines the term "corporate governance" in virtually the same way. And although our focus is on corporate governance, many of this book's principles and observations are also intended for the nation's leaders at the federal, state, and local levels.

In 2004, the Organization for Economic Cooperation and Development (OECD) published a report designed as a non-binding set of principles, recommendations, and best practices for board members and executives worldwide. In this report, the OECD defined "corporate governance" as follows:

Corporate governance involves a set of relationships between a company's management, its board, its shareholders, and other stake-holders. Corporate governance also provides the structure through which the objectives of the company are set, and the means [. . . by which] attaining these objectives and monitoring performance are determined.

While the OECD acknowledged there is no single model of good corporate governance, certain key terms emerge from this definition—"relationships," "strategy," "transparency," "systems," "accountability," and "duty"—and all these terms recur as important themes throughout this book. Corporate governance has two key elements: first, a long-term and dynamic relationship between those who govern and those who are governed, which is focused on checks and balances, trust, values, culture, and transparency; second, a shorter-term transactional relationship, which is focused on objectivity, preparedness, informed decision-making, resource allocation, self-interest avoidance, risk management, conflicts-of-interest avoidance, internal control, and clear definitions of authority. These longer- and shorter-term relationship principles must drive corporate governors' integrity, ethics, compliance, accountability, and shareholder value. Today's directors must recognize that, while truly fiduciary duties extend to the company shareholders and/or owners, decisions made by leaders have direct impact (and create a ripple effect) on thousands of non-owners, including employees, customers, venders, lenders, and lessors.

Risk assessment, management, and mitigation have become some of governance's top priorities. Risks come in a wide variety of shapes and sizes: its sources include the natural world, shareholder activists, computer hackers, disgruntled employees, volatile markets, fierce competitors, hyperactive regulators, rogue financial traders, social media rabble-rousers, political turmoil, sovereign debt crises, nuclear accidents, civil discord, negligence, poor judgment, and plain, old-fashioned human error. Unforeseen risk is all around us. An effectively-functioning board must be at the forefront of predicting, measuring, preventing, and mitigating the consequences of risk. When significant shareholder value is at stake, unexpected surprises and blindsidings are no longer acceptable explanations or excuses. It is insufficient for board members to react passively when problems arise or, even worse, hide under the mahogany table when challenges surface.

Instead, boards must proactively anticipate risks across many disciplines. Contingency planning (i.e., having an evacuation plan, fire-drill map, or "Plan B") is part of strong and effective governance. To craft these plans, board members need to seek advice from outside legal and accounting professionals, as well as from certified risk managers. (For example, board members could consult some of the 21,000 financial and operational risk professionals who are members of the Global Association of Risk Professionals [GARP], based in Jersey City, New Jersey [www.garp.com].) What's the bottom line? If today's board members are going to be held accountable (and, potentially, personally liable) when and if the proverbial shit hits the fan, then they need to learn how to deftly use a shovel.

Those Who Lead			
Government. Boards. Executives. Franchisors. Licensees. Fiduciaries. Trustees. Guardians. Teachers. Coaches. Mentors. Stewards. Parents. Clergy. Deans. Advisors.			
⬇	⬇	⬇	⬇
Gaps Between Expectations, Best Practices, Reality, and Conduct	Lack of Communication and Trust	Conflicts of Interest And Hidden Agendas	Disparities in the Risk/Reward Ratio & Compensation System
⬆	⬆	⬆	⬆
Those Who Are Led			
Citizens. Employees. Shareholders. Players. Students. Mentees. Beneficiaries. Licensees. Franchisees. Families. Congregants. Parishioners. Stakeholders. Clients.			

Great companies come and go. The board members' and executives' primary role is to keep these companies great and well-managed, ready for a sustainable, long-term future. For example IBM recently celebrated its one-hundredth year as a company because it had great leaders who, in turn, had the vision and ability to transform and evolve the company's mission and business model. The only market condition that remains certain is change itself. Board members must keep their eyes on the road ahead and their ears close to the ground: they must be able to anticipate change and redirect accordingly. Remember, the root of the word "director" is also in the terms "direct" and "direction"; the board members must direct a corporation's strategic navigation and have the ability and willingness to make informed decisions, not deflect or delegate their responsibilities.

As a board member, in order to navigate properly, first ask, "In which direction do we want to go and why?" (See Chapter 3.) Then ask, "How ready are we to truly begin and complete this journey?" Apply principles of intellectual honesty and integrity in identifying challenges regarding organizational capacity and readiness. Then ask, "What concrete steps need to be taken, and what responses will we need, to complete the journey?" Having an empty canteen is as about as useful as forgetting to pack it altogether. Then ask, "How do we keep momentum going during the journey?" Many companies stall; it's as though they pull into a rest stop and never get back on the highway, or as though once they began they simply forget to follow a roadmap. Then, their missions derail and their companies unravel. Forward progress is critical. Finally, because life is a journey, not a destination, ask the following question: "How can we, as a board, set new goals and new metrics, and target new destinations, so that our company continues to evolve, grow, and drive shareholder value?"

If every board member commits to asking these five questions on a perpetual basis, I promise you the road to strong governance will be well-paved.

Bethesda, Maryland
March 2012

ENSURING THE BASIS FOR AN EFFECTIVE CORPORATE GOVERNANCE FRAMEWORK

A Model for Best Practices

[Excerpted with Permission from the 2004 OECD Report on Corporate Governance]

EXHIBIT A

The model corporate governance framework should promote transparent and efficient markets, be consistent with the rule of law, and clearly articulate the division of responsibilities among different supervisory, regulatory, and enforcement authorities.

A. The corporate governance framework should be developed with a view to its impact on overall economic performance, market integrity, and the incentives it creates for market participants and the promotion of transparent and efficient markets.

B. The legal and regulatory requirements that affect corporate governance practices in a jurisdiction should be consistent with the rule of law [: they should be] transparent and enforceable.

C. The division of responsibilities among different authorities in a jurisdiction should be clearly articulated and ensure that the public interest is served.

D. Supervisory, regulatory, and enforcement authorities should have the authority, integrity, and resources to fulfill their duties in a professional and objective manner. Moreover, their rulings should be timely, transparent, and fully explained.

I. The Rights of Shareholders and Key Ownership Functions

The model corporate governance framework should protect and facilitate the exercise of shareholders' rights.

A. Basic shareholder rights should include the right to: 1) secure methods of ownership registration; 2) convey or transfer shares; 3) obtain relevant and material information on the corporation on a timely and regular basis; 4) participate and vote in general shareholder meetings; 5) elect and remove members of the board; and 6) share in the profits of the corporation.

B. Shareholders should have the right to participate in, and to be sufficiently informed [about], decisions concerning fundamental corporate changes, such as: 1) amendments to the statutes, articles of incorporation, or similar governing documents of the company; 2) the authorization of additional shares; and 3) extraordinary transactions, including the transfer of all. . . assets that in effect result in the sale of the company.

C. Shareholders should have the opportunity to participate effectively and vote in general shareholder meetings, and should be informed of the rules, including voting procedures, that govern general shareholder meetings:

    1. Shareholders should be furnished with sufficient and timely information concerning the date,

location, and agenda of [each] general meeting, as well as full and timely information regarding the issues to be decided at the meeting.

2. Shareholders should have the opportunity to ask questions of the board (including questions relating to the annual external audit), to place items on the agenda of general meetings, and to propose resolutions, subject to reasonable limitations.

3. Effective shareholder participation in key corporate governance decisions, such as the nomination and election of board members, should be facilitated. Shareholders should be able to make their views known on the remuneration policy for board members and key executives. The equity component of compensation schemes for board members and employees should be subject to shareholder approval.

4. Shareholders should be able to vote in person or in absentia, and equal effect should be given to votes whether cast in person or in absentia.

D. Capital structures and arrangements that enable certain shareholders to obtain a degree of control disproportionate to their equity ownership should be disclosed.

E. Markets for corporate control should be allowed to function in an efficient and transparent manner.

1. The rules and procedures governing the acquisition of corporate control in the capital markets, and extraordinary transactions such as mergers and sales of substantial portions of corporate assets, should be clearly articulated and disclosed so that investors

understand their rights and recourse. Transactions should occur at transparent prices and under fair conditions that protect the rights of all shareholders according to their class.

    2. Anti-takeover devices should not be used to shield management and the board from accountability.

F. The exercise of ownership rights by all shareholders, including institutional investors, should be facilitated.

    1. Institutional investors acting in a fiduciary capacity should disclose their overall corporate governance and voting policies with respect to their investments, including the procedures that they have in place for deciding on the use of their voting rights.

    2. Institutional investors acting in a fiduciary capacity should disclose how they manage material conflicts of interest that may affect the exercise of key ownership rights regarding their investments.

G. Shareholders, including institutional shareholders, should be allowed to consult with each other on issues concerning their basic shareholder rights, subject to exceptions to prevent abuse.

II. The Equitable Treatment of Shareholders

The model corporate governance framework should ensure the equitable treatment of all shareholders, including minority and foreign shareholders. All shareholders should have the opportunity to obtain effective redress for violation of their rights.

A. All shareholders of the same series of a class should be treated equally.

1. Within any series of a class, all shares should carry the same rights. All investors should be able to obtain information about the rights attached to all series and classes of shares before they purchase. Any changes in voting rights should be subject to approval by those classes of shares [that] are negatively affected.

2. Minority shareholders should be protected from abusive actions by, or in the interest of, controlling shareholders acting either directly or indirectly, and should have effective means of redress.

3. Votes should be cast by custodians or nominees in a manner agreed upon with the beneficial owner of the shares.

4. Impediments to cross border voting should be eliminated.

5. Processes and procedures for general shareholder meetings should allow for equitable treatment of all shareholders. Company procedures should not make it unduly difficult or expensive to cast votes.

B. Insider trading and abusive self-dealing should be prohibited.

C. Members of the board and key executives should be required to disclose to the board whether they, directly, indirectly, or on behalf of third parties, have a material interest in any transaction or matter directly affecting the corporation.

III. The Role of Stakeholders in Corporate Governance

The model corporate governance framework should recognize the rights of stakeholders established by law or through mutual agreements and encourage active co-operation between corporations and stakeholders in creating wealth, jobs, and the sustainability of financially sound enterprises.

A. The rights of stakeholders that are established by law or through mutual agreements are to be respected.

B. Where stakeholder interests are protected by law, stakeholders should have the opportunity to obtain effective redress for violation of their rights.

C. Performance-enhancing mechanisms for employee participation should be permitted to develop.

D. Where stakeholders participate in the corporate governance process, they should have access to relevant, sufficient, and reliable information on a timely and regular basis.

E. Stakeholders, including individual employees and their representative bodies, should be able to communicate their concerns about illegal or unethical practices to the board freely and their rights should not be compromised for doing this.

F. The corporate governance framework should be complemented by an effective, efficient insolvency framework and by effective enforcement of creditor rights.

IV. Disclosure and Transparency

The model corporate governance framework should ensure that timely and accurate disclosure is made on all material matters regarding the corporation, including the financial situation, performance, ownership, and governance of the company.

A. Disclosure should include, but not be limited to, material information on:

1. The financial and operating results of the company.

2. Company objectives.

3. Major share ownership and voting rights.

4. Remuneration policy for members of the board and key executives and information about board members, including their qualifications, the selection process, other company directorships, and whether they are regarded as independent by the board.

5. Related party transactions.

6. Foreseeable risk factors.

7. Issues regarding employees and other stakeholders.

8. Governance structures and policies, in particular, the content of any corporate governance code or policy and the process by which it is implemented.

B. Information should be prepared and disclosed in accordance with high quality standards of accounting and financial and non-financial disclosure.

C. An annual audit should be conducted by an independent, competent, qualified auditor in order to provide an external and objective assurance to the board and shareholders that the financial statements fairly represent the financial position and performance of the company in all material respects.

D. External auditors should be accountable to the shareholders and owe a duty to the company to exercise due professional care in the conduct of the audit.

E. Channels for disseminating information should provide for equal, timely, and cost-efficient access to relevant information by users.

F. The corporate governance framework should be complemented by an effective approach that addresses and promotes the provision of analysis or advice by analysts, brokers, rating agencies, and others that is relevant to decisions by investors, free from material conflicts of interest that might compromise the integrity of their analysis or advice.

V. The Responsibilities of the Board

The model corporate governance framework should ensure the strategic guidance of the company, the effective monitoring of management by the board, and the board's accountability to the company and the shareholders.

A. Board members should act on a fully informed basis, in good faith, with due diligence and care, and in the best interest of the company and the shareholders.

B. Where board decisions may affect different shareholder groups differently, the board should treat all shareholders fairly.

C. The board should apply high ethical standards and enforce the core values and mission of the enterprise. It should always act to take into account the best interests of stakeholders.

D. The board should fulfill certain key functions, including:

1. Reviewing and guiding corporate strategy, major plans of action, risk policy, annual budgets, and business plans; setting performance objectives; monitoring implementation and corporate performance; and overseeing major capital expenditures, acquisitions, and divestitures.

2. Monitoring the effectiveness of the company's governance practices and making changes as needed.

3. Selecting, compensating, monitoring, and, when necessary, replacing key executives and overseeing succession planning.

4. Aligning key executive and board remuneration with the longer-term interests of the company and its shareholders.

5. Ensuring a formal and transparent board nomination and election process.

6. Monitoring and managing potential conflicts of interest of management, board members, and shareholders, including misuse of corporate assets and abuse in related party transactions.

7. Ensuring the integrity of the corporation's accounting and financial reporting systems, including the independent audit, and [ensuring] that appropriate systems of control are in place, in particular, systems for risk management, financial and operational control, and compliance with the law and relevant standards.

8. Overseeing the process of disclosure and communications.

E. The board should be able to exercise objective, independent judgment on corporate affairs.

1. Boards should consider assigning a sufficient number of non-executive board members capable of exercising independent judgment to tasks where there is a potential for conflict of interest. Examples of such key responsibilities are: ensuring

the integrity of financial and non-financial reporting, the review of related party transactions, nomination of board members and key executives, and board remuneration.

2. When committees of the board are established, their mandate, composition, and working procedures should be well defined and disclosed by the board.

3. Board members should be able to commit themselves effectively to their responsibilities.

F. In order to fulfill their fiduciary duties and legal responsibilities, board members should always have access to accurate, relevant, and timely information.

Essays on Governance

TABLE OF CONTENTS

Core Principles of Governance

Legal Issues and Challenges In Governance

Key Strategic and Operational Issues Every Board Must Understand

Strategic Planning and Growth Challenges for Directors and Leaders

CHAPTER 1

THE ESSENCE OF STEWARDSHIP

What is "stewardship"? How does it relate to the principles and best practices of effective corporate governance? Finally, why I have chosen this simple yet complex and confusing term as the subject of this book's first chapter?

At its core, the notion of stewardship is rather simple—it is to be in charge of something entrusted to you, but not necessarily owned by you or you alone. In the context of corporate governance, board members, or leaders, are essentially stewards of the enterprise's tangible and intangible assets. They are also stewards of the shareholders' invested capital. Thus, the decisions they reach about the allocation of or use for their company's resources must be made with regard to protecting and building shareholder value. Often this dynamic and its resulting tension are referred to as "the separation of ownership and control": the idea of "ownership" represents the shareholders and "control" the directors. In the context of civil service or the government, elected officials and government workers are stewards of the nation's assets and the taxpayers' contributions

Ultimately, their decisions determine citizens and ecosystems' value. Stewardship is a larger concept, too. In a spiritual context, many different religious leaders have tried to remind us that we are all this planet's stewards. Moreover, we are the stewards of a law-abiding, functional society. Since our time in this world is limited, we are also stewards for the generations that follow us.

When we begin to unpeel these layers of stewardship, in order to define its subcomponents more clearly, things get a bit muddied. To clarify, in the following sections, let's take a look at a few of stewardship's subcomponents.

THE ROLE OF ETHICS

Stewardship and governance share many of the same basic ethical roots and principles, such as integrity, transparency, accountability, compliance, clarity, and responsibility. Boards have defined ethical codes of conduct: these codes, which are designed to meet their legal requirements, also reinforce their roles as stewards. Ethics-based decision-making uses a framework of three types of ethics: the ethics of character, in which clear and pure motives are at the heart of all actions, inactions, and decisions; the ethics of duty, in which rules are followed when decisions are made, both substantively and in relation to protocol; and the ethics of utility, in which decisions lead to good outcomes that are in the shareholders' best interest.

In their roles as stewards and guardians of organizations—and those organizations' missions, goals, boards, and culture—board members must work to establish shared sets of ethical values and agree upon frameworks that will guide their decisions. Often, this is not as easy as it sounds, particularly in today's transparent world, as boards and companies become more global and diverse, and are under greater pressures to perform quarter-to-quarter.

THE ROLE OF RISK

Stewardship, by definition, requires stewards to understand and manage risk related to any potential harm that may come to the asset(s) with which they have been entrusted. If I am the steward (or guardian) of another man's cow, then I must mitigate the risk of any harm coming to the animal, and all my efforts for ensuring shelter, food, safety, and comfort are part of that undertaking. I cannot completely eliminate risk—some circumstances will be beyond my control—but I can manage and mitigate it.

At the corporate level, board members and leaders recognize they must fulfill their obligations as stewards: having an Enterprise Risk Management (ERM) program in place, on an enterprise-wide level, is of critical strategic importance. Increasing numbers of companies are developing these programs, as shown in a recent Risk and Management Society (RIMS) survey: this survey found that between 2009 and 2010, the number of companies which had formal ERM programs rose from 9 percent to 28 percent. The number of programs increased three times in one year; this reflects the volatile world and unstable economy in which boards must serve as guardians of corporate assets. Effective ERM programs remove the typical silos that exist on a departmental basis and look at risk at the enterprise level using a more holistic and strategic basis. The ERM system is designed to identify, manage, and mitigate risk, as well as to identify any of the company's "blind spots" or evolving market conditions that could harm it.

Board members must define their tolerance for risk. Candid discussions must be held and decisions reached. The following hard questions require answers from company leaders:

- What is our appetite for risk?
- How well does (or has) our organization and its culture respond(ed) to taking risks and reacting to crises?
- How much brand or reputational risk are we willing to tolerate? How does this level compare or benchmark with our competitors?
- What are our shareholders' (and other stakeholders') expectations with regard to risk?
- Do we, as board members and leaders, have the skills and resources—and do we have appropriate advisors upon whom to draw—to manage and assess risk exposure?
- How do we define the likelihood of company and/or market-specific risks (e.g., the BP oil spills) *versus* general ecosystem risks (e.g., Hurricane Katrina)?
- What risks are specific to or inherent in our industry?
- In the markets in which we operate, what risks are likely to occur?
- Finally, what current market trends or conditions, which may increase or mitigate risks to the enterprise, are already in place?

THE BENEFICIARY'S ROLE

Whenever I board a plane, the flight attendants (formerly, the "stewards") are always careful to remind me that their primary concern is my safety, not whether I will be able to get up from my chair whenever I want or whether I can have a second gin and tonic.

On a plane, passengers are the beneficiaries of the trained pilots and attendants—the stewards—who are entrusted with the duty of a safe takeoff, journey, and landing.

So, in the context of political or corporate governance, who (or what?) beyond the citizens or the shareholders must be considered when the stewards make decisions? For example, suppose I am a steward of corporate assets, and my company is producing a new widget. I can save two dollars per widget by authorizing the use of a material that might be harmful to the environment or to end-users. In this case, do I maximize shareholder value by using the material, and thus driving better margins, or do I remain accountable to stakeholders, such as the planet and the customers? To complicate matters further, suppose I ignore these competing interests: then, we must consider whether it is fair or right to leave these tasks to regulatory agencies, consumer groups, or the media. Who should enforce laws, norms, guidelines, incentives, or sanctions? We must determine what role(s) corporate citizenship should play in defining a company board's notion of stewardship and guardianship. We must also determine to what extent the corporation will benefit from considering the interests of people besides the shareholders (such as debt holders, employees, and the local community), or considering interests that are separate from increasing profits (such as charitable activities or community loyalty). Finally, we must also determine to what extent corporate law permits these broader considerations.

THE PARADOX OF STEWARDSHIP

By its very definition, stewardship is a paradox of authority. In the case of a company, one party owns the resources and the other party is entrusted with management and care of those same resources.

The stewards are accountable to shareholders in terms of how these resources are deployed and invested; simultaneously, stewards must avoid conflicts of interest or acts of self-interest that are inconsistent with their responsibilities. In turn, the shareholders must be respectful of the stewards' authority and responsibility (e.g., shareholders should be supportive, participatory, and collaborative, but not meddlesome) as long as the stewards do not violate the trust or duty they hold. Each must respect the other's domain, responsibilities, and authorities. Shareholders have a set of defined rights: to inspect company books and records, to participate in annual stockholders' meetings, to vote on certain transactions, and to bring lawsuits if directors or company officers violate their fiduciary duties. The board of directors, as stewards, is invested with the responsibility of the corporation's general oversight and management.

PUTTING STEWARDSHIP INTO ACTION

So, we have grasped that stewardship is made up of guardianship, advocacy, care, diligence, ethics, and risk management, all at the 30,000-foot level (which can be both literal and figurative). Now, we need to put a practical framework around the need for stewardship, creating a method by which we can build a sustainable legacy for an enterprise's leadership and governance. The best framework is an objective Board Evaluation system, which helps ensure alignment of the board members' duties and company shareholders' best interests.

BOARD EVALUATION SYSTEMS

Dedication to a periodic board evaluation process tends to yield boards made up of strong and effective members who clearly understand their roles and responsibilities as stewards; provide strategic guidance to company executives; establish effective controls and mitigate risks; and protect and enforce the company's values, mission, and standards. Board Evaluation systems should enable people to look, objectively and regularly, at key components of board functionality and effectiveness, thus ensuring core stewardship principles are satisfied. These functions include the following:

- Board composition and diversity
- Board processes and decision-making
- New board member training and orientation
- Information and intangible asset management
- Corporate social responsibility
- Enterprise risk management
- Committee effectiveness and composition
- Board terms and director development
- CEO performance and succession planning
- Long-term strategic planning
- Takeover preparedness
- Organizational performance management

Several tools and methodologies can be used to maximize board performance and to reinforce the board members' roles as stewards and guardians, including consulting, training, surveying, self-evaluation tools, benchmarking, trend analysis, prioritization metrics, and peer evaluations. Other methods include fostering open communication lines with senior management and, perhaps, holding annual retreats at which senior management review legal and regulatory developments.

Board Evaluations may also include any or all of the following: third-party governance reviews, conducted by consultants, outside legal counsel, or independent advisors; independent investigations that ensure overall compliance, or address allegations of or beliefs about wrongdoing; audits of the board's dynamics and culture, which ensure that trust, respect, candor, and constructive dissent all factor into board members' deliberations and decision-making; and compliance training and advocacy, in the event of shareholder activism or regulatory actions taken against the company.

Any Board Evaluation process should be guided by Ram Charan's "14 Questions Every Board Member Should Ask," as published in his *Owning Up: The 14 Questions Every Board Member Needs to Ask* (Jossey-Bass, 2009):

1. Is our board composition right for the challenge?
2. Are we addressing the risks that could send our company over the cliff?
3. Are we prepared to do our job well when a crisis erupts?
4. Are we well prepared to name our next CEO?
5. Does our board really own the company's strategy?
6. How can we get the information we need to govern well?
7. How can our board get CEO compensation right?
8. Why do we need a lead director anyway?
9. Is our governance committee "best of breed"?
10. How do we get the most value out of our limited time?
11. How can executive sessions help the board own up?
12. How can our board's self-evaluation improve our functioning and our output?
13. How do we keep from micromanaging?
14. How prepared are we to work with activist shareholders and their proxies?

In addition, by asking certain questions, people can identify early warning signs that the board may be dysfunctional; they may discover red flags demonstrating that the board members may not be embracing their roles as stewards, making the company subject to shareholders' activist action down the road. These questions include:

» Do the board members lack sufficient expertise?

» Are the board members lacking necessary competencies?

» Is the board sufficiently independent?

» Do the board members have little or no stake in the company?

» Can the board members' compensation be perceived as excessive?

» Are the board's chairman and CEO roles combined?

» Is there an unusually low turnover among board members?

» Do the board members have a record of failing to heed the shareholders' will?

» Do the board members have a record of facilitating the board's own entrenchment?

» Does the board have a record of failing to hold management accountable?

Remember, at the core of every director or leader's position—whether he or she is leading a corporate, governmental, non-profit, or religious organization—are stewardship and guardianship. The more leaders can be aligned with their shareholders' best interests, the better governed their organizations will be.

CHAPTER 2

WHAT DOES FIDUCIARY DUTY REALLY MEAN?

Directors of corporations (and certain other business organizations), owe fiduciary duties to their corporations and shareholders. These fiduciary duties, which are legal obligations, generally fall into two broad categories: the duty of care and the duty of loyalty. When directors violate these duties, they can be taken to courts, where they may be made financially liable or their actions invalidated. Perhaps, then, the key starting point for understanding these fiduciary duties' nature and scope is by considering what actions and decisions cannot be altered in court.

Under what's known as the "business judgment rule," we presume directors make business decisions on an informed basis, in good faith, and in the honest belief that their actions are in the best interest of the company. When they do, in fact, act in this manner, directors find that a court will not second-guess their decisions, even if some decisions turn out to be a bad ones. That is, directors' fiduciary duties do not bar them from taking business risks. Generally, courts are not in the business of substituting legal business judgment for the directors', nor do they otherwise engage in substantive evaluations of business decisions or outcomes (with the benefit of 20/20 hindsight). Judges understand that, given their legal background, they do not necessarily possess a monopoly on business insight, business strategy, or the assessment of business risk; thus, they generally reserve scrutiny of business decisions for investors and business managers.

Given all this, when does a court oversee or change a business decision made by a board of directors—or impose liability on such decision-makers? The answer is: when the directors act in a manner contrary to the business judgment rule's presumptions (i.e., when they fail to act on an informed basis, in good faith, or with the honest belief that their actions are in the company's best interests). These are issues that judges and lawyers are in a position to scrutinize; having business expertise is not necessary in order to evaluate them. In such cases, the judicial review's focus, therefore, is on the process undertaken by the board. In particular, the review considers whether that decision-making process was materially flawed, inadequate, tainted, or driven by personal interests. Avoiding these latter concepts is embodied in directors' duties of care and loyalty.

DUTY OF CARE

When making a decision, directors must actively gather material information regarding the company's affairs. Then, they must act upon that information with diligence, care, and skill, all of which are necessary for making a rational business decision. Primarily, board members are entitled to rely on data provided by officers and professional advisers—provided, that is, that the board members know nothing about any possible irregularity or inaccuracy in the information they are given. However, they cannot act in a grossly negligent manner. That is, when board members, remain willfully ignorant of important information (or rush through decisions, which means they cannot reasonably or responsibly evaluate options), they risk breaching their duty of care. In some cases, board members may be held personally responsible for misinformed decisions, if it appears they did not take their duty of care seriously.

DUTY OF LOYALTY

All directors must exercise their powers in the corporation's interest, not in their own, another person's, or another organization's interest. This concept, which is known as the duty of loyalty, can be applied in a number of specific ways. First, directors must avoid any conflicts of interest in dealings with the corporation; they cannot receive personal benefits that differ from those received by all the shareholders. In addition, directors must not step in and remove opportunities or business transactions that are offered to the corporation. For example, say a company director is taking a meeting on the company's behalf when he is offered a great opportunity: obtaining distribution rights for an exciting new type of technology. Trying to obtain those rights for himself, and not first offering them to his corporation, would be a breach of this duty.

Furthermore, directors cannot act in bad faith or in order to do something other than advancing the corporation's best interests. For example, directors cannot knowingly cause the corporation to violate law; they cannot consciously disregard the obligation of overseeing the corporation's activities, which means they could sanction misconduct by the corporation or its employees; and they cannot waste corporate assets.

MEETING FIDUCIARY DUTIES

When individual directors do not observe or protect these fiduciary duties (in particular, this happens when an individual director steals or takes company benefits for himself), they risk personal liability. Generally, however, when an entire board makes decisions, all the board members will be reviewed. Reviewers will consider whether a majority of the directors who made that decision were tainted by problems with duty of care or duty of loyalty. For example, suppose a company has ten directors; only one of them has a personal interest in a certain transaction, and he or she does not control the other directors' decisions. Then, after due deliberation by the full board, including nine disinterested directors, a decision to engage in such a transaction likely would be protected by the business judgment rule: it would not be set aside by a court.

In contrast, if six of the ten voting directors had a personal interest in a transaction and voted to approve it, that decision could be challenged in a court. Under those circumstances, the directors would have to prove that the transaction was entirely fair to both the corporation and its shareholders, despite their personal interests in it. This burden of proof requires a determination, by the court, that the transaction was produced by fair dealing and resulted in a fair price. Yet, suppose a shareholder wished to challenge a transaction that had been approved by an independent, disinterested committee of directors. At that point, the burden would shift back to the shareholder, who would have to prove that the transaction was not entirely fair to the corporation, both in terms of price and process. While other nuances can determine how a court will review a board decision or action (when certain directors are affected by duty of care or duty of loyalty concerns, that is), the above principles generally hold.

Accordingly, to meet the duties of care and loyalty, and to ensure their business decisions are upheld, board members should follow these general guidelines:

- **Work with outside governance counsel** to develop written guidelines for the basic principles of corporate law as they apply to officers and directors' duties. Keep board members informed about recent cases or changes in the law.

- **Work closely with a corporate governance attorney,** as a general rule. If the board members or any directors doubt whether a proposed action is in the corporation's best interests, consult a qualified attorney immediately—not after the deal is done.

- **Keep careful minutes at all meetings** and maintain comprehensive records of information on which the board bases decisions. Be prepared to show financial data, business valuations, market research, opinion letters, and related documentation in case a shareholder challenges an action as "uninformed" or claims it is not the product of a rational process. Well-prepared minutes also serve a variety of other purposes: they are written proof of the directors' situational analyses and appraisals, proof that parent and subsidiary operations are being conducted at arm's length (that is, they are separated), and proof that an officer had authority to engage in the transaction being questioned.

- **Be selective in choosing candidates** for the board of directors. Avoid nominating someone who, while lending a credible name, is unlikely to attend meetings or give any real input about the company's management and direction. This approach only invites claims of corporate mismanagement by shareholders. Similarly, if you are invited to sit on another company's board, don't accept unless you're ready to accept the responsibilities that go with the position.

- **In threatened takeover situations,** be careful: make decisions in the best interests of all shareholders, not just the board members or the officers. In addition, you must be prepared to justify any steps taken to defend the takeover attempt in two ways: first, by proving the reasonable belief that a threat to corporate policy existed; and second, by demonstrating the reasonability of the response in relation to the proposed threat. The adoption of "poison pills," "golden handcuffs," and other common anti-takeover strategies must be considered carefully.

- **Any board member who independently supplies goods and/or services** to the corporation should not participate in board discussions or votes regarding his or her dealings with the corporation. This will help avoid conflict-of-interest claims. A "disinterested and independent" board (or a committee of disinterested and independent board members) should approve proposed actions—after the material facts of each transaction are disclosed and the nature and extent of each the board member's involvement is revealed.

- **Periodically, issue questionnaires to officers and directors** regarding recent transactions with the company so you can assess possible conflicts of interest. Provide incoming board members and newly appointed officers with a more detailed questionnaire. Finally, prior to any securities issuances (such as private placements or public offerings), circulate these questionnaires among all board members.

- **Provide directors with all appropriate background and financial information** relating to proposed board actions well in advance of board meetings. Providing an agenda and proper notice, and selecting a mutually convenient time, place, and date, will ensure good attendance records and board compliance with applicable statutes.

- **Board members who object to proposed actions or resolutions** should either make their votes and ask that such votes be recorded in the minutes, or abstain from voting and promptly file written dissent with the corporation's secretary.

In short, the essence of directors' fiduciary duties is to ensure that the decision-making process is sound. That way, if the process is fully exposed, all that can be questioned after the fact is whether the business decision itself was good or bad. Markets—not courts—are charged with second-guessing the substance of such decisions and judging outcomes. In carrying out their legal obligations to shareholders, directors should—and must—adequately inform themselves, so they are in a position to make reasoned business decisions. They must also identify instances in which their, or other board members', interests diverge from the company's; then, they should structure deliberations so decisions are made—or at least ratified— by those who only have the company's interests at heart.

CHAPTER 3

THE CONSEQUENCES OF RUDDERLESS LEADERSHIP

(The Tao of the Cheshire Cat)

"Cheshire Puss," she began, rather timidly, as she did not at all know whether it would like the name: however, it only grinned a little wider. "Come, it's pleased so far," thought Alice, and she went on. "Would you tell me, please, which way I ought to go from here?" "That depends a good deal on where you want to get to," said the Cat. "I don't much care where—" said Alice. "Then it doesn't matter which way you go," said the Cat. "—so long as I get SOMEWHERE," Alice added as an explanation. "Oh, you're sure to do that," said the Cat, "if you only walk long enough."
—Lewis Carroll, *Alice's Adventures in Wonderland*

Ask any serious boatman whether he can get to his destination without a rudder, and he will look at you as if you are insane. The same concept is true of navigating the corporate world. In the context of governance, the "rudder" is a steering device designed to articulate clearly set goals. With such a rudder, those who govern cannot possibly establish and maintain a culture designed to achieve those goals, and this rudder can also provide a backbone with which to enforce goals and performance metrics. Over the last ten or fifteen years, many citizens and shareholders have become frustrated because our leaders appear rudderless or directionless. This lack of direction resulted in wasted taxpayer dollars and resources, and diminished shareholder value. Now, we want our leaders to pick a clear direction—even if we don't agree with it—just to avoid stagnation, deadlock, and complacency. Otherwise, we risk being hit head-on, like deer in the headlights. Worse yet, we perceive our leaders are behaving like Alice—they are essentially apathetic—in regard to their destinations. They burden us with even greater frustration because they consume resources and get us nowhere.

When Congress members can't reach decisions, boards can't dictate clear strategy, and executives can't effectively lead or motivate, we have a nation run by "Alices." Our economy remains weak, flat, or even broken. If we aim for nothing, we'll be nothing. If we have no clear goals (or seem happy running in place, like a hamster on a wheel), then we'll go nowhere. If we ignore signals that urge us to pro-actively move in one direction or the other, then our ambivalence will act as a cancer: slowly, it will kill our ability to progress. We rely upon this country and our companies to generate tax revenues, innovate, and create new jobs. We cannot allow our governmental or corporate leaders to wander aimlessly from one experience to another, from one policy to another, or from one strategic plan to another. When leaders fall asleep at the helm and their rudders either don't exist or are dysfunctional, empires fall; companies file for bankruptcy.

How does this affect a corporation? Fear, ignorance, ambiva-lence, and insecurity often act as catalysts, shocking us into compla-cency or paralysis. When concerns arise over how stakeholders will perceive a corporate strategy, under scrutiny, or the potential short-term economic punishment associated with those uneasy perceptions about those strategies, change is curtailed and hard questions are avoided. To avoid this, a board of directors must play the important role of rudder, acting in consortium with the management team, to develop a clear strategy and provide for its execution. This clarity is possible because, generally, the board is more objective. An effective monitoring system, proffered by the board, can negate concerns stakeholders have about short-term failure while ensuring long-term success. Board members should establish benchmarks by which they can evaluate results and adjust strategy as needed. Remember, the best boatmen adjust their rudders accordingly as the wind changes and the tide turns.

One of the board of directors' most essential roles is to weigh in each year on the company's overall goals and objectives—and then to hold leaders accountable for achieving these plans. Think of board meetings as checkpoints or tollgates, instances where the company can measure progress or receive navigational help. Board members sit in the same proverbial tree as the Cheshire Cat; they provide navigational tools to the executives responsible for executing strategy. However, unlike the Cat, board members must never tolerate responses or reports as directionless or rudderless as Alice's "I don't know," or, even worse, as "I don't care."

Leadership relies upon informed decision-making that, in turn, is based on a limited amount of information, which is often received either too early or too late. Colin Powell reportedly used a valuable tool for decision-making in the field of battle called the "40/70" rule: if he had less than 40 percent of the data he needed to make a decision, it was probably too early to decide; if he had more than 70 percent, it was probably too late. In the context of corporate governance, I suggest a modified version of Powell's idea, a 55/80 rule, for decision-making to protect corporate assets and drive shareholder value.

Even when board members believe they have the right amount of information to make informed decisions that mitigate risks, they should always be skeptical before they become decisive. Being decisive is critical; otherwise, people wind up like Alice. However, boards and leaders need a system (a voice, a screening, and a filtering process) that confirms they have gathered the right quantity of information and performed the right level of analysis: the board needs a devil's advocate. In other words, when the board members receive advice, someone even higher needs to confirm that all the right questions have been asked. (Speaking of the phrase "devil's advocate," I have long wondered how and when the process of being objective and asking the hard questions became the devil's work.) Asking the right question(s) can help board members better understand their current situation and better position them for evaluating future possibilities. Think of Einstein's notorious phrase, "If I only had the right question." Asking the right questions enables board members to challenge the status quo. The devil's advocate can be a particular board member, members of a board committee, or even an outside board advisor (see Chapter 15 on outside advisors).

Now, let's get back to boards' decision-making best practices. Debate and spirited dialogue must be precursors to board members' decisiveness. Decisions cannot be made by a group of "thinkalikes"; that is, reflective and informed decision-making must always be a part of the process. Such reflection is a best practice, but this requires presence in a realm in which the skeptic's voice and the minority's views are respected (see Chapter 27 on diversity).

The Tao of the Cheshire Cat is simple: if the leaders of an organization does not know where it is going, then any road will take it there. Only after selecting a clear destination do leaders need to begin the devolpment of business and strategic plans. No citizen or shareholder wants to be part of a nation or a company that is rudderless, directionless, insecure, or apathetic. Instead, the productivity of each employee, team, or division should be directly aligned with clear strategic direction, which leaders should communicate on a regular and consistent basis.

CHAPTER 4

LEADERSHIP LESSONS FROM OSTRICHES AND MONKEYS

It seems that, almost every day, news headlines are littered with stories of fallen icons. There are too many to name, and it is too sad to grasp fully. Our society has become tentative in embracing our true heroes, based on the fear that they will eventually let us down.

Reputations and brands, organizations and leaders, are sometimes ruined, not because of a misguided strategy or policy, but because of the conduct of a few who act badly. These few are part of a larger organization, which is held accountable for the conduct of the few, either directly or indirectly. When a wrongful act is first revealed, the old Watergate-type issues (such as what did other members of the organization know, when did they know it, and what did they do to prevent or stop it) all come up for discussion, first in the court of public opinion and eventually in a court of law.

Recently, a group of friends and I debated this complex legal, moral, and ethical issue when tailgating at a Redskins game. One beer-drenched participant remarked, "Yeah, ostriches make terrible leaders . . . you can't properly govern with your head in the sand." This statement is so true, and yet so false.

In fact, governance is based upon accessibility to and responsibility for those who report to you, even if these individuals are several levels down in the organizational chart. You see, after extensive research (including contacting the American Ostrich Association), it turns out ostriches do not bury their heads in the sand. This is a myth that has been perpetuated for years. Instead, while the male ostrich is often seen digging holes, this behavior is either in order to build a nest for the female's eggs or to protect the offspring after delivery. As it turns out, the ostrich is much more accountable and responsible than people think.

The dilemma about to how to treat leaders who have personally done no wrong is akin to the maxim of the Three Monkeys. The Three Monkeys are, most famously, sculpted over the Tosho-gu shrine in Nikko, Japan. Known as Mizaru, Kikazaru, and Iwazaru, they embody the principle, "See no evil, hear no evil, and speak no evil." Traditionally, Westerners' interpretation of this famous sculpture is as a reference to those who deal with impropriety by looking the other way, refusing to acknowledge it, or feigning ignorance. Most of us find this type of behavior morally repulsive; often, laws and professional codes, including lawyers' bar rules, force or strongly encourage leaders to report wrongful behavior as soon as it becomes apparent. Naturally, leaders should gather facts and ensure such behavior is both well documented and verifiable. However, once misconduct is established, leaders of companies must never ignore evil acts, or the resulting immorality, that involve their organizations. To do so destroys an organization's very fabric: it eats, like a cancer, at the core of stakeholder value and trust.

The Eastern interpretation of the Three Monkeys is nearly the polar opposite of Western tradition. To many Asians, the monkeys, as a pictorial maxim, represent a series of reminders: do not listen to evil things, so they do not influence you; do not read evil things, so they do not affect your actions; and, lastly, do not repeat evil things, so they cannot be falsely spread. Other Easterners take the proverb to mean that snoopy, nosy, or gossipy behavior should be avoided. The maxim of these monkeys even appear in Buddhist teachings, in which it advises that if we do not hear, see, or talk poorly about others, then we ourselves shall be spared defamation or criticism.

To connect these Eastern and Western interpretations of the maxim to governance, consider this: it is not enough to report evil activity as you become aware of it. Instead, being a good leader means proactively uncovering concerns within the corporation. While it is good not to spread gossip, acting to avoid seeing evil actions is not. This philosophy ties in nicely with every corporation's legal duty to implement reporting systems; indeed, this seems to be the philosophical underpinning for that area of law. However, this concept goes a step further than legal jurisprudence, leading to the question of what governs us: a legal compass or a moral one? Legal compliance and ethical compliance make up two separate sets of standards: I argue leaders should rely on the latter for guidance in terms of addressing internal-organization morality concerns.

Enron is a great example of the type of problem, described above, that is often at the root of evil corporate actions. In evaluating such cases, we must consider whether it is enough for managers to believe in ethical mandates—whether such mandates will help them recognize evil conduct within the corporation. When the corporation's culture itself incentives evil activity, as was the case at Enron, it is difficult to see how a leader can become the catalyst for change, or, further, whether it is sufficient to have a few pivotal leaders with strong moral compasses. Are legal constraints enough to restrain such behavior? Essentially, we must determine how we apply these maxims at the corporate level, when implementing them at the individual level doesn't always result in ethical outcome. In addition, when it becomes clear that "evil" actions permeated the company culture, we must ask whether there comes a time when a "moral" leader walks away (from a legal and/or a strategic perspective).

Each of these paradoxical interpretations of the Three Monkeys maxim come with its share of wisdom and insights for today's leaders, directors, and board members. On the one hand, as such a leader, you have a fiduciary duty to prevent conduct that harms your company and organization, to act promptly and deliberately when it is detected, and be ready and willing to take accountability for any damage already done. On the other hand, you should be careful not to act too quickly, or to misstep by speaking poorly about others without gathering facts or considering consequences.

Ultimately, today's leaders are probably best served by the wisdom of the fourth monkey, Shizaru, which has its arms crossed. Shizaru, ironically, is often missing from many of pictures and sculptures, yet this figure symbolizes the ultimate principle: "do no evil." Following this precept would certainly be a good start—and would serve as an excellent governance principle.

CHAPTER 5

DISTRACTED DRIVING ON THE ROAD TO GOOD GOVERNANCE

Accidents are a necessary evil in both driving and life. We cannot get behind the wheel without the chance of a collision; similarly, we cannot live without the chance of making a mistake. Each year, more than 40,000 people are killed and over 3,000,000 people are injured in approximately 6,000,000 motor vehicle accidents in the United States. Research indicates that in more than 50 percent of all crashes, driver inattention was a significant factor. When they get behind the wheel, many people seem to be in their own little world; they are focused on everything and anything but the critical act of driving. Now, the number of people who drive as if the road belongs to them alone or as if nobody else is around them (or as if nobody else's destination matters as much as their own) seems to be increasing daily. This is no way to properly drive. Nor is it the right way to live our lives, govern, or lead others. This slow death of common courtesy and the disappearance of a serious commitment to one's safety and the safety of others—both on the road and in life—is a very disturbing trend.

Well, how does driver distraction impact performance? Studies show that for every mile of driving, a focused driver makes approximately 200 decisions. If someone who is going fifty-five miles per hour takes his or her eyes off the road for three to four seconds, the vehicle travels the length of a football field. In fact, texting while driving increases the chances of an accident by 23 percent. Pedestrians who walk into crosswalks and busy streets while texting, talking, or listening to music, compound this risky behavior, thereby increasing the chance of a collision.

Many factors contribute to driver inattention. The most obvious are the following: alcohol or drug abuse, fatigue, reading, weather and traffic conditions, putting on make-up, shaving, texting or messaging, using a cellphone or PDA, eating, drinking, smoking, changing radio stations or CDs, retrieving unsecured objects or cargo, or focusing on a child or passenger in the back seat. We all see these activities in other cars—or in our own—on a daily basis. Less obvious factors include focusing on tough business or family problems, overall stress or anxiousness, running late, engaging in intense conversation, swerving suddenly (to avoid something in the road), using an unfamiliar vehicle, or taking an unfamiliar road.

Given all this, we can learn a great deal about best practices in leadership and governance by observing distracted drivers. If directors and business leaders are distracted or spread too thin, which means they are not focused on the task at hand, then they are significantly more likely to create two problems: first, they will get off course; second, they will hurt others along the way. In particular, they may hurt the stakeholders who, like distracted pedestrians, rely on the drivers to make the right decisions and stay focused behind the (governance) wheel. Stakeholders are further handicapped—beyond mere distraction—because they often cannot attain the necessary knowledge for avoiding the most dangerous intersections, nor can they respond defensively. In the boardroom, there are no warnings. There are no officers pulling people over for rushing or being reckless, which leaves responsibility in the hands of those who lead and govern.

If board members are unfocused, apathetic, or unprepared in board meetings, it is legally and ethically impossible for them to fulfill their fiduciary duties to shareholders. The board members who are more concerned with the menu of the post-board dinner than what's on their agenda are not likely to be effective and engaged. Similarly, board members who spend more time on their smartphones or in sidebar conversations than they do on board dialogues are not likely to make meaningful contributions to dialogue and debate. The board members too distracted by other commitments to read or analyze reports sent out weeks before meetings are not likely to meet the standards of the duty of care. Finally, board members too distracted by their own self-interests or personal agendas are unable to meet the standards of the duty of loyalty. All these factors contribute to distracted boards, which can lead companies straight toward major collisions.

Syrus once wrote, "To do two things at once is to do neither." Stepping aside the perceived strength of multi-tasking skills and the many multi-tasking tools and technologies available to us, by definition, "multi-tasking" means doing multiple tasks at the same time. If board members are multi-tasking, the likelihood of one or more tasks being poorly executed or important details being missed increases dramatically. Even the most talented jugglers can drop a ball. How many times a day do you engage in conversation or take a meeting while also answering an e-mail? Do you find later that you missed something important or typed something you now regret? (In addition, you may have upset the person who was trying to speak with you). The worst-case scenario is a board meeting of six to eight participants in which everyone is only half-listening, dealing instead with e-mails and cell phone calls. Such a gathering is not likely to lead to maximum productivity or results, nor will it protect shareholder value.

As a whole, our society is quickly becoming unable to focus. People are constantly encountering diversions that occupy their time and minds, and this lack of focus and attention is diluting our ability to properly govern, lead and make informed decisions.

Many people—you may be one of them—believe multi-tasking actually makes them more effective. However, the results of a 2009 study conducted at Stanford[1] suggest our perceptions about multi-tasking are false. The brain is not wired to multi-task: it deals with information like a single-server processor would, yet we expect it to operate as a dual-server processor would. We are limited to processing one task at a time; by overloading our brains, we are forcing them to jump back and forth between tasks. Like a computer that has too many applications open, when we take on too many tasks, our minds slow down. It takes more time to process each informational component. This problem is perpetuated by our inability to filter out irrelevant information while we multi-task.

Let's return to the metaphor of driving. Companies are constantly developing sophisticated technology that will aid the distracted driver. Protective measures, like airbags and seatbelts, help mitigate damage to passengers; special sensors notify drivers when they are getting too close to other vehicles or objects. Some cars even park themselves. While advanced technology continues to lessen the chances of risks associated with driving, this is not as true of governance. In governance, a director must act as sensor, airbag, and

---

1   See http://news.stanford.edu/news/2009/august24/multitask-research-study-082409.html.

driver all at once. So, while we see a trend toward accommodating the distracted driver in actual driving, accommodating the distracted director would result in the downfall of the principles of governance we rely upon.

Should stakeholders merely accept the fact that we are all now distracted drivers, and our lack of focus is resulting in the increase of mistakes, failures, and collisions? Alternatively, should those of us who have fiduciary responsibilities seek a greater balance between the actual ability and the perceived capability to multi-task? Only you can decide. Either way, as I discuss below, there are additional lessons from the road worth considering.

LEARNING THE ROAD

It is critical to distinguish between errors in decision-making made because of distraction and because of honest mistakes. If we start with the premise that board members must be well prepared and focused in order to make truly informed decisions, then the business judgment rule (discussed in Chapter 13) should protect most of their decisions, even if these decisions yield poor results. In some cases, boards and executives actually need to learn from their mistakes; this will make them better navigators. Knowing the road ahead can help directors manage potential missteps.

Think about trucks, which, when facing a steep decline shift into a lower gear, gaining greater control and slowing down their pace. This practice has business and life lessons for us all. When we face downward hills in our lives, we can take steps to slow the pace and navigate to a softer landing. Failure to shift gears leads to uncontrollable intensity and pace; it can result in a much more painful impact when a crash occurs. Try to answer these questions: what are you going to do when your brakes fail? What, where, or who is your runaway truck ramp (in other words, your safety net)? You must know when to use the exit ramp. Quitting while you are ahead is not the same as simply quitting. You must learn both discipline and balance.

Over the years, highway patrol statistics have demonstrated that the greatest number of accidents not related to substance abuse happen at dusk. At dusk, it is not clearly night, nor is it day: it's a grayish in-between. At such times, many people have trouble adjusting their vision and perspective. We are able to see more clearly when it is either dark or light. Similarly, we are able to make decisions more easily when things are black and white. Yet things are rarely black and white. At the board level, your ability to make effective decisions will be driven by your ability to navigate through "grayness." The data presented and the consequences' potential certainties are not clear; you must navigate through them without colliding into others. In turn, these others must also operate within the same shades of gray. Skilled board members and company leaders learn to make adjustments accordingly.

Everyone makes mistakes: to err is to be human. However, mistakes need to be made on the basis of good governance, in accordance with the fulfillment of legal duties and obligations. Usually, it is not our errors that get us in trouble; it is the way we conduct ourselves after making them. Failure is merely an invitation to try something again. Each attempt brings you closer to success—if, that is, you learn from your mistakes and react to failures with integrity, humility, and perseverance. There are four classic tragedies of mistake-making: not allowing yourself to act out of fear when making mistakes; not learning from mistakes; making the same mistake twice (or more); and allowing a mistake to destroy your self-confidence or willingness to try again.

Praise can be addictive; many of us will strive to avoid errors in search of praise. Yet, if avoiding errors means creating barriers to your progress or personal growth, then the benefits clearly outweigh the costs. One of my favorite quotations is by the great Thomas Edison, who said, "I have not failed. I have just found the 10,000 ways that won't work." Edison had a great attitude about what he called "failure," and it served him well.

Mistakes come in all shapes and sizes: there are big ones and little ones, ones that cost you time, ones that cost you reputation, and ones that cost you money. There are mistakes that hurt others' feelings and those that hurt only your own ego. Some mistakes have legal consequences and some violate moral codes. Remember, good judgment comes from experience, and experience comes from bad judgment. This is one of the great ironies of life: in order to learn from mistakes, we must make them. Despite our occasional lack of experience, we should always strive to make the right decisions.

MAKING THE RIGHT DECISIONS

So first, let's distinguish between doing something right versus doing something wrong. Most of us can easily distinguish right from wrong, either from a moral perspective or from the perspective of a member of society. For example, it's "right" to help an elderly person with his or her groceries; it's "wrong" to take another person's life. However, as we learned when discussing dusk, things are rarely so clear-cut. Even when they are, there are exceptions. What if that elderly person has dementia, mistakenly thinks that the helper is stealing his or her groceries, and has a heart attack? What if you killed someone, but you had to do so to defend an innocent third party? While these moral quandaries are beyond this book's scope, I share them here as a reminder of the fuzzy lines between what we all typically define as "success" or "failure." A hollow success may not be a true success; it may be a failure. Similarly, a failure accompanied by a deep and meaningful learning experience may end up being considered a success. Perhaps if we focus on the experiences, not on semantics, we will get our answers.

The various ethical frameworks for decision-making have always intrigued me. When we make decisions that have ethical or adverse consequences, each of us considers different types of variables. The hardest decisions are those called "right versus right": that is because when we are making them we are forced to choose between two proper actions. One correct position will be adversely affected. For example, suppose you supervise ten people. You can only afford to allow one an extra day of sick leave the next day, yet two people have requested leave due to severe, and pressing, family situations. In such a case, how do you decide? Unfortunately, not all difficult decisions will enable the convenience of choosing between something that is clearly right and something that is clearly wrong.

These five classic ethical decision-making frameworks will give you some tools for navigating through tough decisions:

Rights Approach: The rights of those affected by the decision or actions are paramount, and concern for this point should drive the final choice. In this example, you would excuse the worker whose absence would have the greatest impact on his or her ability to help family.

Virtue Approach: Decisions and actions must be guided by a principle to "do good above all else." Actions must be consistent with a set of ideal virtues. In this example, you would decide based on your own sense of ethics, family values, and work ethic.

Fairness or Justice Approach: Above all else, actions or decisions should be driven by paramount principles of fairness, justness, and equal treatment. In this example, you would allow both workers to be absent and make other arrangements.

Common Good Approach: The benefit of society, company, country, or community is what needs to come first. If a given action or decision is beneficial for the whole, even if it hurts a few individuals, then it is justified. In this example, you would allow the worker whose absence would least impact the other workers' duties to be absent.

Utilization or Pragmatic Approach: The costs and benefits of each action or decision must be carefully weighed. If a proposed action's benefits outweigh its costs, then it should be taken. In this example, you would carefully weigh the absence of both workers against the costs their absence would cause the company, as well as the impact of not allowing them a day off on their future motivation and productivity.

CAN BOARDS AVOID ACCIDENTS?

The surest way to avoid accidents is to never get behind the wheel. You won't travel very far on the road of life, but you'll be safe. If we lived our lives in fear of collisions, we'd never leave our living-room sofas. Stakeholders depend on more than directors' ability to drive; they also count on their leaders' willingness to do so. For directors, getting behind the governance wheel, so to speak, each day means that we take on the risk: we risk not reaching our destination without a confrontation, a crash, or an injury along the way. Board members and company leaders accept this risk as a cost they pay for the reward of eventually getting where they want to go. Along their journeys, the best leaders develop stronger armor with which to protect themselves when dealing with life's adversities. They also know when to take the exit ramp.

So, if boards and company leaders are incapable of eliminating risk, can they mitigate it? The comforting, and resounding, answer is, "YES!" While the safest road is not devoid of all risks, it is one upon which all drivers accept a certain risk level, exert control where possible, and proceed with goals in mind. The governance best practices discussed throughout this book will reduce the chance of accidents as a company evolves and travels toward its strategic destinations significantly.

That said, it's time to get behind the wheel, put your phone on mute, take out your map, and start driving with focus and purpose.

CHAPTER 6

Governance Lessons Learned from Children's Games

In his seminal book *Too Many Bosses, Too Few Leaders*, Rajeev Peshawaria observes, "Leadership cannot be learned in a classroom, nor automatically acquired by accepting a big title or position of authority. Leadership needs to be discovered and there is no shortcut to the discovery process." Peshawaria argues that leadership is a choice, not an entitlement. Leaders must have the skills both to govern companies and to inspire cadres of supporters—both inside a company and outside it—who understand the organization's goals and mission, and who work to embody them every day.

So, where do we begin our journey of learning the skills and lessons we need in order to be inspired leaders and informed board members? The answer: in childhood. However, leadership is not necessarily learned in the classroom (as Peshawaria observes); it can be learned during playtime. As I always suspected when I was a child, it turns out that recess really was more important than sitting at a desk.

We can learn a lot from playing sports on the field and playing games around a kitchen table. Today, we are also learning from advanced-graphic video games and shared community games that we can play online, using our laptops, tablets, or smartphones.[1]

At a core level, we learn lessons of teamwork, strategy, discipline, patience, persistence, concentration, focus, dignity, respect, creativity, and innovation from sports and games. We find our most effective roles, learn from our mistakes, begin to understand the need to learn (and then either follow the rules or incur penalties), and discover each of our lessons has consequences. Along the way, we discover the joys of winning and the pain of losing; simultaneously, we learn about the lack of control over outcomes, about the role(s) played by luck and chance, about the need to accept and overcome challenges, and, ultimately, about the need for good sportsmanship.

In addition, playing sports and games teaches you lessons about transparency and accountability, which are key traits of a leader or board member. When you miss a tackle or have a basketball stripped out of your hands, there is no place to hide. There are no excuses for dropping that fly ball in center field. When it comes to games, only you can decide whether to practice and improve or determine how hard you will train. Otherwise, you have to accept the fact that others may excel more than you do, because they were willing to invest extra time and effort when you were not. Leaders embrace the facts that games have starts and finishes, winners and losers, and penalties. They are inspired by the challenges and opportunities that sports and games present, and they welcome chances to strengthen their own performance and to commit to being part of a team, both of which are qualities necessary for success.

When playing sports or games, we embrace the joy that comes from spending time with one another. We learn that with some

---

1   Due to my family's addiction to *Words with Friends*, I now have the most limited vocabulary in our household.

coaching, chemistry, cooperation, and communication, a variety of people (folks with varied skills, interests, abilities, and characteristics) can learn to work well as a team. Moreover, these people can commit to compensating for each other's shortcomings; in working together, we learn the sum of the parts can, truly, be greater than the whole. Through games and sports, people learn to leave their egos behind; they also learn the team's best interests must always come ahead of the individual's. Great athletes are less concerned about their individual statistics or performances than they are about the team's outcomes. While the most valuable player, or MVP, is often singled out for leading a team to victory, every team member plays a critical part in that team's success.

From sports and games, we also learn that feedback does not mean failure and that the term "constructive criticism" is not an oxymoron. In addition, we learn that while practice does not always make perfect, it can certainly increase the odds of success. We also learn the importance of role-playing and discover we need different skills to play different positions. Sports and games show us that taking turns is important. For example, if someone is not pleased with the outcome of an at-bat or a spin of the dice, he or she knows not to get discouraged: another opportunity is right around the corner. Finally, we learn from sports and games that success is found in the intersections between hard work and circumstances.

Each type of game gives us some of the basic skills and insights we need for life: *Trivial Pursuit* (remembering facts), *Scrabble* (practicing spelling and vocabulary), chess (developing patience and strategy; thinking ahead), *Clue* (thinking analytically, creatively, and outside the box; connecting the dots to solve a mystery), *Monopoly* (working on negotiation, asset management, and budgeting), *Life* (discovering the reality of your circumstances and of uncontrollable life events, and facing the need to adjust accordingly), *Chutes and Ladders* (learning that we can fall just as fast as we can climb; taking nothing for granted), and *Operation* (having a steady hand and getting things right the first time[2]).

From a leadership and governance perspective, here are a few of my favorite life lessons taken from sports and games:

Whack-A-Mole: for every problem you solve, two or more are likely to appear. So, don't spend too much time celebrating your victories and take nothing for granted.

Monopoly: don't put too many eggs in one basket. In other words, diversify your portfolio. If a strategy begins to yield success, then double down until market conditions begin to change.

Hot Potato: risk shifts back and forth throughout the course of a negotiation or relationship. However, at some point in time, a metaphorical buzzer goes off (e.g., a closing) and someone will be left holding the proverbial hot potato.

Battleship: in every relationship or situational analysis, start by trusting your instincts. As your due diligence yields more facts and helps you understand your circumstances, shift to educated guesses and informed decisions.

Hide and Seek: you can run, but you can't hide forever. Eventually, you will be found and will need to start the process anew. And in our transparent, web 2.0-driven world, all of the good hiding places have been exposed!

Tag: leadership and fortunes will shift. Stay agile and pay attention, and you will never be "it" indefinitely.

Tennis: always keep your eye on the ball, or you risk missing it completely.

---

2   *Operation* also taught me that preparation is far more important than an act itself. As Abe Lincoln often said, "If I had eight hours to chop down a tree, then I would spend at least half of them sharpening my axe."

Blackjack: don't be too greedy, because you may lose everything. You should know when to ask for more and when to stick with the cards in your hand.

Charades: think carefully through what you are trying to communicate to others. Given the right hints and encouragement, they will come to share your vision.

The Last Straw: if you put too much pressure on anyone's shoulders, he or she will break down. Learn to delegate and prioritize key tasks.

Legos: learn to create great things from what you have been given and the tools you have available. Use your imagination and be a visionary.

Street Basketball: if you can't dribble, then learn to shoot. If you can't shoot, then be a great defender. If you want to rebound, learn to box out. If you are not the tallest, then be the smartest or the toughest.

Weebles: life presents us with many challenges. The key is to learn to wobble, without falling down, when you are pushed.

Track and Field: You can never win or lose if you don't run the race.

For insights about being a better leader, go back to your roots. Think about the things you did as a child that were fun or helped you succeed. Then, build on those in the workplace and in the boardroom. Be inquisitive, collaborative, persistent (yet patient), and, always, strategic. Look for ways to win as part of a team. Be a rule learner and a rule follower (unlike *Monopoly*, in life there are no real "Get Out of Jail Free" cards). Finally, by all means, play to win—even if it means losing initially.

CHAPTER 7

THE TRUTH HURTS— DEAL WITH IT

"When regard for the truth has been broken down or even slightly weakened, all things will remain doubtful."

—St. Augustine

Over the past ten years, our nation's government and business leaders seem to have reinterpreted the meaning of the term "the truth" in order to serve their own, selfish purposes. The level of deception, misrepresentation, and spinning—the number of material omissions, misleading statements, and re-interpretation of the actual facts—appears to be an almost daily shock to which we have become numb and which we almost accept as our new norm. The lack of direction, as well as the cloudiness of the forecast ahead, significantly contributes to our prolonged recessionary economy.

However, as Saint Augustine observes, we cannot have certainty without truth: by definition, clarity requires candor and honesty. The truth is often not pleasing to either the ear or the psyche. Yes, some plaid shirts simply do not go with striped pants. Yes, honey, that dress does make you look fat. However, often, rather than be direct and honest, and deliver the news that people really need to hear, we soften such blows with diluted misstatements or outright lies. In such cases, are we really helping? How does a perpetual state of performance review fabrication help advance productivity or the shareholders' best interests? If we don't tell people what they need to hear for self-improvement, it's difficult to determine how we can advance either our society or our companies' performance.

As human beings, we tend to admire those who praise us and disdain those who are critical or scornful. Yet we need to separate the messages from the messengers. The people who offer the most value are the ones willing to be direct, honest, and genuine. Board members telling CEOs that they are doing great jobs (when they are not) or managers telling their teams they are winning (when they are losing) are not observing best practices of governance. The same type of thing happens when teachers give students undeserved grades or voters reelect politicians who have not served citizens well. Often, we are too fearful or too lazy to explore alternatives or to be forthright.

How does this forthrightness extend to the business world? In a finance department, we rely on numbers to tell a story about our financial viability; in marketing, we optimize accounts and campaigns based on consumer response data; and in operations, we increase our efficiency by evaluating internal information. Sometimes the data we rely upon is positive and sometimes it is negative. Either way, that data is valuable because it tells us something important about the company (something that is accurate) and it allows us to take measures to correct mistakes and/or enhance successes. If the data were no longer reliable, or worse, unavailable, what would happen? At that point, would any responsible leader consider making a business decision?

When it comes to human capital, we are slaves to our good behavior. We must consider why companies are investing capital in workforces they are unwilling to optimize. Think of it this way:

telling the truth acts as offering a bid in an open marketplace of idea-sharing, a place in which employees can respond, in real time, to feedback. We need to shift our perspective, shy away from the negative connotations of "constructive criticism," and begin to look more objectively at truths as additional data points that provide useful information for decision-making. To develop a more effective and efficient workforce, tell the truth and tell it often.

Don't get me wrong; I am a huge fan of empathy, diplomacy, and tact. Before you deliver a message, always place yourself in the shoes of the person who will be receiving it and think through your words before you say them. Remember, though, that being tactful is not the same as telling someone what he or she wants to hear just because you don't want to upset or offend him or her. Your body language, the words you select, the verve with which you deliver the message, and your level of empathy and sincerity can all help you remain respectful to the listener without lying or telling an untruth.

At all levels, particularly in corporations, honesty allows for quicker, more informed decisions; it clears up misconceptions; and it allows for realistic expectations and performance. Honesty gives everyone license to think of improvements and suggest them. Without an honest or open culture, employees may fear backlash (or, in the worst cases, termination) for speaking frankly or for sharing critical information with management. Such results build up resentment and bitterness in the workforce.

Leaders must be committed to building a culture in which telling the truth is a core value, both externally and internally. Being direct and explicit must be more important than acting spinelessly or deceitfully. Managers must be rewarded for the courage of their convictions, not the fruits of their spin control, sandbagging, or self-interest. To create such a culture, principles of transparency, accountability, and responsibility must be embraced; the organizational sins of nepotism, turfmanship, and deception must be mitigated or eliminated.

Without truth, we lack clarity, and without clarity, we cannot move toward economic recovery.

CHAPTER 8

MAKING A COMMITMENT
TO COMMITMENT

"The basic philosophy, spirit, and drive of an organization have far more to do with its relative achievements than do technological or economic resources, organizational structure, innovation, and timing. All of these variables weigh heavily in success. But they are, I think, transcended by how strongly the people in the organization believe in the basic precepts and how faithfully they carry them out."

—Thomas J. Watson, Jr.

"Until one is committed, there is hesitancy, the chance to draw back, [and] always ineffectiveness. Concerning all acts of initiative and creation, there is one elementary truth the ignorance of which kills countless ideas and splendid plans: that the moment one definitely commits oneself, then providence moves too. All sorts of things occur to help one that would never otherwise have occurred. A whole stream of events issues from the decision, raising in one's favor all manner of unforeseen incidents, meetings, and material assistance which no man could have dreamed would have come his way. I have learned a deep respect for one of Goethe's couplets: 'Whatever you can do, or dream you can, begin it! Boldness has genius, magic, and power in it.'"

—W.H. Murray

Many of us in today's society seem to have an inability to commit to commitment. Marriage rates have reached an all-time low (less than 45 percent of American adults are married, according to a 2011 Pew Foundation Research Center study report), divorce rates are at all-time highs, politicians make campaign promises only to regularly break them, and CEO turnover rates (and their average terms) are alarming. Moreover, as each new year approaches, many of us make resolutions that will be broken by the following March. We change channels and radio stations so quickly that we can't even tell what show is on or what song is playing. As a nation, our impatience and inability to focus is chipping away at our ability to make long-term commitments and engage in meaningful long-term strategic planning.

A commitment is a promise—one that people depend on—to undertake a duty or obligation, or to promise to do or not do something, the breach of which can have significant consequences for those depending on that commitment. When candidates commit to serve on a board of directors, or executives commit to leadership positions, we expect they will undertake the legal and moral obligations of these fiduciary positions with vigor, passion, and enthusiasm; moreover, as we say when reciting marriage vows, we expect they will do so "in sickness and in health."

Leaders may not be formally required to take vows or make oaths, but that does not mean the consequences of breaking their commitments are not just as significant as the consequences for those who break formal promises of dedicated service to sets of values or defined codes of conduct. In leadership, the commitment to strong, transparent, and effective governance must be unwavering.

I'm reminded of a story about a chicken and a pig that are considering launching a new restaurant. When they start talking about the menu, the chicken suggests they focus on breakfast selections; specifically, they should offer bacon and eggs. The pig is concerned by the unfairness of their potential contributions—after all, he would be fully committed and the chicken would only be involved!

In the context of leadership and governance, board members and executives must be more like the pig—ultimately accountable to the company's success and fully committed to the shareholders' best interests—rather than like the chicken, periodically contributing while merely being kept informed of the company's progress. A willingness to roll up one's sleeves and wade, knee-deep, into the muck is the type of attitude about and philosophical approach to leadership and governance that this nation badly needs right now.

At every level of an organization, commitment is crucial for breeding innovation, developing solutions to problems, and creating internal improvements. A 2009 study found a strong correlation between employees' proactivity levels and their commitment to their organizations. People who behaved like the pig described above were more likely to suggest improvements or implement new initiatives.[1] Organizational leaders can influence proactive behavior and the development of a greater sense of commitment to the organization through implementing programs that create stronger bonds and establish employee identities within the organization, so individual employees feel they are able to contribute to the whole in a valuable manner. This type of organizational structure helps companies avoid the people who, like the above-mentioned chicken, run around offering advice on anything and everything, while lacking adequate information or know-how. Such a structure enables commitment, which is the fuel that turns promises into reality; the accountability

---

1   See http://griffin.zydec.net.au/publications/Strauss_Griffin_Rafferty.pdf.

that separates activity from results; the duty that puts others' interests ahead of one's own; and the manifestation of actions speaking louder than words. Ultimately, having commitment is about having character and integrity, undertaking duty, and having the values to stay the course.

People say that the primary difference between an interest and a commitment is as follows: if you're interested in doing something, then you'll do it when circumstances permit, but when you've committed to doing something, then you'll accept no excuses: only results. Peter Drucker once wrote, "Unless commitment is made, there are only promises and hopes; but no concrete plan of action." To combat a persistent, global recession, we cannot depend on leaders' mere promises to dig us out of our holes. Instead, we need a concrete, implementable game plan.

Let us end here with James Womack's fitting sentiment: "Commitment unlocks the doors of imagination, allows vision, and gives us the 'right stuff' to turn our dreams into reality."

CHAPTER 9

THE PARADOX OF FAIRNESS

Somehow, over time, our society has evolved into a series of ecosystems governed by ideas about "political correctness" and "not wanting to offend anyone's feelings"; these sentiments have become defining principles of fairness and have moved to the top of decision-making priority lists as best practices. To get the productivity and output of our economy and government back on track, these principles of fairness need to move back down to the middle of the pack where they belong. Board members and executives must re-establish "acting in our shareholders' best interests" as the principle that sits atop any strategic priority list ahead of not wanting to ruffle feathers.

Don't get me wrong: fairness is a wonderful tool in governance, and leaders who embrace its principles often win their coworkers' respect and appreciation. Employee perceptions of fairness lead to higher retention rates and greater customer satisfaction, both of which ultimately impact a company's bottom-line and industry competitiveness. To ensure decision-making processes are clear—and that open, honest, and empathetic communication channels for explaining decision-making exist—correct structural supports should be in place. Employees are more committed to organizations that they perceive as fair. This doesn't mean that employees expect all policies to be to their advantage; rather, they expect to have a good understanding of processes by which new policies are established, decision-making procedures, communication channels for decision-making, and expectations of decision-making.

Keeping your workforce informed and offering them input channels is admirable; however, at the end of the day, leaders must lead and make tough decisions, whether or not the affected parties will perceive those decisions as "fair." There is a fundamental difference between a voice and a vote in the decision-making process. If and when companies equate fairness with a vote, and put that fairness at the top of the priority list, effective governance is likely to break down.

The moral and ethical paradox of fairness is this: that which is right isn't always fair, and that which is fair isn't always right.

After all, is it better to be loved or feared? Can leaders be effective and still gain both their employees' respect and attention? A recent HBR study found that it is difficult to achieve both; fairness-based leadership often suffers from a lack of perceived power and the respect that comes with that power.[1] For example, assume you have one hundred employees and ten need to be terminated as soon as possible; the termination number is not negotiable. Should you select the ten most recently hired, the ten with the lowest performance reviews, or the ten from your lowest performance division? Should you select the ten who don't have families to support, or the ten most costly in terms of productivity? Perhaps you should pick ten names randomly from a hat, select the ten you like the least, or decide upon the ten you perceive as the least loyal to the company. In

---

1   See http://hbr.org/2011/07/why-fair-bosses-fall-behind/ar/1.

all likelihood, no matter what you decide, at least ten people, maybe many more, will perceive the consequences of your decision as unfair. As the old adage states, "You can please some of the people all of the time, and all of the people some of the time, but you'll never be able to please all of the people all of the time."

Companies in which executives allow all decisions to be guided either primarily or exclusively by fairness will suffer: their competitors will perceive them as vulnerable, their customers as directionless, their employees as weak and powerless, and their shareholders as rudderless. Tough times require tough decisions. There is no path to take that avoids crossing the sometimes unpopular bridge of unfairness and disparate treatment. Leaders should be prepared to make tough decisions at a moment's notice and be willing to solve problems before they arise, even if those solutions are controversial. As Sir Winston Churchill observed, "Want of foresight, unwillingness to act when action would be simple and effective, lack of clear thinking, confusion of counsel until the emergency comes, until self-preservation strikes its jarring gong—these are the features which constitute the endless repetition of history." Churchill, known for his decisive leadership style, understood that decisions should not be made impulsively; instead, leaders should come prepared, ready to make swift decisions when facing tough consequences.

Communication regarding the consequences of tough or unfair decisions should still be guided by principles of transparency, empathy, and sincerity. Leaders should treat people with dignity and respect at all times. Commitment to a set of shared values, especially when difficult decisions need to be made, is a key pillar of good governance. Yet holding fast to this precept is not the same as putting fairness at the top of a decision-making priority list, which is a decision that, in turn, will unnecessarily skew or delay other difficult decisions that need to be made in volatile and challenging times.

I have always respected those who act with passion and conviction, even if I don't agree with their views. Those whose actions speak louder than their words—who make promises and keep them—are people guided by deep-seated beliefs and strong sets of moral values. They understand and embrace the fact that some other people will always perceive their decisions as unfair, no matter how much time and deliberation went into those decisions. However, governance is not a popularity contest, and executives are not cheerleaders. Governance is hard and challenging work—nobody said it was going to be fun.

CHAPTER 10

STOP WHINING AND START WORKING

As a father of two college-aged adults, a professor at both the University of Maryland and Georgetown University, and a citizen, I must admit that I have some compassion for the recent uptick in protests and uprisings. Occupy, the movement that began on Wall Street, has expanded to occupying virtually everything around the globe. We live in frustrating economic times and face a highly competitive job market. Certainly, the prospect of carrying student loan debt while receiving no income might motivate some people to wear masks, carry outrageous signs, sleep in public parks, or stand in the rain all day. However, as I have always told my own children, be careful what you wish for, because you just might get it. In the case of Occupy, that could mean the disintegration of capitalistic incentive structure and economic stagnation, which could result in a non-competitive, undereducated nation.

Is Occupy's goal really to disrupt the capitalism, entrepreneurship, and innovation that have defined the American Dream and made this country so great for nearly 250 years? Do protestors really think socialism and even communism are better governance systems?

It seems as though there is more than enough historical evidence to demonstrate that an opportunity-driven, capitalistic society offers economic security and quality lives filled with passion and challenges.

I suspect that the people who make up this book's audience fall into many categories. Some are among the 1 percent that everyone appears to be frustrated with; some in the 5 percent that still live pretty darn comfortably; some in the 20 percent that aspire one day to be in the top 10 percent; and some in the 40 to 60 percent that have achieved the American Dream of owning a home and a car, having a good job, and enjoying a quality lifestyle. Life is not a game of numbers; it is about putting your priorities, your energy, and your convictions in the right place.

Ask the immigrant businessman, someone who came to this country with $500 in his pocket, who now runs a highly successful technology company and who is now in the 1 percent, if he sympathizes with these protestors. Ask the African-American partner of a global professional services firm, someone who grew up in the Deep South in abject poverty and who is now in the 1 percent, if she sympathizes with these protesters. Ask the software entrepreneur, someone who has overcome three business failures, whose grit and persistence propelled his fourth company to success, and who is now in the 1 percent, whether he sympathizes with these protesters. Most of the dreaded 1 percent are not hedge-fund managers or fifth-generation silver spooners. Like you and me, they are citizens who have worked very hard to get to where they are and to accumulate what they possess. They, too, had to navigate through frustrating and volatile economic and social conditions to achieve their success. Let's not penalize their efforts with protests, unfair tax systems, or political attempts to create a social divide that could destroy the very fabric of this great nation.

A 2008 study by Prince and Schiff found that 7.6 percent of all U.S. households have a net worth that's between $1 and $10 million. As stated in their book, *The Middle-Class Millionaire*, they found the following: "Overwhelmingly these millionaire households are headed by people raised in ordinary middle-class homes. Through their lifestyle choices and spending decisions, they wield influence in the overall economy in support of the same middle-class values and concerns they were raised with: security, health, self-betterment, family, and community." This class represents people who are more willing to persist when facing potential failure: 90 percent hold the belief that anyone who works hard enough can become a millionaire.

Don't misunderstand me. Governance best practices dictate that board members and executives should *always* be carefully monitoring excessive compensation's viability, risks, and consequences. This is especially true if the rewards given to those who excel are greater than the returns these individuals provide to company shareholders. A CEO who has been making $3.5 million while his company has lost money for the past six consecutive quarters should be singled out and held accountable. In a company whose directors have been asleep at the switch, the annual increase in board fees should be scrutinized. However, the people performing that scrutiny need to be stakeholders who have earned the right to question compensation relative to performance. This scrutiny should not fall to a group of frustrated protesters who have no real connection to the situation.

Recently, when a CNN reporter interviewed one young protester and asked him what he wanted as an outcome of this movement, the protestor responded, "I want someone to pay off my student loans." Really? Really? Well, I might want a Maserati, but I don't see that wish coming to fruition as a result of camping out in McPherson Square. True, *TIME* magazine named "The Protestor" as its Person of the Year in 2011. However, the protestors cited in the magazine were those who helped topple oppressive governments in Egypt, Tunisia, and Yemen, or those who helped start real dialogue for change in Russia, Libya, and other regions. The article did not recognize or endorse whining, nor did it make a declaration against capitalism. In some respects, *TIME* got it right by recognizing "The Protestor" as a representative of the individuals who stand up to oppose oppression and economic tyranny, individuals who hope for a regime in which success, freedom, and happiness are possible. When it comes to those who are committed to real conversations, people who are ready for a unified message and are open to all solutions, I am ready to listen. When it comes to those who deny that discipline, I have no time to listen and no sympathy for the cause. While there are no guarantees, the possibility of wealth via a strong work ethic, entrepreneurship, and accomplishment is what makes this country so great. Nothing fights inequity (or perceived inequality) like achievement, and nothing fights apathy like commitment.

You can debate numbers all day long, pontificating about how much wealth is enough wealth, but our nation's core values—the principles upon which this country were built—are not up for discussion in my mind. Kudos to Mitt Romney who, during the GOP primaries in Florida in January 2012, responded to one of Gingrich's statements by saying, "I have worked hard to accumulate my wealth; I am proud of the money I have made and of the amount of taxes I pay." Let's have pride over protest. Earned affluence is nothing to apologize for; rather, it is an aspiration we must all share. At its essence, governance is about creating the framework for and the resources to foster opportunity for further affluence. So far, we have done a remarkably good job in this, relative to the wealth and median living standards of other nations.

True opportunity cannot be fabricated to appease those who feel hurt by the system because they chose career paths that are already obsolete or are becoming so. Henry Hartman said, "Success always comes when preparation meets opportunity." As members of this society, our goal cannot and should not be to create more success. Instead, we need to focus on generating as much opportunity as possible; as individuals, we should prepare ourselves to meet those opportunities adequately. When prepared individuals meet society's opportunities, success is realized. If market opportunities are drying up, that means we must address the causes of and potential remedies for economic stagnation. However, if the real problem stems from a lack of individual preparation, as I suspect is the case here, then, correspondingly, we must frame the discussion around incentives, education, and retraining; we should not frame it around overhauling an opportunity-generating economic system that has benefited those from all walks of life and helped them in accessions of wealth.

So, let's refocus our efforts, energy, and passion on making sure that this country remains great. Americans are thought leaders, innovation pioneers, and entrepreneurship exporters. That's what we need to wish for. That's what will keep protesters off the streets and help them into good jobs and strong career paths.

CHAPTER 11

The Emperor Needs to Know

Do What You Say and Say What You Mean

"We want to reassure everyone that we're doing fine but that doesn't mean we won't have to make some tough decisions."

—Jeff Joernes

In a famous scene from the film *A Few Good Men*, Colonel Jessep (played by Jack Nicholson) yells at military attorney Kaffee (played by Tom Cruise), "You can't handle the truth!"

How and why does it seem that, over the past few years, this character's words have become a governance standard for brand leaders, CEOs, and even Congress people?

Governance and leadership require prompt, clear, and candid communication with employees, shareholders, stakeholders, and citizens. Whether it is via e-mail, small groups, or larger town-hall meetings, people who are directly or indirectly affected by this information or these decisions (in terms of their health, wealth, safety, or careers) are tiring of spin-control, half-truths, sugar-coating, and long-winded pontifications.

The rule for addressing this is pretty simple: *Do what you say and say what you mean.* Many metaphors and sayings—from "walk the talk" to "where you sit depends on where you stand" to "the truth will set you free"—reinforce this basic principle. However, often it appears more as if our nation's leaders are playing musical chairs, rather than clearly communicating their opinions. In addition, there are those whose opinions are so hardened they forgot governance also concerns compromise and respect for others' positions (remember to "walk a mile in the shoes of another").

The keys to crisis management are honesty and promptness. In 1982, Johnson & Johnson set the precedent for good crisis management when someone in a store tampered with the company's most profitable product, Tylenol; this tampering led to seven deaths in the Chicago area. Even though the company wasn't directly responsible for the deaths, Johnson & Johnson immediately recalled the product from the entire United States market, broadcast multiple announcements to the public, and made the product safer before returning it to the shelves. Above all else, Johnson & Johnson placed public health at the top of the company's priority list, enabling restoration of the Tylenol brand by responding quickly, taking responsibility, and minimizing customers' risk.

In turn, delayed responses and incomplete information can lead to public backlash. This happened in 1999, when Exxon failed to respond to the Alaskan oil spill in a timely manner or take responsibility for the resulting environmental harm. In the public's eyes, Exxon seemed deceitful and unconcerned about the environment.

With the onset of the BP oil spill, Enron accounting fraud, and the United States' financial crisis, the global demand for corporate transparency has increased. Shareholders' and stakeholders' concerns range widely, from environmental and human rights problems to good governance practices to financial reporting accuracy. Ethical and economic considerations, innovation, and learning are all key forces acting on this shift in perspective. Marks and Spencer (M&S), a European retail company, is a leader in its field in terms of sustainable business practices. The company has taken stakeholder transparency and accountability to a new level with Plan A; under this initiative, M&S will reduce its carbon impact and become the world's most sustainable retailer. Rather than acting like a slave to the bottom line each quarter, M&S has put long-term objectives and profitability at its business model's forefront. Skeptics, step aside: this initiative has not just been about "doing good for the sake of doing good." Plan A has directly impacted the company's profits. As a direct result of the initiative, in 2010 M&S saw an additional $70 million in profit. Moreover, stakeholders have been able to see the success, roadblocks, and failures along the way, because M&S is providing them with frequent updates on the company website.

As top brands become more transparent and report on socially responsible initiatives, including how they get it right and how they get it wrong, the rules of the game are changing. For example, The Gap's Global Compliance and Integrity Department shares data on its website regarding violations of its code of vendor conduct in various categories, such as management systems, environment, labor, and working conditions, all broken down by region. Overall, providing easy-to-understand, honest, and balanced information generates trust and brand vitality. For instance, the Global Reporting Initiative's (GRI) mission is to "make sustainable reporting standard practice for all organizations." In 2010, the United States achieved the milestone of becoming the world's largest GRI reporting country, with 183 reporting organizations (this meant a 30 percent increase from 2009).

Today, forums for communication are more vibrant than ever before. Technology is beginning to solve the collective action problem faced by disparate groups, the members of which would like to have voices in public discourse and responses to those voices. Online social media is bringing the citizens even closer to decision-makers. In July 2011, for example, President Obama held the first-ever live Twitter Town Hall, in which citizens could tweet him their questions and receive responses in real time. In September 2011, the White House launched a program called "We The People," which enables individuals to petition the government. All petitions that receive 25,000 signatures in thirty days are guaranteed a public response from the White House. Our national and corporate leaders have all the tools in place: they merely need to step up to the plate with the truth.

Whether people like what you have to say or not, most value the individuals who are willing to tell them the (bitter) truth. Clarity of message trumps intent. Truth-telling, candor, and compassion must be part of a company's culture; moreover, the company's governance and leadership, as embodied in its leaders, must trust in the shareholders' ability to digest and understand material information as it develops and unfolds, not weeks or months later, when it is too late for anyone to react accordingly.

Perhaps you've heard of the children's story, "The Emperor's New Clothes." In this tale, a ruler is convinced by a shyster tailor that the latter's suit of non-existent clothes is the finest in the land. The ruler puts on the suit and then proceeds to parade down his village's crowded streets in order to show his outfit to his community. People are horrified by the sight but are too afraid to say anything; they fear that their words will offend him or that their honesty will result in negative consequences. Finally, a small child speaks up and tells the emperor the truth.

This story offers us many insightful lessons about leadership and governance:

1. *Conduct due diligence on key advisors.* The tailor in this story was clearly unqualified—where was the effective vetting process?

2. *Trusting your instincts will overcome bad advice.* The emperor suspected that his new suit of clothing was non-existent, but followed the advice of his new tailor anyway. If something seems too good to be true, then it probably is.

3. *Restrain your vanity.* Even if the emperor truly believed that he had been made the finest suit of clothing, did he really need to parade around the village to show it off?

4. *Create a culture in which truth is validated.* The saddest part of this story is that none of the villagers spoke up. They were too concerned about telling the king what they thought he wanted to hear, instead of focusing on what he needed to hear. A culture like this one, built on a foundation of such a "cheerleader syndrome," will always lead to poor decision-making and weak leadership and governance. The culture must encourage people to speak the truth without restraint or fear of retribution.

5. *Do not build a society that depends on childlike innocence to point out flaws.* After embarrassing himself and offending everyone around him, the emperor, somewhat randomly, relies on the voice of a small child to uncover the truth. Really? Come on, we can do better than that. Let's take off the rose-colored glasses and see things as they truly are.

6. *Be true to yourself.* Know your true strengths and weaknesses; don't try to hide them or deny that they exist. Rely on the advice of professionals, people who will help you

capitalize on your strengths and be honest about your (or your organization's) weaknesses.

7. *Friends don't let friends drive drunk.* Build relationships based on trust and candor. True friends and objective advisors don't let leaders operate on the basis of vanity, ego, pomp, or circumstance.

The bottom line is that the Emperor needs to know the truth (and so do his people).

CHAPTER 12

THE ROLE OF THE GOVERNANCE LAWYER

By Lizanne Thomas, Jones Day

I am a governance practitioner. I started my career about twenty-seven years ago, doing public company mergers and acquisitions (M&A), and my career has morphed into a governance practice. I like to tell people that I practice governance, teach it, and live it.

By living it, I mean that I serve as a director of a tiny little company with a big name: Krispy Kreme Doughnuts. Serving as a director for Krispy Kreme Doughnuts has been a great experience. It has informed my perspective on how I should advise companies regarding governance issues. It has also changed the way I approach governance issues. In this essay, I am not going to address the problems of our nation's financial institutions directly, although I will tell you that I think the meltdown the financial industry experienced in 2008 and 2009 has had a ripple effect in terms of how decision-makers determine choices throughout corporate America.

My client base does not come from New York, like much of the financial industry's does, but rather from the heartland—from those who make widgets and those who provide services to those who make widgets. I want to start this essay by telling you a story about the first time I began to realize the limitations of my contribution to good governance as a lawyer, and how this awareness has informed my perspective. A number of years ago, I was representing a company that was very much in a state of crisis. At a real turning point in its corporate history, we were negotiating a transaction that would have been a transformative one. The negotiations, I am sorry to say, were not going well. My colleagues and I were in New York, having completed these negotiations, and we were not satisfied with where things had landed. As a result, we all trooped back to the corporate jet to fly home, feeling as though the negotiations had stalled. We were not sure what direction the company would take from there.

Our group included the CEO; myself, a very vocal and talkative lawyer; the CFO, who had very strong opinions about these stalled negotiations' financial implications; and a marketing person—a PR person—who had her own views about what ought to happen next. The latter three of us yammered, and yammered, and yammered at this CEO for half of the flight home, each of us speaking from our own particular perspectives about what he ought to do and what recommendation to the board he ought to make.

Finally, there came a moment when he said, "Stop. I've heard enough. I don't want to hear anymore." He turned to me and said, "L.T., I'm going to make a decision that's a legal one, but it's not going to make you happy." He turned to the CFO and said, "I'm going to make a decision that I think is prudent financially, but it's not going to make you happy." Then, he turned to the marketing person and said, "And I'm going to make a decision that takes into account what you said, but it's not going to make you happy either."

Then, he said, "What I'm going to do is more than what is defensible. I'm going to do what is right."

I remember that moment. I paused, and said to myself, "Don't forget this message, because this is the lesson that should guide us in corporate decision-making going forward"; particularly, it should guide those of us who intend to be corporate advisors in the future.

So, that is my theme in this chapter—*what we need to do is to move beyond that which is defensible and toward that which is right.*

As a public company lawyer, I live in a place called "business-judgment-rule land." I try to place my clients within the business judgment rule, or I try to move them as close to that rule as I possibly can. I hope most of you know what that means. The "business judgment rule" is a legal presumption that protects corporate decision-makers from liability. It is a presumption that board members have fulfilled their fiduciary duties if they have acted in good faith and fulfilled their duties of loyalty and due care. Now, we could spend weeks parsing out how the business judgment rule really works. However, my point here is that even well-intentioned people have, over time, allowed our focus on staying within that rule to cause us to emphasize process, when what we ought to be emphasizing is substance. I think we have lost focus. In losing focus, we have lost great meaning.

I doubt there is a public company director, C-level officer, CEO, CFO, or chief legal officer today who could not recite for you—quite well—the business judgment rule that I just referenced. These individuals hear about those concepts all the time from chatty lawyers like me. I am in boardrooms probably about a hundred times a year, and I can vouch for the fact that the people who talk the most are the lawyers. So, our clients can recite those business judgment rule precepts well.

However, you will get the same prevaricating response from any director if you ask him or her, "What are the three most important drivers for your business, right now, and what are the most specific risks to each of those drivers?" Directors are not as conversant about, nor as focused on, the substance of what drives their businesses, and we are less aware than we should be of the risks connected to all those decisions. In my experience, most directors, decision-makers, managers, and even lawyers are earnest people. They intend to fulfill their duties and do their jobs very, very well. Of course, there are pockets of unfettered greed and arrogance. However, most corporate people and most corporate leaders are neither fundamentally greedy nor fundamentally arrogant. Yet, here we are, faced with such a degree of earned distrust that we must move at light speed if we are to get ahead of efforts to legislate or regulate trustworthy corporate conduct, and it may be too late.

Now, I am not challenging the concept of regulation in the financial services industry. I am really more focused on whether or not general corporate conduct is going to be regulated into trustworthiness, and, to that, I am unabashedly opposed. As I told my teenage sons when they went on their first dates, "Trust is hard to earn, easy to lose, and nearly impossible to win back." That describes the governance situation we are in today, at a time of crisis, navigating through turbulent financial markets and an ever-changing regulatory environment. What can governance lawyers do to be part of the solution, not part of the problem? What can corporate lawyers do to try to earn back the trust that we have lost? I have three suggestions, two that are general and one that is snatched from today's headlines:

1. Remember, relish, and assert your role as an independent advisor.
2. Never allow clients (board members or a management team) to approve what they do not understand.

3. Take the lead in advocating fundamental change in
   executive compensation.

Let's talk about each one of these points in a bit more detail.

REMEMBER, RELISH, AND ASSERT YOUR
ROLE AS AN INDEPENDENT ADVISOR.

As an independent advisor, I really hate it when I hear a lawyer say, "That's a business decision, so it's not really my space"; this is particularly bad when I hear it too early. Our clients are paying for our experience, our judgment, and, importantly, our independence. They are paying for our professionalism, which may be just as important. If we, as lawyers, are going to assert the right to continue to be self-regulated, then we are called upon to act with the kind of independent judgment that earns self-regulation.

Now, what that sometimes means is that we must speak the truth to powerful individuals. A mentor of mine once told me one of his philosophies. He said, "You know, I love being in the private practice of law. I just love it. I love the independence of it. I love my role as a counselor, and I love the fact that I can tell a client something he or she doesn't like. I can get fired by a client, and I can come to work the next day, and I can go find another client. I love that independence."

It was such a positive, enthusiastic description of our role that I will never forget it.

Another general counsel made quite an impression on me not long ago, when we were talking about a moral conundrum with which she was dealing. (She works for a company that is very much in the headlines right now.) She said, "You know, I know how I'm going to answer this particular issue. I know how I'm going to deal with this because I'd rather be unemployed than unemployable." She was going to hold on to her reputation, if not her job, by making sure that the advice she was giving to her client was right, if unwelcome.

So, my rule number one is this: seize and hold on to that role as an independent counselor. Celebrate it.

NEVER ALLOW CLIENTS TO APPROVE WHAT THEY DO NOT UNDERSTAND.

Rule number two, which might actually be my favorite, is this: never allow your clients to approve that which they do not understand. Look all the way back to Enron, to WorldCom, even to Disney (the infamous Michael Ovitz case) and certainly to this most recent meltdown. This has all been just as much a function of not understanding—a lack of comprehension—as it has been a function of greed and opportunism. I guarantee this: had some of these companies' and failed investment banks' board members really appreciated the long-term consequences—and the fact that the dance would have to end—they would have engaged in different kinds of conversation, which would have caused different results.

I have two stories to share in that regard. First, I want to talk about the CEO of another corporate client that I had the privilege to represent. He is an incredibly plainspoken man; he does not even have a college degree. Yet, he is the CEO of a New York Stock Exchange-traded company that is and has been at the top of its industry for quite some time.

He understands his business and is always ranked as the number one CEO in that particular industry; the company itself performs at as high a level as well. He has a policy—not because I taught him, not because anybody else taught him, but because it is the right thing to do—that he never allows any proposal to go to the board without specifically delineating the top three risks it presents, and he does this delineation in the simplest little PowerPoint presentation you can imagine.

He offers up three risks of the plan. Sometimes, when he has presented those risks, the board has said, "We hear you on that. The risks scare us more than they scare you. Don't do this deal." However, the point to this story is that the CEO provides real clarity and real sharing of information, and I think it improves the board members' decision-making.

For those of you reading this chapter who are lawyers (or those of you who are maybe considering a law career), one of the concepts I want you to understand is that you are joining a profession that is not, strictly speaking, defined by legal issues or legal demands. Another client's general counsel told me she does not consider herself head of the legal department. She said, "The department that I run is the department of difficult issues," and in her company, it is true. It does not matter where the issue originates. If the issue is hard to figure out, it ends up with the lawyers. That, I believe, is because their intelligence, their discipline, and their judgment is internally respected.

My partner, Bob Profusek, who heads our M&A practice, said it best. Regarding the responsibility to really understand what we are doing, he said, "This stuff is hard, and this stuff is multifaceted. You have to know the business backwards and forwards. You have to know the industries and you have to know the risks, and the people who can handle the hard stuff are hard to find. They need more than a pedigree from a top-flight business or law school. They need to have a little dirt under their fingernails as well."

ADVOCATE FUNDAMENTAL CHANGE
IN EXECUTIVE COMPENSATION.

Let us turn to executive compensation. Credit here goes to Frederic Cook, one of the nation's leading compensation consultants, for coming up with a phrase that I think is going to catch on—that is, if we have even the most remote opportunity of getting ahead of legislated solutions on executive compensation, beyond the TARP-benefited institutions. Cook calls this "pay for sustainable performance."

I like how this phrase plays on the green concept, but I also like what I think it means—that is, that rich rewards for a short-term bounce, particularly when the backside of that bounce is something we do not yet know, are no longer acceptable by any standard. They are no longer defensible, no longer right. While that sounds terrific, I want to issue a warning about the concept of sustainable performance and the move away from "short-termism" in compensation. Note that this concept——focusing on longer-term, sustained performance for executive compensation—is in actual conflict with what shareholder activists have wrought. We have eliminated classified boards. We have implemented the majority vote. Proxy access is well on its way. All of these have resulted in potential for rapid, year-over-year turnover in corporate leadership.

So, while we want short-termism removed from executive compensation, we seem to want short-termism in corporate governance. I think the two are in absolute conflict, and, while I feel that I am a bit on my own on this point, I believe I will soon be vindicated. Over the next five years, this conflict is going to crystallize. I argue that those on the side of good corporate governance need to pick one model. Pick long-term or pick short-term, and stick with it, but do not leave this in conflict. I hope that some of you have seen a documentary, which shows up from time to time on PBS, called *The Corporation*. It explains, as you all know, that a corporation is deemed to be a person, as a legal matter. However, as a person, so this documentary says, a corporation is effectively a psychopath. The documentary argues that corporations themselves are devoid of internal moral codes. It makes sense that a company, arguably, will do what is right only in order to avoid penalties and negative sanctions, rather than to do what is right out of a sense of moral duty.

I do not see it quite so starkly. If you have not already gathered it, I believe in the corporate enterprise. I think the board members and management are the company's conscience. To you lawyers out there, remember: you are the little voice inside their heads. Board members and management, when relying on your advice and independent counsel, should be animated by a much more subtle and moral understanding of what maximizing shareholder value means.

I hope we have now learned, once and for all, that shortcuts, workarounds, untrammeled greed, feelings of entitlement, ignored risks, or worse, un-comprehended risks, all ultimately impair shareholder value. If you are devoted to paying attention to those considerations, you will advise your clients in a way that ultimately will yield maximum shareholder value. To the lawyers reading this essay, your mission, and mine, is to advise not merely that which is defensible, but that which is right.

ABOUT THE AUTHOR

LIZANNE THOMAS is Partner-in-Charge of the 150-lawyer Atlanta office of Jones Day, where she also heads the firm's global corporate governance team. While her roots are in M&A law, Thomas practices, teaches, and lives corporate governance. As counsel to a number of public companies, she participates in more than 100 board meetings per year. She has lectured on Dodd-Frank to leading business organizations, companies, and universities throughout the world. She represents special committees in going private and other control transactions, as well as in internal investigations involving issues ranging from financial restatements to allegations of executive misconduct. Thomas is also experienced in public and private mergers and acquisitions, takeovers, takeover preparedness, and executive compensation.

Thomas is a member of the Board of Directors of Krispy Kreme Doughnuts, Inc. (NYSE: KKD), upon which she serves as chair of the Governance Committee and member of the Compensation Committee, and previously served as co-chair of the Special Committee, which was charged with investigating a variety of allegations relating to the company.

Active in the community, Thomas serves on the Georgia Research Alliance's Board of Trustees, the Metro Atlanta Chamber of Commerce's Board of Directors' Executive Committee, and the Atlanta Ballet's Board of Directors. She holds various leadership roles at the Woodruff Arts Center and is a member of both the Rotary Club of Atlanta and the United Way Tocqueville Society. She is a Trustee of Furman University and former president of the Law Council for Washington and Lee University.

CHAPTER 13

GOVERNANCE AND THE LAW: 101

"The next ten years must be an era of transparency in government, in governance, and in our relationships with one another. We have a lot of damage to repair and it cannot be accomplished overnight."

—Arthur Leavitt

"It is better to be hated for what you truly are than to be loved for something that you are not."

—André Gide

"What lies behind us and what lies before us are small matters compared to what lies within us."

—Ralph Waldo Emerson

The laws establishing guidelines for the formation and management of corporations (and other entities that provide liability protection and/or facilitate capital formation) are more than one hundred years old. Yet, despite their longevity, we are still trying to embrace fully the laws' true legal, moral, and ethical consequences from a governance perspective.

At their core, laws governing corporations and the roles of and relationships between board members, executives, and shareholders shift into high gear as soon as a single share of stock is issued. This statement is especially true if some owners will not be involved in the company's day-to-day management. The notion of a "passive" owner means that the "active" owners have an obligation—and a duty—to govern their company in a manner that is fair to all types of owners. It's true that a company's charter and bylaws provide mechanisms for organizing intra-company affairs privately and shareholder agreements further enable shareholders to negotiate tailored protections. However, state corporate laws typically "fill the charter and contractual gaps" by articulating certain minimum (sometimes mandatory) standards of conduct expected of all directors and officers. These standards are expected whether or not a set of corporate legal documents clearly articulates them.

In the early days of corporate governance laws, people abided by the original, essentially "laissez faire," framework, which set forth a few basic duties. Then, if and when a shareholder brought a lawsuit against a company officer, alleging a breach of a fiduciary duty, this framework would leave it to the courts to determine whether that individual had met the obligations attached to these duties. For the most part, courts remained careful not to second-guess boards' business decisions unless or until the breach of a particular duty. This type of approach, still used today and now known as the "business judgment rule," has protected and continues to protect board decisions made in good faith and in accordance with governance best practices. The stock market crash of 1929 led to the creation of two new pieces of legislation, the Securities Act of 1933 and the Securities Exchange Act of 1934, both of which created new obligations for board members and leaders of companies with publicly traded shares.

Then, for a period of about sixty years, the United States saw very few significant shifts in governance law and policy. Of course, major cases received decisions, but we can leave discussion of those to the law students. In the 1980s, the pace and increase in the volume of merger and acquisition (M&A) transactions added new twists to the business judgment rule. At that point, the rule had to ensure that companies allowed no self-dealing and that board members worked hard to ensure that shareholders were getting the best value. These changes led to increases in the amounts of third-party valuation reports and fairness opinions gathered.

Then, everything changed.

The dot-com bubble burst; people uncovered accounting nightmares at WorldCom, Tyco, Enron, Adelphia, and many other corporations; and Congress people began to rethink the effectiveness of governance law essentially being left to the fifty states, rather than being a federal matter. In 2002 and 2003 came the first round of "federalization of corporate law": this included the passage of Sarbanes-Oxley and various new rules made by the SEC, FINRA, the NYSE, and NASDAQ. The latter directly impacted publicly held companies. It also indirectly influenced, and placed additional burdens upon, the officers and directors of privately held companies, trade associations, foundations, universities, and even government agencies. The country also experienced a significant uptick in shareholder activism, as proxy advisory firms (such as RiskMetrics Group's ISS; Glass, Lewis & Co.; Egan-Jones Proxy Services; Macro Consulting Group; C&W Investment; and ProxyTell, LLC)—in addition to large, typically passive institutional investors and specialized private equity and hedge funds—began expressing views and bringing shareholder-level legal actions, thus enforcing principles of fairness, transparency, and accountability. Board composition dynamics, board committee functions, the extent of board compensation, and the terms of service were all changing and all under close scrutiny. Simultaneously, Web 2.0 and social media platforms had just begun to hit their full stride.

The resulting changes' central themes included more objectivity in board member selection; more independence and autonomy for auditors; more control over financial reporting: stiffer penalties for abuse of laws and regulations pertaining to corporate governance, accounting practices, and financial reporting; and new rules ensuring fair and prompt access to information and current events that affect a company's current status and further performance.

These events led to an age of scrutiny: we entered an era of validation and verification. We refined, reexamined, and retooled the roles of a board and its committees. Nine years later, we rewrote the set best practices, procedures, and protocols; the implementation costs have become burdensome and high. Companies have redesigned internal controls and systems to ensure compliance with the rules, while holding managers accountable for enforcement and results. Job descriptions of CEOs have come to read, "Forget the gravy, where's the beef?" In other words, they include less pay, fewer perks, and less power in exchange for more performance and less tolerance of error or abuse. These CEOs live in an era featuring more accountability and shorter tenure. Events such as the collapse of the financial markets, the failure of Lehman Brothers, the housing market meltdown, the Stanford and Madoff scandals, the federal debt debate, and the Standard & Poor downgrade of the credit rating of the United States, have not eased these concerns in any way. In this era of scrutiny joined with distrust, leadership and good governance are more important than ever. Investors must have confidence that company leaders will be guided by strong ethical and moral values, integrity, transparency, fairness, and respect for fiduciary obligations to shareholders.

In the mid-2000s, the markets and companies began digesting these new rules and obligations. Some companies embraced them, spending millions on compliance systems and overhauling their internal controls and reporting systems. Others rejected the costs and burdens; they took their companies private, merged with other firms, or even went out of business. People debated the subjects of executive compensation, board effectiveness, and corporate social citizenship openly, as anti-management and anti-leadership bias snuck into Main Street America. Since 2007, distrust—of Wall Street, big company CEOs, financial institutions, and the federal government—has been a recurring theme in policy and political debates. These factors became exacerbated by the market crash and mortgage meltdown in 2008-2009, when government bailouts (and the failures of Lehman, Countrywide, and other major lenders and investment banks) led to the prospect of the Dodd-Frank Act. Thus, the federalization of corporate and governance laws' second wave took place a short seven years after the first.

What events or developments will trigger a third wave? Is it possible leaders and markets have finally learned their lessons, and no more major regulation will be needed for a few decades? Time will tell, but these past few years have certainly been exciting and volatile times for corporate and transactional lawyers.

THE FUNDAMENTALS OF CORPORATE LAW 101

In a corporation, a legal entity (as opposed to an individual) owns a business' assets and is liable for that business' debts. The distinguishing characteristics of a corporation include:

Continuity of life: all state corporation laws stipulate that a corporation will continue existing until articles of dissolution are filed (or the corporation is merged out of existence), even if the owners (that is, the shareholders) die, go bankrupt, retire, or give up their company interests.

Limited liability: a shareholder isn't personally liable for corporate debt or claims against the corporation except in special circumstances, such as misusing the corporation to perpetrate fraud.

Free transferability of interest: shareholders may generally sell all or part of their interest to any buyer without the other shareholders' consent.

Centralized management: the board of directors (as elected by the shareholders) has authority to make independent business decisions on the corporation's behalf.

The details of corporation formation vary from state to state. However, virtually every state requires that you file articles (or a certificate) of incorporation. Once you choose the state in which you'd like to incorporate your business, you'll have to meet a number of registration requirements. Doing so will enable your company to obtain (and maintain) corporate status and enjoy the protections that state affords corporations. Observing all these legal formalities will help protect shareholders from personal liability.

Shareholders own a corporation. These shareholders may be individuals, partnerships, trusts, or even other corporations: there is no limit to the number of shareholders a corporation may have.

A corporate entity is separate and distinct from its shareholders, and the shareholders' personal assets aren't available to satisfy corporate obligations. When seeking payment, the corporation's creditors may only look to the corporation's assets. This is a type of protection commonly referred to as the "corporate veil." If a corporation is involved in a number of business lines, separate corporate subsidiaries (that is, corporations owned by another corporation) may be created to protect the assets of one business activity from the liabilities of the other(s).

Management responsibility is vested in the company's board of directors, which is responsible for overall policy decisions as well as the company's general direction and business plan. The board appoints officers to manage day-to-day operations.

Unlike partnerships, a corporation is a tax-paying entity; based on the corporation's profits, federal and state tax returns must be filed and taxes paid (unless the corporation elects an "S" status, as discussed below). Losses are not passed through to the shareholders, but they may be carried forward as an offset against the corporation's future income. The board members may choose to distribute after-tax profits to the shareholders as dividends; then, the shareholders are taxed at their individual rates (a process known as "double taxation").

If a corporation meets certain IRS requirements, its leaders can choose to place it under "S" status, which affects how the corporation is federally taxed. An S corporation must meet specific requirements: first, it can have no more than one hundred shareholders who (with very few exceptions) must be both individuals and United States residents; second, it can't have two classes of stock with different financial interests. Management responsibility is the same as that of a regular corporation (which is taxed under Chapter C of the Internal Revenue Code), but the S corporation doesn't pay federal tax on its income. Rather, the corporation passes profits and losses through to the shareholders, who declare them on their individual tax returns. The main reason to elect S corporation status is that doing so avoids double taxation, which is inherent in a Chapter C corporation.

We can think of the corporation as a nexus of contracts, one that brings together various stakeholders: shareholders, directors, officers, employees, and third parties. The relationships connected at this nexus are managed in several ways: through a combination of enabling and mandatory provisions in corporate law (from statutes and case law), by the company's internal governance documents, through best practices, and by these constituencies' personal and political dynamics. Let's take a closer look at the internal governance documents. These consist, primarily, of the company's charter (also known as the certificate of incorporation or articles of incorporation) and its bylaws. The charter, the foundational document, establishes a corporation's legal existence and serves as its constitution. In addition, the charter sets forth core terms, such as the number of shares authorized for sale, whether directors can be freed from paying damages if they violate the duty of care, and so forth. As such, the charter cannot be superseded by other corporate documents; it can only be amended after receiving approval from both the board members and the shareholders. The corporation's bylaws are of secondary importance compared to the charter: the bylaws address varied, detailed governance processes, (such as stockholder meeting times and procedures; directors' election, resignation, and removal; officer appointments, and so on). While stockholders have an absolute right to amend the bylaws, the board of directors may also receive this right (that is, if such a power is stipulated in the charter). Still, the bylaws cannot exceed the charter's scope.

While the charter and bylaws have an important role in shaping governance, mandatory and enabling provisions (under corporate law) are certainly more influential. Under state corporate laws, the board of directors is charged with managing the corporation's business and affairs. Because directors receive managerial powers, a classic tension develops between shareholders and directors. This tension is known, more formally, as the "separation of ownership from control." To manage this tension, state corporate laws constrain directors' authority. Specifically, this constraint appears through the fiduciary duties of care and loyalty directors owe to the stockholders (discussed in Chapter 2).

The business judgment rule (the legal presumption that, in decision-making, the corporation's directors acted on an informed basis, in good faith, and in the honest belief that action was in the company's best interest) balances these fiduciary duties. This rule both presumes that business decisions are made in this manner and protects the ones that are. Usually, when directors act in good faith, with an honest belief they do so in the company's best interests, and on an informed basis, they are protected from judicial scrutiny and second-guessing—that is, if the systems and documentation in place demonstrate informed, objective, and rational decision-making. If a board of directors is acting without self-interest, then, typically, courts and regulators won't substitute their business judgment for the board's judgment (in other words, "no harm, no foul"). However, in this new age of scrutiny, acting without self-interest must be carefully documented. The business judgment rule's protections apply when affirmative decisions to act or refrain from acting are made; it does not apply to mere inaction.

To satisfy the business judgment rule, in each relevant scenario directors must remain informed about all material facts. Directors must investigate and comprehend all information related to the transactions they consider; moreover, they should understand the company's operations, business model, and strategic direction. Boards should not undergo micromanagement (this is not required or recommended); however, if a board member has doubts, he or she should ask more questions. If reasonably reliable and competent employees present directors with internal reports (such as those on financial topics), directors are entitled to rely upon those reports when making decisions. Similarly, directors are entitled to rely on the reports of reasonably qualified outside advisors.

These fiduciary duties, along with the business judgment rule, serve as corporation directors' broad guiding principles. The duties and the rule themselves do not mandate ways in which they should be carried out, yet they strongly influence how directors adopt many best practices. Developing informed directors who satisfy the business judgment rule starts with comprehensive director orientation and training programs. The basic orientation program, for example, is a full-day meeting the directors take with the company's CEO, CFO, business unit heads, general counsel, and auditor. In general, every training and orientation program should include discussions of the following: the company's mission, vision, and values; the company's history and culture; industry trends and forecasts; key challenges and objectives; responsibilities and expectations; committees and structures; intellectual capital management; and harvesting of such capital. The company should also develop a board manual: a handy reference guide that includes important information and company documents.

The board's assembly and operation affects its members' ability to make sound decisions that, in turn, are protected by the business judgment rule. Board members should have financial acumen and strong business experience; they should be racially and culturally diverse individuals. Board selection should not be an experiment in nepotism and cronyism, but, rather, should be an opportunity to include independent members. Instead of passively accepting presentations, board members should encourage interactive board dialogue and participation. In addition, board members should reconsider the composition of executive committees, encouraging participation by all members. When analyzing significant board issues or complex problems, or when working to overcome the hurdles that temporarily halt the company's growth these board members should be proactive, not reactive. They should create and enforce codes of conduct. Moreover, they should hold an annual strategy retreat to reassess, regularly, both the above and other issues.

In addition, though directors' fiduciary duties are broadly stated, such duties also impose several derived responsibilities upon the directors, by necessity. Most obviously, when carrying out their fiduciary duties, directors must maintain general responsibility for corporate governance and leadership. Directors have to establish both the corporation's general strategic vision and its direction, ensuring they develop both growth and innovation strategies. For example, they have the authority to decide whether the corporation should engage in major transactions, such as a merger or sale of assets. Indeed, they are guardians of those assets. Furthermore, when protecting those assets, their responsibility includes overseeing operations: such oversight includes instituting internal controls, auditing functions, and ensuring installation of proper risk management and mitigation systems. Ultimately, directors drive any corporation's culture. If they do not set the proper tone, exemplify ethical conduct, or promote compliance with applicable laws, the corporation, as a whole, will fail to develop a compliance culture, resulting in exposure to unnecessary risks.

How a board of directors lives up to these responsibilities, and functions accordingly, is driven by a number of variables. The board's composition, including members' areas of experience and ethnic and/ or racial diversity, plays a major role. In addition, the board's charter is influential because it sets forth the board's mission and values, role and authority, and scope of committees to be formed. The charter also determines other details, such as the meetings' number, format, and agendas. Another factor, certainly, is the board members' commitment, which should start with good faith and requires the following: setting clear expectations, requiring or encouraging attendance at meetings, encouraging input and participation, and setting terms and rotation. Board members cannot underestimate the required devotion to cultivating communication channels. Those directors who confer regularly with the management team (and advisors, if any) will be better informed and able to defend their actions. Finally, the board members will have to consider the issue of their compensation (for instance, the extent to which compensation will be direct or indirect, in kind or in the form of expense reimbursement, and so forth).

Directors carry out their responsibilities in several ways. First, they adopt resolutions by which to accomplish the corporation's formal actions and set company policy. Second, they work with management to adopt policies and procedures that employees will follow when acting on behalf of or within the corporation. These policy and procedure documents, when added to the charter and bylaws, operate as both the corporation's internal legal system and set of governance principles. Third, directors also exert their influence over the corporation by interacting with key parties or individuals within the governance structure. For example, they work closely with the corporation's officers. The officers, who receive delegated authority, take responsibility for the company's day-to-day affairs and implement the directors' strategy and policy decisions. They communicate directly with both senior management and other non-equity stakeholders.

The Puzzle Pieces of Governance

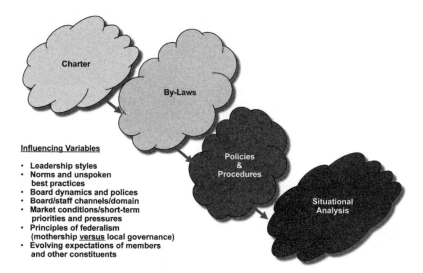

Influencing Variables

- Leadership styles
- Norms and unspoken best practices
- Board dynamics and polices
- Board/staff channels/domain
- Market conditions/short-term priorities and pressures
- Principles of federalism (mothership versus local governance)
- Evolving expectations of members and other constituents

Box 13-A: The Puzzle Pieces of Governance

The Board's Essential Responsibilities

Box 13-B: The Board's Essential Responsibilities

Key Issues In Board Structure

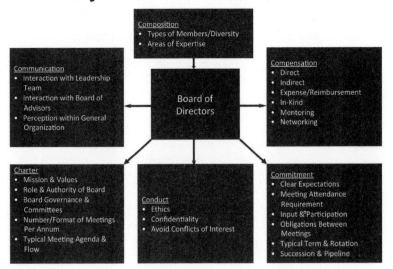

Box 13-C: Key Issues In Board Structure

Corporate Governance Structure

Box 13-D: Corporate Governance Structure

CORPORATE GOVERNANCE IN THE
ERA OF INCREASED SCRUTINY

As discussed above, several recent events—the Enron, Tyco, and WorldCom scandals of the early 2000s; the 2007-2008 financial crisis; Lehman's collapse; and the AIG meltdown—have ushered in a new corporate governance era of increased scrutiny. As many commentators have considered, a number of conditions and factors led to these governance failures. The 2007-2008 financial crisis, for example, raised concerns about possible breaches of trust made by public companies' officers and directors; this led to a loss of confidence in the markets. Many onlookers asked whether company leaders were asleep at the wheel or knowingly participated in wrongdoing, while

135

others wondered whether some of the governance failings could be ascribed to ego and skewed incentives. After all, some CEOs and other company leaders received overcompensation and encouragement to engage in risk-taking in order to increase monetary rewards; thus, they put pursuit of economic interests above the preserving the company's well-being or shareholder value. Other onlookers might suggest, perhaps, that just the sins of a few such leaders have been inappropriately attributed to the rest of corporate America.

Another explanation is that public companies have been, simply, plagued by short-termism. The market demands that companies meet earnings targets, or improve performance, on a quarter-to-quarter basis. Even leaders with good intentions, therefore, feel pressure to concentrate on making the next quarter's goals rather than planning for the next quarter century. Other additional factors directors may have faced include economic cycles, stock-market corrections, and political pressures.

Whatever the contributing factors, we must now conduct corporate governance in an era of increased scrutiny. Exposure of wrongdoing, and its resulting economic downturns, has given rise to a number of legal and policy objectives. Congress members have reacted to these perceived abuses by trying to restore or rebuild trust and confidence in both companies and markets. One major area reformers have focused on is the requirement of greater transparency and truthfulness in financial reporting, ensuring investors are provided with complete, relevant, and reliable data. A related issue also under consideration is that of full, fair, and prompt disclosure of material developments. More generally, legislators have sought to protect objectivity and accountability in board operations and executive decision-making; they are working to combat perceived cronyism. All this new legislation raises the stakes, increasing the risks and the magnitude thereof, for officers and directors of public companies. Government officials are emphasizing these new mandates and using political maneuvering to create budgets that support vigilant enforcement, such as increased SEC funding.

In this new regulatory environment, leaders' mantras must include greater accountability and transparency. Creative reengineering of a company's balance sheet will no longer be tolerated. Instead, government and shareholders alike expect all companies to have in place appropriate systems, controls, and checks and balances. We expect board members to address and then take decisive action in response to ethical failures or compliance breakdowns. Integrity-based risks no longer fall into the "head-in-the-sand" category; they are not merely the CEO or HR department's problem. Instead, today's directors must embody values that support new levels and expectations of oversight, such as consensus building, trust building, exhibiting strong moral fiber, "walking the talk," collaborating, and proffering mutual respect.

More broadly, boards of directors need to self-assess, honestly, their own individual values and group dynamics and/or culture, in their positions as the company's shepherds. Today, board members have explicit responsibilities with regard to establishing and enforcing corporate culture. A company's leaders are expected to serve as employees' beacons of, catalysts for, and sources of inspiration and motivation. Employees, customers, strategic partners, and other stakeholders may even view them as patriarchal figures or financial providers, particularly in times of economic distress. To promote the above-mentioned ideals, both board members and CEOs are embracing and enforcing new codes of ethics.

These leaders also have to look to the future and consider inspiring and mentoring their successors. Companies must allocate resources to training and developing human capital. People in leadership positions must commit to grooming the next generation of leaders and developing succession plans that will ease those transitions. In addition to navigating internal demands and expectations, either the directors or other company leaders have to manage external pressures. Directors of public companies, for example, must manage their businesses in a fishbowl, facing scrutiny from both Wall Street and Main Street. More and more, leaders have to manage and mitigate risks posed, precisely, because of their companies' public identities.

Such increased pressures on boards of directors often drive governance policies, pushing them beyond the simple maximization of shareholders' values. Board members consider other goals and constituencies: many companies, for example, are committing to larger amounts of community and social responsibility. In addition, companies have begun to promote environmental objectives, finding creative ways of merging sound environmental practices with their economic self-interests (for example, through strong environmental practices, companies can achieve efficiency or cut costs). Another current area of interest is diversity: companies seek to achieve internal diversity and promote that diversity externally by favoring suppliers who show commitment to such a policy. Indeed, in this era of scrutiny, boards of directors may need to reevaluate their relationships with third parties (that is, consider the fairness of the company's relationships with vendors, suppliers, subcontractors, and partners), ensuring they show respect for other companies' intellectual property rights.

To meet these challenges, boards are becoming stronger and more independent, engaging in increased communication with employees, investors, and other stakeholders. In order to participate in such a strong board, members must have enough confidence and self-responsibility to challenge the company's senior leadership. These members must work together, both as a board and in separate committees, using shared values, allocating responsibility and workload fairly (that is, no freeloaders), and creating a climate of trust and respect. They must watch the company's culture—its integrity and effectiveness—closely. Board members must institute best practices and policies based upon principles of validation and verification, and they must establish systems for documenting decision-making. To assist themselves in this process, board members or directors should retain the best possible professional advisors and, when in doubt, should not hesitate to get second opinions. Under these new standards and heightened shareholder expectations, those leaders who take their responsibilities lightly will be held accountable and face increased risks of civil, even, criminal liability for breaches of duty.

WHAT DID WE MANAGE TO ACCOMPLISH?

At this point, we can ask ourselves the following questions: Did we create adequate checks and balances in corporate governance? Did we improve our national public companies' accountability and transparency? Did we restore trust in financial markets and public company leaders? Have we really moved the "fraud prevention needle" by a significant margin, in light of the Madoff, Stanford, and Satyam scandals? Have we mitigated the risk of corporate governance abuse, and have we created effective consequences for noncompliance? Only time will tell; for now, we must watch as new chapters of board members and executives' obligations continue to unfold.

CHAPTER 14

THE CORPORATE GOVERNANCE AUDIT

Best Practices in Quality Control and Insurance Coverage

with Bernard Bell, Jones Day

A natural way to begin reviewing and analyzing an organization's corporate governance practices is through a legal and operational audit. This audit focuses on an organization's compliance with current laws, ensuring its governance, decision-making systems, and internal processes are in place and comply with applicable laws, regulations, and best practices. The legal audit should include recommendations for improvement and provide a series of compliance training programs for officers, directors, and managers who have significant financial or reporting responsibilities; in addition, it should include a review of the company's current quality and internal control programs and a review of its insurance coverage scope. (Bernard Bell contributed the last section of this essay, which discusses reviewing a company's current insurance policies.)

Topics and questions that should be examined and discussed during a Corporate Governance Best Practices Audit include the following:

- The board's size and composition, along with the relationship of its composition to company performance. (At present, we are seeing a definite trend of smaller boards and higher ratios of outside directors.)
- The audit committee's independence and objectivity, which must meet Sarbanes-Oxley requirements.
- The compensation committee's knowledge, skills, and discipline.
- The overall structure of executive compensation and stock options plans. Current issues related to this topic that will require examination include the following: whether pay is, or should be, linked to performance; whether pay is generally fair; whether rewards are linked to accomplishment of strategic objectives; whether perquisites are excessive, or if they should be reduced; whether the board is willing or able to stand up to the CEO; and so on.
- Existence of information and reporting systems within the organization, the presence of which ensures board members are doing the following: remaining fully and promptly informed, adequately performing their oversight role, have processes in place to manage and mitigate enterprise-level risks, and can address red flags in a timely and proper manner. A written statement of corporate governance policy must be in place.
- Review, identification, and assessment of the risks (legal, market, operational, and other) that might materially affect the company. With the board members' oversight

and review, management should analyze risks according to division, department, or business practice; then, management should develop management and mitigation plans tailored to each division. This process should culminate in adopting policies and procedures that guide and govern employee conduct in each space.

- Closeness and effectiveness with which the board members monitor integrity and accuracy of the company's financial statements and reports (without micromanaging).
- The board members' compensation system and the extent to which it may influence their objectivity. For example, are directors required to own a specific amount of company stock?
- Communicative transparency with shareholders and representatives of financial markets. Are the requirements of Regulation FD being met?
- The effectiveness of the board members' strategic and business planning skills. Have they set clear goals for the executive management team? How well is the team implementing these goals, and how closely is their performance being monitored?
- The risk management procedures that are in place. This audit should include a comprehensive review of officer and director liability insurance policies, as well as a review of other types of risk management (such as information/data security, physical security, and so on, as set forth later in this essay).
- The succession plans in place for both board membership and executive management.

- Evaluation of how well the various board members' skills match up with the company's current medium- and long-term strategies. Have changes to the company's business model caused shifts in its focus? Has this triggered need for new directors, who have different sets of skills? What procedures, in place for replacing directors, may now be obsolete?

- Any proactive steps board members are taking to maximize shareholder value, such as leveraging intellectual assets.

- Whether the board has a nominating committee. If so, are its policies and criteria clearly articulated, and how closely are these policies followed? What due diligence is carried out on prospective candidates?

- Whether there is a performance-review process for board members. Why or why not? If there is, how effective have such reviews been in improving individual members' or the overall board's performance?

- Whether board meetings are held both with and without the CEO present to encourage candor and objectivity. Who selects and appoints committee members? Members of the board, or the CEO? Do the bylaws allow for a non-executive chairman? If so, have the differences in the chairman's and CEO's responsibilities been clearly articulated? Is there good chemistry between the chairman and CEO? Why or why not? Are periodic meetings held with only independent directors present?

- The frequency and effectiveness of board meetings. Who sets the agenda? Are there minimal attendance standards? How often do committees meet? How many committees are in place, and how well do they function? Are they reporting to the entire board adequately? Is the delineation of authority from the committees to the entire board clearly established?

- Any contingency plan put in place by the board in case the company becomes financially distressed. Does the board understand its fiduciary responsibilities may extend to other stakeholders, such as creditors and vendors, if the company should become insolvent?
- Whether the board has a formal orientation program for new members. If so, when was it last updated?
- Whether the board's composition reflects gender, ethnic, and racial diversity. How many international members does the board have? What are the board members' ages?

Both privately held and publicly held companies must have a corporate governance process in place: one that upholds the integrity of the company's leadership to both shareholders and employees; creates truly-informed board members, who have power to act based on timely and accurate information; and protects the board's authority while fostering its members' courage to take whatever action is necessary in order to fulfill fiduciary obligations. When reexamining board members' roles, functions, and responsibilities, we find it is no longer sufficient for them merely to make periodic, meaningful contributions to the company's strategic direction. Instead, now directors must be proactive, defending the best interests of the shareholders, employees, participants, and beneficiaries of the company's pensions, 401(k)s, and stock option plans. Board members and corporate leaders should assume their meetings will be held, metaphorically speaking, in rooms with glass walls; that is, their actions will be microscopically examined.

QUALITY CONTROL AND THE BOARD OF DIRECTORS

A Corporate Governance Best Practices Audit is an important method for identifying and managing a company's legal, market, operational, and other risks; it's also important for testing the integrity of the company's governance infrastructure. However, such an audit can also facilitate examination of current quality control and internal control processes: issues that are also critical to sound stewardship of any business. For example, in 2011, nearly one billion Big Mac® sandwiches were served at McDonald's® restaurants around the globe. Imagine the quality controls, operational systems, and processes that must be in place in order to serve the same thing in the same way—one billion times—at tens of thousands of different locations, which are owned and run by thousands of different people from nearly two hundred different countries.

To think about quality control in terms of governance, consider, from a strategic standpoint, what happens when effective systems of increasing consumer satisfaction, brand loyalty, market competitiveness, product consistency, and healthy margins are in place. Specifically, from a compliance and protective perspective, ask any leader of a company that has faced a product recall (or a product-liability lawsuit, a product regulatory ban, a media or social group-led product boycott, or an FDA investigation) whether quality control systems are important for protecting and promoting shareholder value.

Boards often include an executive committee, a nominations committee, a compensation committee, and an audit committee. Certainly, these committees perform critical functions for good corporate governance. However, some of the most important functionality areas that increase and protect shareholder value—such as innovation and creativity, quality control and brand loyalty, culture and diversity, and effective maintenance and growth of strategic interdependent relationships, to name a few—are left to company executives' discretion and responsibility.

So, what should board members know about quality control basics?

Let's start with a quality control program's key components: components that, ultimately, connect to overall enterprise risk management's (ERM) core discipline, as discussed elsewhere in this book. A company that does not maintain or enforce an effective quality control strategy is not likely to survive the competitive marketplace. The strategic principle that "a chain is only as strong as its weakest link" applies directly to this aspect's importance within an overall business system. When a company establishes and enforces quality control standards, it not only assures uniformity of quality; it also satisfies the statutory obligation (imposed upon owners of a trademark by the federal Lanham Act) assigned to direct or licensed brand use. If company representatives fail to monitor or control the operations of a licensee, their actions could result in the statutory abandonment of company rights to the trademark; at that point, the trademark may no longer distinguish a particular product or service from those offered by others in the market.

DEVELOPING AND ENFORCING SYSTEM STANDARDS

The glue holding a typical quality control system together consists of the uniform policies, procedures, and specifications all its employees must follow; licensees; channel partners; and stakeholders. The system's rules and regulations, which are typically found in the company's training programs, systems, processes, protocols, and operations manual(s), must be carefully planned and developed;

clearly articulated by all stakeholders, both initially and on an ongoing basis; accepted by those affected by the system as understandable and reasonable; consistently applied; and rigidly enforced by company representatives (typically, field support staff conduct such enforcement). Obviously, developing uniform standards is not very useful unless systems for monitoring and enforcing these standards, as well as noncompliance penalties, are in place (all these are typically found in the business agreement).

Compliance with quality control standards requires mutual respect by and among the company workers and stakeholders. Development and enforcement of the company's system standards must be reasonable, and the affected stakeholders must understand reasonable standards are in the best interests of all network partners. (Remember, licensees, channel partners, and other affected parties typically have love-hate relationships with system standards. On the one hand, they love reasonable standards that result in happy consumers and eliminate noncomplying partners. On the other hand, they detest standards that are unattainable; vaguely communicated; or enforced arbitrarily, too rigidly, or randomly.)

Board members and company leaders should ensure the company's operations manual, and its other written and electronic communications, describe and detail system standards. Company materials should address, among other topics, the following:

- Required and authorized products or services to be offered and sold, and (subject, of course, to local antitrust laws), the prices at which business may sell these authorized products or services;
- Manners in which businesses may offer and sell these products or services (including food and beverage

preparation, storage, handling, and/or packaging procedures);

- Required images and appearances of facilities, vehicles, and employees;
- Designated and approved suppliers, and supplier-approval criteria and procedures;
- Types, models, and brands of required operating assets (such as equipment, signs, furnishings, furniture, and vehicles) and supplies (such as ingredients, packaging, and ancillary items);
- Use and display of trademarks and service marks;
- Advertising and promotional programs, along with the materials and media used in them;
- Sale and delivery terms and conditions for items a business acquires from the company and its affiliates;
- Levels of staffing and training;
- Days and hours of operation;
- Participation in market research, testing, product, and service development programs;
- Payment, point-of-sale, and computer system standards;
- Reporting requirements;
- Insurance requirements;
- Health and safety procedures; and, finally,
- Customer interaction and/or satisfaction.

To protect and ensure quality control on a true and continuing basis, directors and leaders must monitor system and marketplace developments, and then initiate any necessary changes. A company must build up a culture in which change is inevitable, expected, and warmly embraced, all from the very beginning. Changes to the system must be viewed as positive evolutions of the company, not as burdens or daunting challenges. To accomplish the above, however, the company must function within a culture of trust: all stakeholders will need assurance that these changes are both reasonable and necessary. If a change involves new products or services, affected partners will need assurance that these new concepts were developed through adequate market research, and that they are not ideas or strategies of the month, created merely on a whim.

Over the course of any partnership-channel relationship, change may be triggered by periodic events or trends, such as new competitive conditions, alterations in territorial policies, technological innovations, additions or losses of key suppliers, introductions of alternative locations, and mergers or acquisitions. Alternatively, change may come from rectifying deficiencies in extant business agreements, particularly in cases related to system change. (Such events may require all parties' consent, either formally or informally.)

Directors and executives may deploy a wide variety of strategies and methods to ensure maintenance of certain quality levels: license, franchise, and distribution agreements; operations manuals; initial and ongoing training programs; financing arrangements; approved-supplier programs; and dispersal of field support personnel, who establish, ensure, and maintain quality control. In such cases, leaders must also consider potential limitations imposed by antitrust and related laws, with respect to the types of control that may be imposed upon any given channel.

WHEN QUALITY CONTROL NEEDS A BACK-UP
PLAN: THE ROLE OF INSURANCE COVERAGE

Board members and business leaders need to understand insurance is a critical component of any corporation's overall risk management program; moreover, maintaining such insurance may also be an important factor of attracting or retaining independent directors. In a 2012 survey by Towers Watson, boards of 400 publicly-held companies increased their average policy limit coverage from $80 million to $87 million to protect against lawsuits and unforeseen liabilities. And as the cost of these premiums increase for the coverages purchased, it is critical that the board knows what they are paying for and what may be excluded. This section outlines, in general terms, some of the important factors about corporate insurance to consider from the positions of executives or directors charged with oversight responsibility. The section also summarizes—in grossly simplified form—some principal types of insurance commonly sold to corporations.

Broker selection

Corporation representatives typically purchase the corporation's insurance through a broker or agent. Therefore, it is wise for the insurance buyer (depending on internal capabilities to do so) to ensure his or her outside expert is familiar with current market conditions, especially the coverage requirements for other entities with similar risk profiles. The buyer should also understand the means for the broker's compensation, including any commission basis, or whether the broker has any incentive to favor one insurance provider over another. Ultimately, a corporation requires insurance that is most appropriate for its needs, not its broker's needs. Finally, a corporate buyer using a smaller brokerage firm should not be bashful about asking for details regarding the brokers' own errors and omissions coverage. (This last point is not of great concern for corporate buyers working with the largest international brokerage firms.)

The larger picture

Those responsible for corporate insurance should remain informed in terms of what coverage the corporation has decided not to purchase, in addition to reviewing obtained coverage. Responsible parties should be informed about what additional coverage may be available, and at what cost. In some cases, gaining additional coverage may mean gaining additional types of policies; alternatively, it may mean endorsements that broaden a corporation's existing coverage. Another important consideration is limits adequacy, especially when we consider the stratospheric legal costs of defending certain types of litigation (for example, securities class action suits can be tremendously expensive). Experienced brokers can assist in benchmarking limits, based on those of peer groups, for the different coverage types.

Legal advice can add value at the point of purchase

Cynics may say an insurance premium is simply the price you pay for the right to sue an insurance company. That may (or may not) be an exaggeration. Even so, often, it is prudent to consult an experienced insurance coverage attorney to discuss a potential coverage plan's scope and contours. Such a consultation is especially important in regard to business continuity insurance or directors' and/or officers' liability insurance. Ultimately, the insurance buyer retains responsibility for the business judgment of selecting a particular coverage plan (he or she must weigh costs and benefits of various coverage enhancements), but receiving legal advice from an experienced practitioner (in conjunction with receiving help from an experienced brokerage, as noted) is helpful for developing an understanding of a balanced plan. This is especially true in cases of business interruption insurance and directors' and officers' insurance, all of which may qualify for non-standard policies—policies that can vary widely from insurer to insurer and from year to year.

Think about claims handling, not just upfront premium costs

By buying corporate insurance, you are paying for a promise. However, the promise is not worth much if the insurance company making it does not have the financial strength to support—that is, pay for—claims. Even if an insurance company is financially sound, its promise to pay is not worth much if it routinely resists paying covered claims. Unfortunately, there is no commonly accepted way to measure a company's amount of claims resistance. However, asking professional advisors for their candid opinions on this topic is worthwhile. In addition to the claims themselves, claims handling matters—that is also what you're buying.

Protection against rescinding claims

Any type of management liability policy should protect the insured parties (also known as "insureds") against an insurance company's attempt to rescind coverage of all insureds based on misrepresentations or omissions made by one or more parties in the process of obtaining the insurance. Protection against such an attempt is particularly necessary for situations such as bankruptcy, in which an organization cannot necessarily protect its directors or officers through reimbursement.

TYPES OF INSURANCE FOR CORPORATE ENTITIES

General Liability

Virtually every business will purchase commercial (sometimes called "comprehensive") general liability insurance. Such insurance protects the business against claims from third parties alleging liability for physical injury or property damage that resulted from the company's operations and products, or incidents on the company's premises. In addition to covering these claims, general liability insurance policies also cover the cost of defending or settling such claims. The policy limits may include defense costs; when this happens, typically, the costs of defense costs used are debited against the available amounts for paying settlements or judgments. Conversely, however some policies may force insurers to defend the insured party until the policy's limits are exhausted in the payment of settlement or judgment. This policy covers all risks that are not expressly excluded, including risks not thought about by either party.

This type of policy may also include coverage of advertising and personal injury liability. Such a liability subset covers certain offenses committed either by the corporation itself or an employee while conducting business. Typically, these claims include libel, slander, disparagement, or copyright infringement in advertisements.

General liability insurance may also include coverage for risks presented by products' potential liability. Typically called "products/completed operations" coverage, this insurance will protect a company against liability risks that come from product distribution, after the products leave the insured party's control and premises.

General liability policies provide coverage for damage resulting from "occurrences." In the insurance field, a prevalent definition of the term "occurrence" is "an accident, including continuous or repeated exposure to conditions, which results in personal injury, property damage, or advertising injury [that was] neither expected nor intended from the standpoint of the insured." One notable feature of this type of "occurrence"-based coverage is that such policies may cover claims asserted long after the policy period itself is over. Such coverage is distinguished from "claims-made" coverage, which only covers claims made while the policy period is in effect.

Business Property

Business property insurance covers damage to the company's real and personal property, including buildings, their contents, and equipment. It is a type of what's known as "first-party" insurance, because it covers the insured's own property; thus, coverage can be requested without a claim from a third party. Under property policies, insurance companies will typically pay for direct physical loss of or damage to the covered property. An "all risk" policy provides insurance against all types of risk involving direct physical loss; a "named peril" policy insures against specific risks, such as fires or floods.

The two most common types of commercial property insurance are replacement cost coverage and actual value coverage. The first, replacement cost coverage, pays for replacement of damaged property through costs for new property of a roughly similar quality. Actual value coverage pays for the property's replacement costs, minus depreciation costs based on factors such as wear and tear or aging. Some policies, when measuring a loss, use a combination of both types of insurance.

Business Interruption

Typically, a property damage policy covers the cost of repairing or replacing buildings and equipment, but it does not cover income lost during the time between when the damage occurred and when the repair was made. Property policies usually exclude coverage of indirect economic losses that may arise from damage to property. However, for many businesses, their loss of income due to an (insured) event may be much larger than the cost of repairing, replacing, or even rebuilding the damaged property. As a result, many property programs also include insurance that covers what are known as "business interruption losses." Commonly, to qualify for coverage, losses must be direct results of the property damage type against which the business is also insured. The intention of purchasing business interruption insurance is keeping the company in the financial position it would have had if no damage, or resulting loss, had occurred.

Employment Practices Liability

Employment Practices Liability Insurance (EPLI) covers traditional, employment-related claims, including lawsuits filed by a company's employees, former employees, and employment candidates. This type of insurance coverage commonly protects a company and its directors, officers, and other employees from expenses associated with alleged violations of employment rights, such as acts of discrimination or wrongful termination. Under this type of coverage, an insurance company will reimburse the insured company for the expenses it incurred in the defense of an employment-related lawsuit or claim. While EPLI policies also cover the cost of settlements or judgments the company is required to pay, they usually do not cover criminal or civil fines, penalties, or punitive damages.

Directors and Officers (D&O)

Directors' and Officers' (D&O) insurance covers claims against insured individuals. As its name suggests, this type of coverage includes directors and officers; however, this type of insurance also covers other employees and executives. In fact, D&O insurance may cover the entire company itself, as an entity: this is especially true in certain cases of securities law exposure. Under a traditional D&O policy, an insurance company agrees to pay, on behalf of the individual directors or officers, all amounts those individuals have become legally obligated to pay; that is, in such cases of covered claims arising from a "wrongful act" committed in their directorial capacity. The definition of a covered claim varies both from insurer to insurer and from year to year. Such differences can matter greatly in a corporate context. Such claims almost always include lawsuits and criminal proceedings; usually, they will also include other written demands for relief and formal administrative or regulatory proceedings and investigations. When selecting a policy, the corporate buyer should take care in matching the organization's exposure to such things as informal SEC investigations or agency subpoenas, for example, against the offered coverage. The definition of "wrongful acts" usually includes acts, errors, misstatements, omissions, neglect, or breaches of duty committed by individual directors or officers, while they were acting in their capacities as directors or officers.

Unlike occurrence-based general liability insurance, D&O insurance is usually on a claims-made basis; this means it only covers claims made (and, sometimes, only claims both made and reported) against the insured during the relevant policy period. When providing most D&O policies, insurance companies do not have a duty to defend (although, for some smaller and/or non-profit organizations, that option is available). Instead, an insurance company will reimburse the insured for the defense costs.

D&O policies commonly exclude coverage for certain situations, including the following:

- If the company sues its own director or officer, there may be no coverage.
- If a particular director or officer is judged guilty of deliberate fraud or unlawful personal profit, there may be no coverage for the judgment costs; moreover, the director or officer may have to repay defense costs incurred by the insurance company on the corporation's behalf.
- There is usually no coverage for taxes, or for civil or criminal fines and/or penalties, that a director or officer is required to fulfill.

Significantly, D&O insurance should protect directors and officers from liability in case the organization files for bankruptcy. This complex topic of particular liability coverage includes many technical points that are beyond this essay's scope. Suffice it to say that a corporate buyer should pay thorough attention to this matter when purchasing the insurance, and the topic should be reviewed, in detail, every year during insurance renewal. Nobody wants to sort through such issues immediately prior to a bankruptcy filing. Including D&O coverage is an important element of director recruitment.

The overall points regarding the value of experienced brokers and coverage counsel discussed earlier in this essay must be emphasized with respect to D&O insurance. D&O insurance is a highly complex area; the types of coverage offered, and the cases of law in which that coverage is interpreted, are evolving rapidly.

Professional Liability/Errors and Omissions (E&O)

Professional liability insurance protects the insured against loss resulting from (as claimed) negligent acts, errors, or omissions when performing professional services. Different types of professional liability insurance have specific names: medical malpractice insurance and legal malpractice insurance are perhaps the most well known examples. Coverage used by other professional service providers (e.g., accountants, architects, and engineers) is often called Errors and Omissions (E&O) insurance. Many general E&O policies do not apply to specialized professions; rather, they can cover any professional within an insured organization. Like D&O coverage, usually E&O insurance is provided on a claims-made basis.

Fiduciary Liability

Organizations that provide employees with benefit plans frequently obtain insurance to cover breach-of-duty allegations, according to regulations imposed by the Employee Retirement Security Act of 1974 (ERISA), or to cover other claims that may stem from the company management's fiduciary service under the plans. A fiduciary liability insurance policy, for example, protects the fiduciary's personal assets in the event a claim is made regarding the breach of fiduciary duties. What, precisely, does this mean? A breach of fiduciary responsibilities may include illegal use of funds, failure to diversify investments, conflicts of interest, funding insufficiently, or otherwise failing to act prudently. A fiduciary may also be considered liable for the actions of persons who or entities that provide services to a plan, such as law firms or management investment firms. Therefore, fiduciary liability coverage frequently extends to third parties' wrongful acts for which the insured is legally responsible.

Workers' Compensation and Employers' Liability

Workers' compensation provides wage replacement and medical benefits to employees injured in the course of employment, but this provision is granted in exchange for mandatory relinquishment of the employee's right to sue the employer. This insurance plan awards compensation rates according to a strict liability system. Within this system, the employee receives damages regardless of whether or not the injury directly resulted from an employer's negligence.

Many corporate entities select such insurance for themselves under applicable state workers' compensation laws, covering payments for physical injury (including death) because of accident or disease. Entities also frequently purchase employers' liability insurance to cover work-related injuries or illnesses not covered by workers' compensation. Often, workers' compensation and employers' liability insurance are offered together, as packages.

COMMERCIAL VEHICLE FLEET INSURANCE

Finally, a commercial vehicle fleet policy insures commercial vehicles owned or leased by businesses from loss due to accidents involving these vehicles. Just as a personal car insurance policy will exclude coverage of the vehicle for commercial use, a commercial vehicle policy will establish a definition of commercial use. Under commercial policies, businesses have the option of collision coverage, comprehensive coverage, and other variations based on specified conditions.

ABOUT THE CONTRIBUTOR

BERNARD BELL is a Partner in Jones Day's Washington, D.C., office. He has decades of experience in civil litigation as a trial lawyer and, for the last eighteen years, he has concentrated his practice on obtaining insurance recoveries for corporate policyholders and their individual directors and officers. His practice covers the full range of insurance claims, from property damage and business interruption losses to claims arising from alleged directors' and officers' liabilities to employment, environmental, fiduciary (ERISA), product, professional, and toxic tort liabilities. He uses his extensive experience with contested claims to assist clients in coverage placement. Bell is a frequent author of articles and is a frequent speaker on insurance coverage issues.

CHAPTER 15

You Are Not Alone

(The Role and Critical Importance of Advisory Boards and Special Advisors to Boards and Leaders)

To whom do board members and senior management teams turn when they need advice or guidance? Who provides a company's leaders and executives with the general policies and directions around which a specific growth plan is built and executed?

One group to turn to is a board of advisors. While a board of advisors is often confused with a board of directors, the two types of boards actually play very different roles and have very different responsibilities from one another. As discussed in previous chapters, the members of a board of directors owe very specific fiduciary duties to the corporation's shareholders (this is a requirement under virtually all applicable state corporate laws). In a basic governance structure, the shareholders elect the directors, who in turn appoint officers. The directors' role is to set the company's broad goals and policy objectives, which will benefit and protect the shareholders' interests, and the officers' responsibility is to develop and implement plans for meeting these goals and objectives.

In contrast, the members of an advisory board do not owe the shareholders fiduciary duties under state corporate laws (which means they cannot be held as responsible, in general, for their acts or recommendations), so the advisory board can be much more informal in terms of how many meetings it holds or what agendas those meetings cover. While an advisory board can be assembled for general purposes, a series of different advisory boards can also be set up for specific purposes, such as technical review, marketing strategy, recruitment and compensation, or research and development. Relying on an advisory board can also be an excellent way for a board of directors to get a second opinion on certain matters without interrupting existing relationships. For example, suppose a group of directors may want access to a highly respected business lawyer, but are reluctant to terminate the relationship with the company's current law firm. Asking that lawyer to serve on an advisory board can be a good compromise.

In connection with its business and strategic growth plans, or its capital-formation process, a growing company will often set up an advisory board. This action demonstrates to the business plan's prospective investors that the company's officers have access to credible and objective sources of advice and contacts, while some of the precious, few board of directors' seats remain available. Initially, seats on the board of directors are usually set aside for co-founders and investors; many prospective advisory board members may be reluctant to accept the responsibility that comes with a seat on the board of directors, especially at the outset of their relationships with a company. Of course, the showcase value of collecting many important people who barely know the company, and who will never show up for any meetings, dilutes the value of the boards' credibility. When making their final decisions, prospective investors place varying amounts of weight on the board of advisors' strength and composition. Often, they will request direct access to advisory board members, as part of their due diligence process, and wish to ascertain the depth of the advisors' commitment.

One critical difference between a board of directors and an advisory board is that corporate management can accept or ignore any advisory board's recommendations. However, the management does not have this luxury when receiving a mandate from the board of directors. In addition, because members of the advisory board do not owe the same duties to the company and the shareholders as members of the board of directors do, they can be used to mediate disputes by and among officers or between officers and directors. Advisory board members can also be used to help identify potential candidates for the board of directors, or their board may become be a recruiting ground for the directors' board.

Since the rules governing a board of advisors are not set forth in a corporate law statute or in case law, a corporation's representatives must be very clear about the corporation's expectations of each advisory board member and how each of them will be compensated. In the early stages of a company's development, rewards for advisory board members should be structured in a manner that encourages long-term commitment and provides for proactive, not merely reactive, contributions to the company's growth plans.

GETTING SOLID GROWTH ADVICE: TIPS FOR HIRING EFFECTIVE OUTSIDE ADVISORS

One critical success factor for effective governance is the board members' and company leaders' need to screen for, recruit, and maintain dynamic relationships with teams of advisors, such as attorneys, accountants, consultants, and other external professional advisors. The last group should come from a wide variety of business disciplines (such as marketing, sales, finance, administrative management, strategic planning, computer systems, manufacturing, production, advertising, operations, or personnel). When creating this team of advisors, the company's leaders (and where applicable, the in-house legal department) must manage relationships in order to ensure cost-efficiency and internal team compatibility; in addition, they must ensure that tasks and problems are assigned to advisors with appropriate background and expertise.

As a general rule, companies hire professional service providers and business consultants to fill a particular need for any or all of the following:

- Expert advice in a particular field of knowledge;
- A readily available pool of human resources to supplement the lack of full-time employees;
- Identification and solution of specific problems with or barriers to growth;
- Stimulation or implementation of new ideas, technology, or programs;
- Sounding boards (or shoulders to cry on);
- Access to contacts and resources;
- Insights into other, similar companies' successes and failures.

Once the exact reason, specific project, or detailed problem has been identified, certain key questions must be addressed when selecting the appropriate advisor or service provider (either an individual or a firm), such as:

- How does this particular advisor's background, education, and experience relate to the task or problem at hand?
- How does this professional advisor charge for services? What billing options, if any, are available? Is any creative billing option offered, such as equity for services (see below), deferred fees, reduced rates, project-specific discounts, or contingencies? How do this advisor's rates compare to others'? How much will it cost to accomplish this specific project or resolve the problem?
- Which of the advisor's staff members will actually be assigned to this project? What are particular members' fields of expertise? Will the advisor provide access to other members of the firm who have specialized expertise, on an as-needed basis?
- What is the firm's anticipated timetable for completing the work? What progress reports will be provided? What input from the management team will the service provider require?
- What is the service provider's representative client base? What references can be offered? Does the firm have any actual or potential conflicts of interest? How does the company you represent compare to the firm's current client base?

In addition to answering the above questions, certain misperceptions and myths regarding the use of outside advisors must be done away with before any relationship commences.

COACHES AND MENTORS

A rapidly increasing number of executive leaders (and, in some cases, even board members) are turning to coaches and mentors as sources of guidance, insight, and business advice. These coaches and mentors can also serve as a strategic sounding board.

Mentors are individuals who, typically, give back to the business community by selecting one or more protégés with whom they can share wisdom and advice. They tend to be older, are successful in their careers, and were beneficiaries of mentorship that helped them significantly during their own careers. They enjoy sharing their knowledge and experience with protégés; usually, the depth of their advice is at the macro, big-picture level. While mentors can be paid, the bulk of mentor-protégé relationships are either unpaid or deploy a structure in which the mentor receives an equity stake in or a board seat at the protégé's company. Mentoring can be formal and required by regulation, such as those in connection with the federal government contracting 8(a) set aside program. Mentoring support can be part of a national network, such as the Service Corp of Retired Executives (SCORE) or be regional in focus, such as the Venture Menoring Service run by MIT.

Mentor-protégé relationships can be formal—with sets of defined rules, expectations, and scheduled meetings—or informal, with meetings and interactions held on an ad-hoc or as-needed basis. Finding a mentor is not easy, and there is not really any formal network upon which a potential protégé can draw. Instead, most mentor-protégé relationships are based on some current or prior connection. Early on, the mentor and protégé should establish a natural rapport of trust and confidence. Such a rapport cannot be forced. If the mentor-protégé relationship is not a good fit for either party, then they should end the relationship immediately. Both parties should be clear about their aspirations to and expectations for the relationship, which can be short-term, long-term, or driven by either a special set of circumstances or a pending transaction. Mentors may have multiple protégés (though they must preserve each individual's confidentiality), while protégés may have multiple mentors for a variety of different purposes or to gain different perspectives.

In turn, business coaches, similar to their athletic counterparts, can be sources of wisdom, guidance, training, and discipline for their clients. Business coaches are, essentially, paid mentors; however, often they are more focused on a specific area that needs improvement or guidance, as opposed to most mentors, who provide general counsel. For example, a coach could focus, with laser-like precision, on improving an entrepreneur or executive's leadership skills, team-building skills, or marketing expertise, etc. Alternatively, a coach could act as a general sounding board and guide, pushing the entrepreneur to his or her overall optimal performance. A coaching agreement's scope, which should be clearly defined, could include one or more of the following tasks:

- Offering general strategic support and guidance;
- Acting as a sounding board: being a source for an outside perspective and independent viewpoints;
- Playing the skeptic or devil's advocate—challenging the CEO or entrepreneur's views and decisions in ways that his or her employees may be unwilling or afraid to try (especially if the company's culture is similar to that of the "Emperor's New Clothes" framework);
- Helping a client develop specific skills, such as leadership, delegation, time management, communication,

organizational skills, interpersonal skills, negotiation, and so on.

Coaches come in a variety of shapes and sizes. Some have the same characteristics mentors do, while others are themselves entrepreneurs trying to build thriving coaching practices; in other words, they are not acting solely out of the goodness of their hearts.

Bear in mind that most coaches do not view themselves as consultants. Their focus is on a person, not an organization. Coaches are brought on board to inspire, not do the work for someone else. They are not there to solve problems, but rather to help their client solve a problem. Let's return to the idea of athletics again: a coach may inspire someone to run a few extra laps but will not run them for the athlete. The same principles apply to business coaching. So, as with mentoring, it's critical to detail clear expectations about the coach-entrepreneur relationship's scope and goals when that relationship begins.

The essence of business coaching lies in listening, observing, recommending, questioning, and encouraging. Many coaches of professional athletic teams (remember, the professional athletes on these teams make millions and millions of dollars) no longer even view themselves as coaches in the traditional sense. They view their coaching role as establishing goals and challenges, and then offering up the strategies and resources to reach those goals (subject to the players' feedback). Effective business coaches often mimic this approach: they draw on their database of knowledge and experience, coupled with their strong listening and questioning skills, and offer the entrepreneurial leader a range of possible solutions to the specific or general problems being faced (often, they offer a healthy dose of encouragement, when needed and where applicable, that the problem can and will be solved in some fashion).

Many of the above observations about rapport, trust, and presumably fit regarding mentors also apply to coaches, with one big difference. If you, as a client, hire a coach, then you are paying that individual just like you would any other professional advisor. Thus, your expectations can be more formal and more defined. In a coaching relationship, you can be more demanding than you can be in a volunteer-based mentoring relationship. Bear in mind that you are not paying for the coach to be your new best friend and cheerleader, any more than you are paying your personal trainer to tell you that you look great in those spandex shorts. The coach is there to provide objective, pragmatic, and effective advice: either to help you develop a specific skill set, solve a specific problem, or serve strategically as a sounding board.

CHAPTER 16

WHEN BAD THINGS HAPPEN TO GOOD COMPANIES

Nine Critical Questions Every Board Must Ask

By Henry Klehm and Joan McKown, Jones Day

About a decade ago, it seemed as though large companies—some of which were considered industry leaders—were imploding, if not every day, at least every month: Enron, WorldCom, Adelphia, Parmalat, and a string of others were among them. As commentators have noticed, in recent years the number of headline-grabbing corporate failures caused by C-suite corporate malfeasance has fallen substantially. The decline is attributed to such various causes as improved internal control, following the Sarbanes-Oxley Act; heightened regulation of public company auditors; an increased focus on business ethics and compliance; and increased probability of enforcement by government actions.

However, there are probably very few business leaders who still believe their companies are immune to such issues. Bad things still happen at good companies. For example, maverick employees go "rogue," taking unauthorized chances that put huge sums at risk.

Some eager business unit managers stretch too far to make quarterly numbers. Alternatively, financial reporting systems have hidden problems, sometimes building up over years, which lead to inflated profits. Well-meaning professionals can get complex, revenue-recognition accounting principles wrong. Finally, senior executives even occasionally agree to deals, an action that subsequently gets them arrested.

Corporate board members learn about these problems in a host of ways. Internal and external auditors bring issues to the surface, sometimes before an issue becomes material and sometimes not. General counsels receive government subpoenas, triggering internal investigations that uncover bribery and corruption. Company representatives follow up on anonymous hotline calls, frequently discovering poor human resource practices or, less frequently, financial problems.

Now, in the wake of the Dodd-Frank Act's changes to government whistleblower programs and reinvigoration of law enforcement, chances of corporate misconduct being detected or reported to the government have increased exponentially. The Securities and Exchange Commission's (SEC) Enforcement Division has prided itself in moving from a reactive, regulatory agency to a proactive, forward-thinking, law enforcement program. Assisting these efforts is an enhanced whistleblower provision, which, in all enforcement actions wherein monetary sanctions are more than $1 million, requires the SEC to pay 10 to 30 percent of the financial recovery to whistleblowers who have turned in original information regarding a related securities law violation. With sanctions often reaching tens of millions of dollars, it is not surprising to hear SEC officials state that they are now receiving, on average, one significant complaint a day—compared to the average of one per month, prior to the Dodd-Frank whistleblower provision's enactment.

Regardless of how corporate misconduct comes to company directors' attention, board members must ensure that the company's process for dealing with malfeasance and negligence protects the shareholders. Simultaneously, the process must root out the real problem and minimize business disruption, reputational impact, and potential for either harsh government enforcement action or expensive private civil litigation outcomes. State laws regarding directors' oversight duties and independence also set minimum standards against which to balance these factors. When civil and criminal law enforcement programs, such as the SEC and the Department of Justice (DOJ), get involved, board members must ensure the company's representatives can answer these four basic questions: First, did the company self-police through its systems to find the problem? Second, did the company report, to both investors and the government, on an appropriate and timely basis? Third, did the company take effective remedial measures? Finally, did the company cooperate with the government? (Here, the definition of "cooperate" includes sharing the results of any related internal investigation.)

In our experience, the questions listed below are those that are most frequently asked, or those that should be asked, when bad news about corporate behavior arrives in the boardroom. Of course, every situation is different: perfect answers hardly ever appear. The most successful responses to these questions, though, come from advance planning—planning begun before any sign of bad news appears, and when neither a shareholder nor a government crisis is not looming.

WHO IS IN CHARGE—THE MANAGEMENT, BOARD MEMBERS, OR A BOARD COMMITTEE?

When bad news arrives, the first—and potentially most important—decision is assigning the responsibility to oversee and manage the situation. This decision shapes the government's view of everything that follows. There is no one right answer, and the answer can change in the initial stages of assessing the problem as the company learns more about the facts. To maximize government credit for the company's response, and to minimize the possibility of successful shareholder derivative action challenging that response, the internal investigation must be appropriately separate from any managers involved in the problem. Ultimately, the board members remain responsible for overseeing the problem, but can choose to delegate this responsibility to the audit committee, and/or a special committee, when necessary.

Day-to-day management of the investigation can be determined by considering where the problem lies on a spectrum. Does the problem appear to be isolated, limited to the wrongdoing of a low-level employee? Then, most likely, this is a problem that can be investigated by internal audit staff. However, if, after further investigation, it becomes clear that the problem is more serious, widespread, or involves more senior management, the company's general counsel must become substantially involved; moreover, the general counsel needs to inform the independent audit committee members and, often, the external auditor. At this point, the audit committee members should quickly decide whether the matter falls within their charter and, as such, whether the matter should be subject to the committee's management. If the potential misconduct falls at the more serious end of the spectrum, there is no question that an independent audit committee—and, in some instances, a special board committee—should manage the investigation in order to demonstrate its independence.

Of course, the initial answer to the question of who should be in charge can change as the matter progresses. The facts ascertained during an independent, properly scoped, and thorough investigation (in which investigators search electronic communications and interview witnesses) can implicate more senior employees and managers. Directors charged with overseeing the matter must constantly reassess initial oversight and management decisions to maintain the investigation's independence. If the government's representatives do not believe the investigation is appropriately independent from management or potential wrongdoers, the company's investigators will be perceived as protecting management or the company. The benefits of conducting an internal investigation will be diminished, according to government enforcers, and shareholders may challenge directors to demonstrate the appropriate fulfillment of their state-mandated legal duties.

WHO IS GOING TO DO THE INVESTIGATION AND WHAT IS GOING TO BE INVESTIGATED?

Much like the investigation oversight and management decision described above, the answer to this question can substantially impact both the government representatives' view of the company's response and the outcome of shareholder litigation. Investigators must be independent of influences that would be perceived as skewing the outcome or acting improperly to arrive at that outcome. The investigators must also have the appropriate knowledge, skills, and experience required to address the problem and its causes, and to formulate remedial recommendations. Thus, the answer to this question should also be determined based on the above continuum. The more serious or widespread a potential problem is, the more likely an investigation needs to be conducted by counsel, consultants, and accountants who remain independent from management.

Additionally, both the investigation's scope and initial steps are critically important. Whoever is assigned to investigate must have the authority to do so properly. When the investigation starts, the company must make certain that all evidence, especially documents of any form (including electronic communications), is preserved. Any actions that might create the appearance of a cover-up must be prevented.

HOW LONG WILL THIS TAKE AND
HOW MUCH WILL IT COST?

Time and money, which are always important issues, must be balanced against the need to resolve the investigation quickly. The above are fair questions that can and should be asked of the investigation team. The investigation itself should be run in a strategic, cost-effective manner. Typically, time pressures come from a variety of factors: business issues; the need to complete audit work, either to file quarterly or annual periodic reports; pressure on the government investigators, who are themselves measured in part on how quickly they conclude investigations; and the legitimate desire just to move on.

There are a host of factors that determine an investigation's length. At the top of the list are the substantive focus' complexity and the involvement of international locations. For example, revenue recognition issues regarding complex software contracts can take years to sort out, as can corruption investigations involving multiple subsidiaries located in foreign countries. From the government's side, authorities can press for results if a matter involves topics of enforcement significance, but then they can be called on to other priority matters for months, or occasionally years, at a time. Other factors include: how extensive and pervasive the problem is, how local or global the problem is, how high up in the organization the problem reached, and how long the misconduct continued. Unforeseen elements can result in additional delays. For example, key employees and government investigators move on to new positions for one reason or another. To provide directors with a reasonable estimate of how long it will really take to get to a conclusion, all of these factors need to be assessed. Even then, directors should understand that making an estimate is somewhat like predicting next week's weather.

Handling costs with the investigation team also requires finesse and care. Directors and management should avoid sending any signal that a cut-rate, less-than-thoughtful, or incomplete investigation will be acceptable when the stakes are high. There is no requirement for a corporation to account for every penny; both the law and most applicable auditing standards require reasonability. The government investigators will analyze whether the internal investigation was appropriate in terms of scope and thoroughness; conducting a less-than-complete investigation in an effort to limit costs will likely be discovered when the government investigators assess the investigation's reliability. Since even a limited investigation can be quite costly, it makes little long-term sense to be penny-wise in resourcing and scoping that investigation, only to end up with no credit from the government.

To manage both the cost and the length of time an investigation takes, board overseers and managers should maintain focus on receiving regular reports from the investigators. Reports should cover progress, delays, and changes in scope. The overarching objective should be efficiently to do what is necessary in order to give the best possible answers to the questions of what happened, why, by whom, whether it is fixed, and how can it be prevented in the future. Such an objective holds true regardless of where the answers lead.

WHAT REMEDIAL STEPS SHOULD WE TAKE?

The board members' responsibility to address remediation, in the wake of problems, addresses a host of sources. Directors' state law duties generally require appropriate responses to indications of legal compliance problems. Both the SEC and DOJ have policies regarding bringing and resolving enforcement actions that take into account the effectiveness of steps a company has taken to remediate problems. Federal Sentencing Guidelines explicitly address the need to remediate both the harm caused to third parties by misconduct and the organizational processes that allowed the misconduct to occur. Public company auditors will seek to document the appropriateness of controls, books, and records remediation in order to provide necessary opinions about financial statements and internal controls going forward.

Appropriate remediation should address correcting books and records, updating systems and processes, and addressing financial losses. When conducting remediation, board members should also address the often-difficult issue of personnel actions. On the one hand, personnel actions should not be taken lightly. Disciplining or terminating lower-level employees will quickly call into question the company's entire response to the problem. If government officials view a person in a senior position as a culpable participant in wrongdoing, and the company continues to employ that person, it can become extremely difficult to negotiate a resolution for the company, which may increase the amount of sanctions the government representatives seek. On the other hand, the "kill 'em all" approach should be avoided. Risks of private employment litigation can be minimized by thoughtful evaluation of each individual's conduct within and responsibility to the organization.

Additionally, remember that thorough remediation, implementation of appropriate new systems and processes, the right ongoing auditing, and correct monitoring of controls (to demonstrate effectiveness) can be costly. However, government organizations are showing increased willingness to rely on credible evidence of corporations' self-imposed remedial steps. Nevertheless, the associated costs are likely to be less than the cost of a government-imposed, independent, corporate monitor or consultant charged with reviewing compliance and internal controls, conducting auditing, and recommending enhancements. Monitors are expensive and they can impose controls that the company representatives believe are costly and unnecessary.

Responding weakly to problems within an organization can also have a detrimental effect on the company's culture. If employees believe issues are swept under the rug, they are also likely to believe the organization's leaders do not take wrongdoing seriously. Thus, the employees become less likely to report potential issues at an early stage—when the problems are still small. Not only should directors make sure that management takes appropriate remedial steps, they should also ensure that employees know the seriousness with which the board members and management approach these issues.

Many board members are well schooled in taking a lesson-learned approach to business decisions that go wrong. By studying mistaken business strategies, those that resulted in losses, board members hope their future business decisions will be better ones. The same principle applies to control lapses and misbehavior. A well-considered, lessons-learned approach will incorporate such results into the company's enterprise risk management program, and the organization itself will emerge stronger from the crisis.

SHOULD WE REPORT THE FINDINGS TO THE GOVERNMENT?

While government officials would always like the answer to this question to be, "Yes," and offer a mechanism through which to do so, "self-reporting," the reality is that this question is typically among the board members' most difficult and complex decisions. Doing so risks the matter becoming public, either through self-disclosure or through public enforcement action, which can result in business and reputational consequences, as well as private civil litigation. When self-reporting, a company also gives up the potentially significant ability to control the matter's outcome. In exchange for self-reporting, the government offers the chance for a company to avoid prosecution, or at least to reduce the sanctions. However, there are no guarantees.

The law has no broad requirement for companies to self-report problems to the government, although there are some limited exceptions. Generally, as a matter of state corporate law, the board members' decision is protected by the business judgment rule. In short, so long as the directors act on an informed basis in good faith, their decisions will not be subject to claims of breaching fiduciary duty.

To reach business judgment requires a nuanced consideration of specific facts. First, among others, making such a decision may not be entirely within the company's control. If the company has determined that a whistleblower or other informant has gone to the government or a media outlet, then the decision to go to the government likely becomes an affirmative on an accelerated timetable. Second, once they are aware of material financial reporting problems, the company's auditors are under a statutory obligation to consider whether the company's response is appropriate before they sign off on financial statements. Given the vigor with which both the SEC and the Public Company Accounting Oversight Board have pursued auditors in recent years, it is not surprising that auditors are reluctant, to say the least, to sign off if misconduct has not been reported. Third, board members need to consider reactions of shareholders and other constituencies, in addition to reputational consequences, if the board decides not to self-report and the matter later becomes public. For example, companies with meaningful government contracts that do not self-report and are later exposed risk substantial business consequences, including debarment, from subsequent enforcement actions. There is never a perfect answer.

However, suppose the decision is made to self-report: the next question is when. Board members must consider the possible actions of uncontrollable actors, such as whistleblowers or auditors, described above. A company should not self-report until its representatives have done as much as possible to determine the problem's scope and likely consequential issues. This does not mean waiting until the problem is completely investigated and remediated. Rather, the company's objective should be to demonstrate an aggressive and proper response to the allegations. If the company waits until considerable time has passed since the allegations first surfaced, a response looks less than aggressive. As seasoned business executives know, problems are rarely limited to one issue, one person, or one contract. If the problem's contours seem apparent, that may be sufficient knowledge for a timing decision. Again, this is not a decision that will be perfect.

Finally, not every problem needs to be or is disclosed to the government. Plain mistakes happen: sometimes problems get caught before the money involved becomes significant, and sometimes board members make the business decisions to deal with such problems internally. Most likely, serious violations of law, widespread and systematic misconduct, or senior management involvement should be self-reported. The likelihood that these types of problems will forever remain hidden from the government is no longer a substantial one. Terminating a named executive officer, for example, requires disclosures be filed with the SEC. Misstating the basis for an executive's departure will only compound the problems. In summary, to compare this problem to the current wave of extreme reality TV shows, deciding to self-report or not should be done with the assistance of seasoned professional advisors in order to avoid serious injury.

WHO SPEAKS FOR THE COMPANY TO THE MEDIA?

Dealing with the media during a crisis is, of course, important for both reputational and legal reasons. Typically, the person speaking— and it should be one person—must be someone who can speak with both knowledge of and credibility about the company and the issue. The spokesperson must be completely free of association with the problems. Sometimes, he or she can be the company's CEO or chief communications executive. Only in the most rare cases should an independent director take on this role. If there is no other available choice, a director who has a pre-established leadership role within the board, such as a non-executive board chair or a lead independent director, may be the best option. Whoever it is, the board must be in full agreement this individual speaks for the company. It is hard to imagine anything more demonstrative to external constituencies of internal strife than independent directors having a public disagreement about a corporate crisis. Most corporate crisis PR experts will also say independent counsel are rarely, if ever, effective spokespersons. In times of trouble, shareholders and the media want to hear from a company representative, not third parties.

However, one mistake to avoid is that of viewing public relations as purely a media issue. Communications professionals must coordinate with investor relations managers and the legal team to avoid public statements that damage the company's relationship with the government or, in the worst case, create new legal issues. A well-seasoned media consultant will be used to working with lawyers to help the company put out the best message.

IS THE COMPANY GOING TO BE
SUED, AND IF SO, BY WHOM?

The answer to this question is: not always, but it is best to plan on potential suing and to be well prepared. Not every company that self-reports problems to the government gets sued by both the government and private plaintiffs. At the outset of problems that have litigious possibilities, board members should make sure the company takes steps to adequately protect the investigation, and related communications and deliberations, from eventual plaintiffs' scrutiny. An ounce of proper planning that protects both attorney-client communications and the investigation itself from eventual discovery can be worth a ton of later aggravation. In the last several years, governmental policies about the need for corporations to share possibly privileged investigation results, in order to maximize credit for cooperation, have softened. Nevertheless, regardless of whether the company's representatives later decide to share possibly privileged information with government officials, carefully protecting communications will avoid issues in any subsequent private civil litigation.

In actuality, every year the government closes many investigations without undertaking public enforcement action. The ultimate outcome for a company engaging with the government largely depends on the problem's seriousness, the senior management's involvement, and the government's enforcement priorities. However, with regard to the difficult situations in which the company is likely to be sued, the company's response is important. By responding to the problem aggressively and appropriately, a company can have an enormous impact on the sanctions the government insists on, in terms of disgorgement, penalties, charges for fraud, undertakings, or monitors.

Additionally, the likelihood of private civil litigation is important. Regarding significant problems that are disclosed to the public, certainly, private plaintiffs' lawyers are likely to announce company investigations as precursors to class actions or derivative shareholder claims. Remember, whenever an employment action takes place, the prospect of employment litigation exists. A frequent strategy deployed by plaintiffs' lawyers includes casting or recasting the facts to suggest that the disciplined employee was a whistleblower and his or her role in any wrongdoing was minimal. Under the still-to-be published rules following Dodd-Frank, which mandate that stock exchange listing standards require companies to broaden clawback compensation claims from employees who may have benefited (financially) from any wrongdoing, companies will need to evaluate the claim of any employee seeking repayment of compensation that, no doubt, could eventually be part of a civil litigation suit.

The bottom line is: while litigation does not necessarily result in every case, the prospects for civil litigation abound. Preparation is key.

DO WE, THE BOARD MEMBER, HAVE PERSONAL LIABILITY?

The answer is maybe, but rarely. Directors should understand the reality of this matter. The board members' key duty, under state law and important government policies, is to have processes in place that can uncover misconduct at an early stage and make sure it is stopped. Federal Sentencing Guidelines state that board members must be knowledgeable about the company's compliance program and "exercise reasonable oversight with respect to the implementation and effectiveness of the compliance and ethic program." Directors also have oversight "Caremark" duties developed through case law and various other sources, such as stock exchange rules, the Sarbanes-Oxley Act, and audit committee charters.

As a result, despite seemingly endless prospects of private civil litigation, few enforcement or derivative actions against independent directors in recent years have been successful. True, the SEC is bringing more cases of failure to stop senior officers' misconduct against independent directors. In addition, in what were at least derivative actions against directors following the financial crisis, a

Delaware court determined that shareholder plaintiffs had brought together sufficient facts to suggest supposedly independent directors had participated in a long-running scheme to overstate financial results.

Directors will not always be able to avoid being named in private civil litigation. However, the simple fact is that when directors affirmatively and appropriately respond to indications of trouble, their prospects of facing personal civil liability or being named in a public enforcement action are considerably reduced.

ARE WE INSURED?

The answer here depends on the terms of your company's Directors' and Officers' policy. Such a policy should be reviewed early on in any investigation, especially in an investigation that appears to be broad in nature. Some policies require that the company inform the insurer of an investigation at an early stage, and some policies will cover the investigations' costs. Every good crisis management plan should include a careful review of all policies. There are, however, limits to what can be insured. In any subsequent resolution with government representatives, an insurer can reimburse the company for disgorgement payment or ill-gotten gains, but not for any fines or penalties the government collects. (For more on insurance coverage issues, see Chapter 14.)

CONCLUSION

Possibly the best piece of advice is to start thinking about possible answers to these questions in advance, rather than trying to determine answers during the heat of a crisis. Each crisis has its own complexities, but there are constants in each problematic situation. Well-prepared board members will be thinking about who will be speaking for the board and to whom the board will turn for outside counsel, should a situation arise in which outside counsel (apart from the company's regular outside counsel and other advisors) is necessary. The time to begin developing relationships with such advisors is well before the onset of tensions associated with problems such as the ones described in this essay. While every answer to these questions cannot be written out in advance, contingency plans should be considered in calm settings. Finally, as they would for any evolving business situation, directors should recognize that the answer to each question can and will change as the problem's scope becomes clearer.

ABOUT THE AUTHORS

JOAN McKOWN is a partner in the Washington, D.C. office of Jones Day. She is the former longtime chief counsel of the Division of Enforcement at the U.S. Securities and Exchange Commission. During the twenty-four years of her career at the SEC, she played a key role in establishing enforcement policies at the agency and in reviewing proposed enforcement actions before they were recommended to the Commission for approval.

As chief counsel for seventeen years, McKown worked closely with the Commission and senior SEC staff. Her substantive experience extends across the full range of Enforcement Division matters. During her tenure, she reviewed all enforcement recommendations sent to the Commission and actively participated in the Commission's consideration of all enforcement cases. She oversaw the drafting of the Enforcement Division Manual and played a significant role in the Division's organizational changes.

McKown also served as a key liaison between the Enforcement Division and other SEC staff and regulatory authorities. She had the primary responsibility of formulating the Enforcement Division's legislative priorities, as well as rule proposals and other important policy matters. She frequently represented the Division in dealing with other regulators, including the Commodities and Futures Trade Commission, federal banking regulators, and state securities regulators.

McKown has counseled SEC commissioners about enforcement policies and practices, spearheaded implementation of the Sarbanes-Oxley Act's (2002) enforcement-related portions, and been involved in hundreds of SEC enforcement cases' settlement negotiations.

HENRY KLEHM is a partner in the New York City office of Jones Day. His practice focuses on regulatory examinations, investigations, enforcement actions, other proceedings with United States and foreign regulators, and corporate governance matters. Klehm also counsels boards, corporations, and financial institutions on internal investigations, crisis management, and effective compliance and ethics programs.

Klehm recently represented financial institutions and senior corporate officers in government investigations involving the trading of CDOs and CDSs, insider trading, the Foreign Corrupt Practices Act, and money laundering. In addition to global banks, he represents senior financial and risk officers in investigations related to accounting for contingencies, fair value, and related disclosure matters.

Prior to joining Jones Day, Klehm was the global head of compliance for Deutsche Bank, AG. From 1999 until 2002, he was the deputy general counsel and the senior regulatory lawyer for Prudential Financial. Before joining Prudential, he was with the Enforcement Division of the Securities and Exchange Commission for ten years, serving as head of the enforcement section for the northeastern United States for five years. At the SEC, Klehm investigated, litigated, and supervised more than 500 enforcement actions, including insider trading, financial frauds, Ponzi schemes, rogue traders, market manipulations, investment companies, and advisor matters.

Since 2006, Klehm has served as an independent director and chair of the audit committee of RenaissanceRe Holdings, Ltd., a NYSE-listed catastrophe reinsurance firm. He frequently lectures on financial services, regulatory issues, and corporate governance, and provides training for public company directors on duties and liabilities.

CHAPTER 17

THE ART AND SCIENCE OF DUE DILIGENCE IN AN ERA OF ACCOUNTABILITY AND TRANSPARENCY

Following the collapses of Enron, WorldCom, and several other major, multinational companies, capital markets experienced the Era of Accountability 1.0: this era included passage of the Sarbanes-Oxley Act ("Sarbox") in 2002. Sarbox brought new standards for conduct and governance to public-company boards of directors and officers, including new and more stringent reporting requirements, stronger internal controls, and stiffer penalties for non-compliance. This legislation also influenced the focus and depth of M&A due-diligence standards, which began to delve even more deeply into issues of financial reporting, objectivity, and verification.

Less than a decade later, we have entered the Era of Accountability 2.0. Events in this era—including Barack Obama's election and his administration's commitment to transparency; government roles in bailouts, including TARP; failures of banks and automobile companies; Dodd-Frank's passage; MF Global's collapse; the Madoff and Stanford scandals; the severe global recession; and mistrust in Wall Street—are collectively contributing to an increase in staffing at the Securities and Exchange Commission (SEC), the expectation of vigorous government enforcement activities in a variety of areas, and the possibility of new GAAP standards. These evolving developments, in turn, are elevating, expanding and refining the portfolio of due diligence best practices in M&A, financing, and other core business transactions.

I am not implying that the movement from accountability 1.0 to 2.0 involves a tectonic shift in due diligence best practices. Rather, M&A and related transactional best practices and documentation will always evolve in small increments because they involve changes in human behavior—how we think, how we interact, how we ask questions, and how we analyze the answers. There are occasional exceptions to these rules, such as the fairly rapid and widespread move to electronic data rooms. Responses to sweeping legislative and regulatory developments, too, are necessarily fast-paced. The government interventions of the last few years, triggered in large part by excesses that exploited a flawed regulatory regime—and fueled by intense, enduring public outrage—is so sweeping that due diligence best practices are bound to respond to these challenges. Buyers and sellers now live in a more highly regulated economy, one in which they are subject to intense public scrutiny and microscopic examination by vigorous government enforcement. While this response should, in large part, encompass the reaffirmation of existing best practices (and, as such, much of the below discussion emphasizes these practices, arguing they prevail in the Era of Accountability 1.0), the new environment in which these best practices continue to develop merits a 2.0 designation. That is, while we expect the anticipated changes in practices to be incremental, the ever-expanding government regulations and enforcement activities present a qualitative change in environment.

BEST PRACTICES IN DUE DILIGENCE IN
THE ERA OF ACCOUNTABILITY 2.0

First, boards of directors and company leaders must embrace the notion that due diligence is both an art and a science. Moreover, it is a process, not an event. In this new era, due diligence requires an increasingly creative and strategic approach, not just mechanical methodology. For example, conducting due diligence in a M&A transaction requires company leaders to dive into the company's history, mission, values, culture, and intangible assets; it does not mean moving through a mere formalistic review of key contracts and corporate housekeeping documents. Due diligence must be focused on avoiding the characterization of "failure" attributed to 30 to 70 percent of all M&A transactions (such a characterization is derived by using post-closing metrics that include reduced shareholder value). Businesses, large and small alike, continuing to cope with the current economic conditions, must surely try to avoid foundering again, this time on the rocks of failed M&A endeavors. Lawyers, accountants, investment bankers, industry specialists, and strategic consultants must reaffirm existing best practices; they must commit to higher, more inquisitive standards of due diligence conduct in this, the Era of Accountability 2.0.

THE QUEST FOR THE "INFORMED DECISION"

One of this essay's critical aspects is reinforcing the point that board members and executives, "as the stewards of corporate assets and as the strategic drivers of shareholder value," have a fiduciary duty to make informed decisions. Understanding and embarking on the latest best practices for effective due diligence will go a long way toward ensuring that their obligations have been satisfied.

Today's directors and executives must be disciplined and rigorous in their analyses and scrutiny of issues: they must prepare and ask many good, relevant questions; they must insist on clear and honest answers; and they must verify those answers' veracity. Just like the title character from the children's book *Curious George*, we must have the persistence of that little monkey while getting to the bottom line.

Patience Matters

Remember Columbo, the detective that the late Peter Falk played during the 1970s? Columbo always solved the crime through his last question, the "one more question" that he had almost forgotten to ask, stated just as he was walking out the door. While running a business may not be about solving crimes, it requires similar inquisitiveness and a tireless pursuit of accurate information. Often the truth is not readily apparent, and eliciting it requires asking that one last question, just like Columbo. While directors do not have a duty to set up a system of espionage in order to ferret out wrongdoing or misinformation, they should, at a minimum, avoid charges of being uninterested or of blindly accepting information; instead, they should strive for Columbo's healthy skepticism and thorough analysis. The company will be better for it, and the directors will satisfy their obligations because of it.

Returning to an M&A transaction (or any other transaction in which board members and executives must rely on extensive data gathering and analysis to support their decision-making), the due diligence process involves a review (legal, financial, and strategic) of all the seller's documents, contractual relationships, operating history, and organizational structure. Due diligence is not just a process. It is also a reality test: it tests whether the factors driving the deal, making it look attractive to the parties, are real or illusory. Due diligence is not a quest to find the deal breakers; rather, it is a test of the values underlying the transaction. In other words, conducting due diligence is like making sure that the inside of a house is as attractive as the outside. Once the structure and interior have been inspected, the facts can be used to support a deal that makes sense. Otherwise, the buyer should leave the unsuitable property to be disassembled or remodeled; that way, he or she avoids committing to a transaction that is operationally, financially, or strategically imprudent. Understand, too, that in the Era of Accountability 2.0, due diligence will typically be more expansive—and probe more deeply—than ever before. Accordingly, conducting the diligence will take longer and cost more, especially if the prospective buyer is a company that is either public or has plans to go public within the next eighteen months.

Remember, don't rely solely on fairness, opinions, or independent valuation reports instead of effective due diligence if your instincts are telling you there's a problem with the proposed transaction.

As stated earlier, effective due diligence is both an art and a science. Its art comes from having the style and experience to know which questions to ask, as well as how and when to ask them. This is the ability to create feelings of both trust and fear in the seller, a combination that encourages full and complete disclosure. In this sense, the due diligence team is also on a risk-discovery and assessment mission, looking for potential problems and liabilities, finding ways to resolve these problems prior to closing, and ensuring that risks will be allocated fairly and openly after closing.

The science of due diligence comes from preparing comprehensive and customized checklists of specific questions to present to the seller, maintaining methodical systems for organizing and analyzing the documents and data a seller provides, and in quantitatively assessing any risks connected to the problems discovered through the due diligence process. One of the key areas to focus on is detection of the seller's obligations, particularly those that the buyer will be expected or required to assume after closing. The prior concern is especially relevant for a stock purchase transaction or comparable merger. Contrastingly, in an asset purchase, parties must specifically define purchased liabilities, subject to a few successor liabilities that cannot be avoided contractually. The due diligence process is designed to accomplish two things on behalf of the buyer: first, to detect the existence of any obligations; and, second, to identify any defaults or problems in connection with these obligations that will affect the buyer after closing.

The best way for a buyer to ensure that the potential purchase has been thoroughly checked is through effective due diligence preparation and planning. Astute buyers typically employ comprehensive due diligence checklists, which are intended to help buyers accomplish three goals. First, the checklists guide the company's management team while its members work closely with counsel to gather, and review, all the legal documents that may be relevant to the transaction's structure and pricing. Second, the checklists help the buyer's team assess potential legal risks and liabilities following the closing. Third, the checklists enable the team to identify all of the consents, approvals, and notifications that may be required from or to be given to third parties and government agencies. The most common form of third-party consent is the type required in connection with existing contracts; such consent cannot be changed or otherwise transferred without the other party's prior approval.

A due diligence checklist, however, should be a set of guidelines, not a crutch. The buyer's management team must take the lead in developing questions that pertain to the nature of the seller's business. These questions will set the pace for the review's level of detail and adequacy. The key point here is that every type of business has its own types of issues and problems, so a standard set of questions is rarely sufficient. Moreover, there are no substitutes for taking face-to-face meetings with key leaders While reviewing documents online is a good start, it is not nearly adequate enough to meet today's due diligence standards.

The Era of Accountability 2.0 is not simply a time of increased government regulation and scrutiny. It is also a time in which the increased threat of shareholder litigation, and the challenge of dealing with that threat, must be addressed. By most measures, commercial contract dispute and M&A-related litigation filings have increased over the past few years, perhaps substantially. Of particular importance here are two points: first, a greater percentage of relationships and transactions are being challenged where they fail to meet the original objectives; and second, each individual transaction is being challenged by an increasing number of suits. Instead of one or two firms filing suit, as happened in the past, a transaction announcement could be met by more than a handful of suits filed by different law firms in multiple jurisdictions. Companies engaging in M&A, therefore, face a greater likelihood of litigation being initiated against them. To make matters worse, they also face a greater difficulty in defending against such litigation on multiple fronts, each with a different judge who has a different level of corporate law understanding.

These cases can impose significant costs (most obviously, litigation expenses) and can jeopardize a transaction's closing, which gives the opposing side's plaintiffs both holdup and settlement value. (Many of these cases may lack enough merit to result in director liability, but that is somewhat beside the point.) In addition, by filing in multiple jurisdictions, plaintiffs stack the deck; they need only persuade one court that their claims are meritorious and should be litigated (in that forum). The best way for any board to avoid this threat is to treat every transaction as though it will be challenged and subjected to a court's scrutiny. With that mindset, the directors can engage in and oversee due diligence in a manner that exemplifies best practices and strives to set a standard that is above legitimate.

CHAPTER 18

Corporate Governance and Corporate Communications

Challenges and Opportunities in a Changing World

By Dave Groobert, U.S. General Manager, Environics Communications

Governance board members are used to their discussions, deliberations, and debates taking place in private, behind closed doors, and under a cloak of confidentiality. Yet their decisions impact thousands, or even millions, of people outside the boardroom. How and when decisions are communicated, and how public input can shape what happens inside the boardroom, is the function of corporate communications. Knowing and understanding how corporate communications works, and how it can help or hinder a board's effectiveness, is critical—especially in today's world, in which forms of social media empower the masses to learn, disseminate, and respond to information quickly.

WHAT IS CORPORATE COMMUNICATIONS?

Quite simply, "corporate communications" means using an assortment of communications tools and tactics to disseminate news and information, and by doing so inform, educate, and often motivate a corporation's various internal and external audiences.

Traditionally, corporate communications have included two general categories of activities: marketing and public relations. Marketing included branding, paid advertising, sales promotions, special events, and similar activities designed to build awareness (and, often, to generate increased sales or public support for a cause or specific point of view). Public relations became defined as media relations (working with reporters to interest them in writing stories that would favorably position a product, service, organization, or idea), as well as investor relations, financial and industry analyst relations, employee communications, and crisis communications. All these traditional activities had a primary goal of one-way communications: sending information downstream to an audience.

Yet it's not that simple any more, with today's social media platforms changing communications from one-way information disseminations into two-way conversations between individuals and groups. Dan Tisch, chairman of the Global Alliance for Public Relations and Communication Management, explained this well in a *New York Times* article: "In a world where the ordinary consumer is walking around with global publishing power in his or her pocket, the role of public relations and corporate communications has shifted from creating content to attempting to influence the content that's created by others."

Tisch is referring to an individual's ability to share information quickly and easily via social media platforms, such as Facebook®,

Twitter®, and countless others. However, social media channels empower the public to go beyond just sharing to supporting pro-actively—or challenging aggressively—news and information. Just look at how citizen involvement via social media has rapidly changed the political landscape both at home and abroad. You can see the dramatic power these social media platforms provide to the masses to influence those who govern.

The power of social media, combined with the migration of news publication to the Internet, has also led to another dramatic shift: the twenty-four-hour news cycle. Before the Internet, the time in which an organization could disseminate information and expect it to be circulated was clearly defined by traditional media outlets: daily or weekly for newspapers, weekly or monthly for magazines, and hourly or nightly for broadcasts (with an occasional "news bulletin" that could interrupt regular programming at any time). Today, because of the Internet, news dissemination is instantaneous. Traditional media outlets are now online, and people continually rush to post news at any hour of the day or night. Additionally, the public, at large, has become an army of roving reporters who can instantly transmit news stories directly to others or forward those stories to traditional news outlets.

The power of the Internet and social media means two things for leadership and governance: news travels at the speed of electrons, and people can reply to news just as fast as it appears. This develop-ment changes both a corporate communications program's role and the board members' responsibility in the corporate communications process.

REQUIREMENTS OF A GOOD CORPORATE COMMUNICATIONS PROGRAM

Before discussing the board members' specific role, any business leader involved in corporate governance or management of an organization's intangible assets must first understand three key attributes of an effective corporate communications program: honesty and transparency, consistency of message, and need for rapid response.

First and foremost is honesty and transparency, which is a simple concept, but one that is often ignored, at great peril. The newspapers and the Internet are littered with remnants of businesses and nonprofit organizations that have been publicly dishonest and suffered the consequences. There is a misperception that communications professionals can "spin," or turn, a negative situation into a positive story, or hide the truth behind a veil of obfuscation. Life simply doesn't work that way. Reporters are paid to get to the truth, not to be mouthpieces for organizations. Now, bloggers also see themselves in this journalistic role; some have successfully investigated and reported breaking news stories, challenging both businesses and nonprofits directly and effectively.

Honesty includes transparency, which is a communications buzzword in the social media era. Bloggers and others online are quick to assess when an individual or organization is being upfront about, or trying to obscure, who they are or whom they represent. Organizations that have tried to hide involvement in a communications effort—by having third parties surreptitiously carry messages, for instance—end up being discovered and eviscerated in short order. Facebook® officials learned this the hard way when people discovered the company had secretly hired a PR firm to try and smear Google®'s reputation in the press and the blogosphere.

The second requirement of a good corporate communications program is consistency of message. A changing explanation is a recipe for disaster. The Susan G. Komen for the Cure organization found this out in 2012, through its highly controversial decision (later reversed) to stop funding Planned Parenthood. As the controversy grew, the organization changed the publicly stated reasoning for its board's decision. The media and Komen's detractors quickly seized upon this inconsistency, further inflaming the situation and causing even more potential damage to the Komen brand.

Finally, the third requirement is the need to respond quickly to news and information that circulate online or in traditional media. Thanks to social media, ordinary citizens can react to news and generate news of their own (which might or might not be fair or accurate) in a matter of seconds. As explained above, postings by ordinary citizens can quickly "go viral" on the Internet and spread globally. Corporate communications personnel must, therefore, continually monitor social media channels and be prepared to respond. This idea does not mean denying or challenging posts that are truthful. Instead, it means making sure that honest and accurate information is made available, inaccurate information is addressed, and organizational opinions and reactions are shared in a way that is appropriately responsive and respectful.

WHAT ALL THIS MEANS TO A GOVERNANCE BOARD

Corporate governance and corporate communications go hand-in-hand. Ultimately, a leader's governance role is to analyze information and make informed decisions that are in the best interest of the organization's stakeholders. Corporate communications' role is to explain these decisions so that they can be accepted and enacted most efficiently and effectively. This is a symbiotic relationship and those who govern need to treat it as such.

Governance board members, at their regular meetings, hear reports from various departments: financial/accounting, legal, executive, regulatory, and others. Yet the corporate communications department is often left off the regular reporting agenda (unless there is a crisis underway). This is unfortunate, because a timely report from corporate communications can help board members understand how important constituencies are viewing the organization internally and externally. In fact, a report from a communications executive can be an early warning sign of trouble that requires board consideration, since issues that often appear in employee communications, in the media, or online subsequently explode into crises if they are not addressed promptly and thoroughly. If they have this information, the board members can be proactive in addressing concerns and setting the course for how the organization is interacting with its constituencies, in good times and in bad.

The Global Alliance for Public Relations and Communication Management explains this point further. The Alliance discusses organizations operating under the "stakeholder governance model," about which it says: ". . . [such a model] implies that a corporation's board of directors—as well as the elected leadership of a social or public sector organization—has the responsibility to define, monitor, and implement relationship policies with all primary stakeholder groups." In its 2010 Stockholm Accords, which represent a call to action for public relations and communication in a global society, the Alliance members write: "Organizations operating under the stakeholder governance model empower their board members, elected officials, and non-profit organization leaders to be directly responsible for deciding and implementing stakeholder relationship policies."

In other words, boards need to consider how their decisions will be communicated and received by those who will be affected by such communications. A corporate communications professional can tell them. A senior professional in corporate communications at a for-profit or non-profit organization can easily assess how traditional and online media will analyze and portray a decision. He or she can predict what questions will be asked, as well as how different constituencies inside and outside the organization will interpret and respond to the news. (There are many stories of corporate board members not seeking guidance, or not listening to counsel they received from communications professionals—and subsequently regretting not giving communications more forethought.) Governance board members also need to engage stakeholders in dialogue about how the organization can report to and communicate meaningfully with them in order to maximize these communications efforts and minimize the likelihood for problems.

For this reason, it is critical that board members charged with governance view the corporate communications function as equally important to that of other executive-level departments, and turn to corporate communications professionals as part of the decision-making process.

I am not suggesting that communications personnel create or change decisions made at the board level, or that a governance body should let public reaction prevent leaders from making tough but necessary decisions. However, those who are appointed to govern an organization should recognize the importance of communicating their decisions effectively, and seek counsel from communications professionals in this regard specifically. Then, once a decision is made, governance board members should turn to communications professionals in order to develop and implement a plan to announce the news. This means informing the communications professionals (that is, giving them as much information as possible without violating board confidentiality) about how and why the decision was made.

This strategy is easy to implement when times are good and governance decisions are popular. That isn't always the situation; many times, a decision can lead to controversy or board members are responding to a crisis that is already underway.

IN TIMES OF CRISIS . . .

So, what happens to the communications function in times of crisis or controversy? Often, at these moments, the lawyers take control, and the internal communications experts are shunted aside or severely restricted from being able to do their jobs.

Jonelle Birney Sullivan, who headed corporation communications at MCI through numerous business transactions (including the collapsed merger with British Telecom), quickly summed up what happens in these types of situations. In a recent blog posting about corporate communications during times of crisis, she writes:

> As pressure mounts, lawyers hunker down as the outside experts struggle to get up to speed and add value quickly. In many cases, the trusted communications executive is marginalized or comes under fire internally, while still having to play the role of the organization's face to the media." Sullivan points out that the person who could be most helpful in these situations—the internal corporate communications expert—is often mistakenly "marginalized" or completely shut out of the internal process, while simultaneously being expected to explain and defend the company to news outlets.

One of the main reasons the above scenario happens is the "say nothing" strategy endorsed by the legal counsel. This strategy simply doesn't work, because if a crisis is underway, it's too late to say nothing. Others are already saying a lot—just Google your organization's name, for example, and you'll see for yourself! If an organization releases nothing in response, then the story is defined completely by others; the organization's total silence connotes acceptance that the story is true, along with the possible implication that the organization is wrong, acting unfair, or is guilty. Instead, legal counsel and communications counsel must work together, along with board members, to balance the need to protect the company with the need to communicate, recognizing that these objectives can coexist without causing further harm.

Sullivan's statement also refers to another knee-jerk reaction to a crisis: bringing in outside communications counsel (an action often taken by governance board members), as emergency consultants. This can add value, as outsiders can provide a fresh perspective, but should be done to supplement—not replace or supersede—the experienced internal communications team.

In times of conflict or crisis, governance board members also need to speak with one unified voice. The most effective representative of the board is typically the chairperson, CEO, or executive director (assuming that person is a board member). Organizations are consistently criticized when, in times of controversy or crisis, the most senior executives are not made available to speak publicly. The rest of the board members, quite simply, need to support the organization by keeping quiet. While individual board members might vehemently disagree with board decisions in private, once a decision has been made they must publicly support it or, at a minimum, remain mum. Returning to my earlier point about consistency of message, note that nothing can be more harmful than a board member going on record with or whispering in the background about (as it still becomes a part of the story) an opposing view. Going off message is, quite simply, a public violation of the basic governance principle of unity outside the boardroom.

The other governance question that often arises is how much information to disclose publicly, when that information is negative. In my opinion, based on years of experience and years of watching situations come to light in both traditional and social media, the answer is simple: all of the information, all at once. Delaying the release of negative or harmful information only delays the inevitable. In other words, pulling the Band-Aid off slowly doesn't lessen the pain but, instead, prolongs it. When board members have a tough decision or bad news to share, they should work with communications professionals to craft a strategy and key messages, and then get all their news out right away.

SUMMARY

When considering your corporate communications responsibilities inside the boardroom, think about how you're receiving and reacting to news in your day-to-day life. Most likely, you're reading newspapers, watching television, talking to friends and business associates, reading blogs, friending other people on Facebook®, posting photos on Flickr®, and maybe Tweeting.

So, outside the boardroom, you're consuming traditional and new sources of news, information, and opinions; you're also making judgments about businesses, corporations, associations, and non-profit organizations, along with the people who run them. You're forming your opinions based on what is communicated to you, along with when and how you receive the information. You're deciding which organizations are credible and trustworthy, which are treating their employees and constituents well, and which are achieving their missions. You're also deciding which organizations are poorly run, which might be wasting money or treating others unfairly, or which might even be breaking the law. Throughout all of this, you're making decisions based on combinations of facts and opinions coming to you through dozens of sources, all day and all night.

Many of the positive and negative reactions you might have to news are not only based on what's being said, but also on how effectively (or ineffectively) the news is being communicated by its respective source. As a member of a board, you have direct responsibility for decisions. However, you also can have a positive role in how these decisions are communicated by using honesty, transparency, and professional counsel from communications personnel to accurately disseminate news and to engage in conversations with constituents that further explain and support your mission.

ABOUT THE AUTHOR

DAVE GROOBERT is the U.S. General Manager for Environics Communications, a North American public relations agency with offices in Washington, San Francisco, Toronto, Montreal, and Ottawa. He has more than twenty-five years of public relations experience, including working with numerous national and international corporations, associations, and non-profit organizations. He has also served as director of public relations at COMSAT Corporation, a global, publicly traded satellite communications company acquired by Lockheed Martin.

CHAPTER 19

CORPORATE SECURITY

By Robert Dodge and Bruce Wimmer, Pinkerton Global
Consulting and Investigations

Corporate security is a key function that can be easily over-looked, pushed off, or assumed away. Thus, this essay is focused on why your company's security profile must be part of your board's oversight agenda. Today's business risk environments have become increasingly more severe, complex, and globally interdependent. Effectively managing these environments is a fundamental require-ment of business; the important activity of assessing risk must be in place in order to protect both the company's tangible and intan-gible assets, as well as to mitigate risks of violent workplace incidents or of external threats to company leaders. Shareholders, boards of directors, key stakeholders, and the public all expect organizations to identify and anticipate areas of risk, as well as to set in place a cohesive strategy (across all functions) to mitigate or reduce those risks. In addition, these groups expect management will respond in a highly effective manner to the events and incidents that threaten the organization's assets.

A proactive strategy for mitigating the risk of loss ultimately provides organizational profitability with a positive impact and is a key organizational governance responsibility of both senior management and governing boards. It is critical board members provide the comprehensive review and support necessary for protecting lives and assets. These lives and assets might not be just those belonging to your own organizations; remember the damage caused by the Bhopal, India, disaster, or by the recent Gulf oil spill. These corporate mishaps greatly affected nearby communities. Having the right people and the risk profile, plan, preparedness, and execution ready will, through prevention, make many responses unnecessary and minimize losses related to incidents that actually occur. Throughout this essay, there is an implied idea of "God forbid"; nobody wants to deal with employee casualties, destroyed facilities, business evaporation, or any of the other horrific situations that could occur. We must all acknowledge that organizations have to deal with these risks every day, and board members' decisions can have a huge impact on effective outcomes.

Take a minute and put this into personal terms: How many of your family members, friends, or acquaintances have experienced a devastating event that they hadn't planned for? Whether it's a heart attack or stroke, a major crime, a natural disaster, or another event, the lack of planning can have major impacts. It can have a far-reaching effect on global corporations because of all the interdependencies that have evolved around the world—some part of the organization can be at grave risk every hour of every day. Hiring the right people—and insisting on accountability, planning, preparing, and responding effectively—will at least benefit your organization, or at most save it in extreme circumstances.

Effective leadership within an organization's top levels, and its related security functions, is imperative. All of the following rely in some measure upon the effectiveness of an accountable senior executive: organizational reputation, uninterrupted reliability of technical infrastructure and normal business processes, protection of physical and financial assets, safety of employees, and shareholder confidence. Traditionally, what has been previously lacking is a single position at the senior governance level: the person in this position should have the responsibility of crafting, influencing, and directing an organization-wide protection strategy. In many organizations, this type of accountability is dispersed, possibly among managers of several different departments who have potentially conflicting objectives. Today's diverse risks come within a complex matrix of interrelated threats, vulnerabilities, and consequences; therefore, the safeguards against these risks must also be interdependent. Thus, for an organization to be able to influence business strategy and address matters of internal risk exposure, it must have a Chief Security Officer (CSO) at the appropriate internal level.

We at Pinkerton recommend that the CSO report to the organization's most senior-level executive, which will ensure a strong liaison with the board of directors and its operating committees. Such a liaison will signal both top management commitment and the security program's legitimacy. The board members should be involved in hiring the CSO—this is not a case of simple delegation. Rather, the CSO position should be filled by a key hire: a person who possesses a long list of criteria, chemistry, and personality items. The person who fills this position should meet the demand of top-level assessment and agreement. The person an organization chooses can figuratively make the difference between its employees' life and death, particularly in some of the more dire circumstances possible in today's world. Experience is important, albeit secondary to personality and fit within your organization. The CSO must be someone who is strategic and tactical, decisive and collaborative. He or she needs to herd all the business' various segments toward lower risk profiles and proactive planning.

Some critical success factors and characteristics to look for in establishing the CSO position are the following:

- The ability to create sustainable, competitive advantages through pragmatic, innovative security solutions;
- High-quality analytical skills enabling the individual to marry top-level strategies with organization-wide, detailed deployment;
- Exceptional management experience and relationship management at all organizational levels;
- Expertise in communicating recommended courses of action for innovative, business-oriented responses;
- Global experience in the core functions that most impact the organization;
- Passion for excellence and the desire to find all the unturned stones in an organization's plans;
- A strong sense of urgency that can be distributed to all levels in the organization in terms of managing risk.

Hiring is only the beginning—most likely, you will have to spend a considerable amount of time integrating the CSO into the organization, insuring that he or she understands the unique risk picture, critical protection points, and how to execute maneuvers in a critically-timed situation. If the CSO is coming from a long career in law enforcement or the military, he or she may be highly qualified in terms of some very specialized security capabilities, but also almost completely devoid of the business understanding necessary to integrate into the organization and understand priorities in risk tradeoffs. If the CSO is coming from a different industry, many of the risks will be different. The CSO will have to establish new relationships and understand how to get things done effectively inside the organization. In these areas, board members can provide invaluable context.

We had the opportunity to work with a retired general who had had a very long military career and, over the course of thirty years, ended up managing over 100,000 people. After several hours of reviewing a private company's structure, performance, and operations, he had just one question: "What's 'ROI' mean?" Once we regained our composure, it was easy to explain the term meant, "return on investment," because he had an inherent understanding of tradeoffs and short-term and long-term people investments. However, this incident underscores the important differences across corporate and industry cultures. Don't assume they get it. Make sure.

UNDERSTANDING YOUR RISK PROFILE

Do you really understand your organization's appetite for and exposure to risk? If you work for a global equipment manufacturer, the organization's risks are vastly different from those of a regional accounting firm. That said, the process of determining security risks, and the relevant terminology, are often misunderstood. The term "risk" is often wrongly interchanged for "threat." Even though a global manufacturer may have a presence in some geographic locations with higher threat levels, that does not mean the organization automatically faces higher risk. Threat is only part of the risk equation. If a company (wisely) takes the high threat into consideration, enhances security effectiveness in regions where the threat is higher, and thus lowers it vulnerabilities, the company's overall risk might actually be lower than that faced by a regional accounting firm located in a low-threat environment. If an organization's supply chain covers thirty-four countries (including some very dangerous places), the risks might be multiplied. However, if the company recognizes the potential increase consequences and/or the business impact of diverse locations, and ensures resiliency, its risk may actually be lower than that faced by a business that places all its suppliers in a single country. For example, say all a company's suppliers are in Eastern Japan—the recent earthquake and tsunami would have totally disrupted the supply chain.

Like many board topics, the details of this subject can be mind-numbing; however, the right people who have gone through the right process and truly determined the risk can deliver the topic's essence clearly and concisely. Security approaches should be risk-based and the company should ensure representatives are correctly calculating the risk. Demand risk-based security. Risk is likely an area in which corporate security workers will interface heavily with members from other parts of the organization—the same ones that they will have to work with in an emergency—so friction is a harbinger of later problems.

Making plans around your defined risk profile never ends; only events that cause the need for revised planning interrupt the process. Just like a business plan, a risk mitigation plan is a living document, one that is continually being shaped by the present and future. An initial plan will likely consider the impact of a pandemic, while the hint of an emergent virus will cause re-planning and impact analysis. Additionally, we recommend doing an after-action study and analysis of events to capture lessons learned. Investigations should always be analyzed to capture problems. If a violent workplace incident took place, or a manager discovered a purchasing VP's involvement in a purchasing kickback scam, corporate security employees should evaluate the incident and look for the vulnerabilities that allowed it to occur. Even if an emergency evacuation went well, for instance, the security team may still be able to take away some "lessons learned" from that real-world incident. All of these incidents or possibilities can be captured through analysis in order to make corrective actions and fine-tune plans for even more effective responses in the future. Plans, policies, and procedures can be improved and enhanced.

The board members likely represent the broadest set of experiences in an organization. Applying their oversight, along with this exposure, to many different situations, scenarios, and approaches to problems will broaden the overall thought process concerning risk mitigation and increase organizational preparedness. Board members should be comfortable and assured that the overall security plan considers the entire range of possibilities, and they should feel compelled to ask very hard, probing questions. In addition, it helps for a company to hire an outside firm or advisor to critique and/or review the top-level thinking, major assumptions, and response scenarios within the security plan. If this outside entity could also become a contingent response provider in an emergency, including its representatives in the review process will proactively get that entity up to speed, and build partnerships necessary for a comprehensive response down the road. Remember, it doesn't cost much to validate!

Being prepared, which includes holding serious exercises, gives a company an idea of how the plan is going to hold up when something real occurs. Individuals might have backup communications in the plan, only to find out, through an exercise, that satellite phones weren't charged or an account had been de-activated through oversight or nonpayment. Depending on the risks' scope, a preparedness plan has to involve everyone at the organization, while also assuming that some of the key people will be absent most of the time.

For example, a senior executive at a global enterprise, which we recently worked with, had been the CIO for a company in the Snowbelt that had a large facility with telemarketing, distribution, and corporate data areas all under one roof. The company did work for national clients that demanded highly available, twenty-four/seven responses. One afternoon, while the executive was returning from a customer visit, he got word that a delivery truck had taken out the facility's main power line. Heavy snow had caused the line to sag a couple of critical inches: this, combined with the six inches of snow under the delivery truck, made for a stunning collision and a complete loss of power. The good news was that the organization had a contingency plan for this type of problem, and therefore had an entire local generator (that, sure enough, started on cue). Activities across the business continued, except for some new equipment (high-growth expansion gear) the company needed integrated. The key response individual jumped into action and installed most of the equipment. Then, a server rack slipped onto a raised floor panel and tipped. The rack didn't tip over, but the panel slid several inches, nipping off the end of the response person's finger. Ouch—didn't see that coming! While the company recovered from the incident, this event underscores how easy it is to rely on one key person. The company's future plans insured multiple people had familiarity with key recovery processes. When an event with risk potential happens, individuals need to be able to react in a manner that does the organization the most good. Despite great planning, circumstances have a way of negating a completely scripted approach; however, the effort behind a plan will ensure that you have most of it right. It's also important to understand tradeoffs in advance.

Start with the worst-case scenarios. What could really impact your business and ruin your day? 2011, the worst year ever in terms of catastrophic expense, included natural disasters that resulted in almost $380 billion of damages. Fortunately, the year's fatalities were below average; possibly, this decrease was due to better preparedness and greatly increased, near-real-time communications, capabilities enabled by millions of mobile phones, tablets, and other devices. After the worst has been identified the worst, assess the probabilities and look at the plan.

Organizational security is a key area, impacting an organization's very survival. It is easy to minimize these efforts, but we urge executives and board members to insist on implementing an active risk management program, along with hiring and empowering a great CSO. Validate and understand the current risk and security strategy, and get outside opinions if any doubt remains about whether the plan is comprehensive, complete, and tested. Monitor on an ongoing basis, paying particular attention to real incidents that occur and the quality of response. Make sure executives and board members are providing the necessary oversight to the management team and CSO.

ABOUT PINKERTON

For over 160 years, the Pinkerton name has evoked memories of America's first detective agency. Today, Pinkerton Consulting and Investigations is a leading global provider of security, investigations, and risk management services, with offices located in North America, Latin America, Europe, and Asia. Pinkerton is a division of Securitas, a global leader in security services with 295,000 employees in over fifty countries. See www.pinkerton.com.

ABOUT THE AUTHORS

ROBERT L. DODGE, CPP, is a Vice President with Pinkerton Consulting and Investigations. He has been involved in security management, investigations, and security consulting for twenty-three years. In his current role as VP with Pinkerton, Dodge is responsible for managing operations for the Western United States and client needs globally, along with Pinkerton's Global Supply Chain Security Division and Pinkerton's Global Risk Group. During his career, he has conducted and managed numerous investigations and security consulting projects in more than fifty countries around the world.

BRUCE WIMMER, CPP, is the Director of Global Consulting and Logistics at Pinkerton Consulting and Investigations. Wimmer has nearly forty years of experience in government and the private sector. For most of his twenty-two years in government, he was a Special Agent in the U.S. Air Force Office of Special Investigations. He has lived and worked for eighteen years outside the United States, in Vietnam, Thailand, the Republic of Korea, Japan, the Philippines, the People's Republic of China, Hong Kong SAR, the United Kingdom, Germany, and Honduras. He has worked in nearly sixty countries around the world and in all fifty states.

Information Systems and the Chief Information Officer (CIO)

By Neil Evans, (former CIO) Microsoft, and Pete O'Dell,
Swan Island Networks

The Chief Information Officer's (CIO) role is vastly different across organizations in terms of reporting, responsibility, authority, centralization, and budgetary controls. In all cases, however, this role's function has a large impact on the organization on both an operational and strategic basis, and requires strong board oversight to ensure that its comprehensive expectations are set and met.

The CIO who is meeting today's needs may not be equipped for the rapid technological changes taking place or understand the new responses based on shifts in a company's core business. Nothing in corporate America has changed more in the last forty years than the increasing reliance on technology, and this areas is showing no sign of slowing down; you are quick or you are dead. The growing number of cyber-threats is another big concern board members should be involved in.

Data processing, information systems, information technology, or knowledge management—whatever you want to call it, this function has grown dramatically in the last fifty years, and continues to change at a very rapid rate. A large organization likely has systems conceived and deployed both in the 60s and every decade following—a complex spider web or network of disparate capabilities. Today's environment of mobility, cloud computing, and cyber risk defines an entirely new set of challenges that must be addressed, since Moore's Law is now on steroids, figuratively speaking. If the constant set of changing demands in technology make you a little queasy or apprehensive, you are probably paying attention at the right level. It is rare that an organization needs a tactical and detailed technician, a strategic visionary, and a vigilant guard all in the same person; but this is the reality that must be dealt with when assessing a CIO. Recruiting for this position was difficult before the start of major cyber attacks; now, it is an even more complicated scenario.

Members of an organization will have many opinions about the role of technology within the organization, and how well the IT organization is meeting them. We recommend a comprehensive survey, written in business language, done by an outside company that will assess both perceptions and overall health of the current environment. This assessment—coupled with interviews of key executives across the company, strategic planning from the existing CIO, and a strong, all-in financial assessment of how much technology is costing the business in total—will give board members the material needed to assess the current situation. In some organizations, spending of significant amounts of dollars takes place outside the CIO's control, but these factors are still important to consider in the overall technology assessment.

CRITICAL RISKS AND STRATEGIES

As board members, are you cognizant of the risks that the IT department has to guard against and that could significantly harm the organization? Each industry has its own elements, but several are pervasive across all organizations.

1. Continuity: Few organizations could set up a manual shop outside an earthquake zone, like Bank of America did after the San Francisco leveling in 1906. Systems have to recover and work under an increasing number of situations, any of which can knock them out. In addition, systems are becoming intertwined with outside providers, so maintaining their continuity becomes an increasingly faceted problem. The CIO isn't the only one involved in this effort, we hope; this is a key risk area that demands attention. Exercises to test assumptions and validate plans are critical, and outside validation is also recommended.

2. System data security: Each year, directors and board members find out through the press that their systems suffered a major breach or break-in, putting the entire organization at risk. RSA, Sony PlayStation, and STRATFOR are three recent examples of such incidents. While technology is making the physical security world better—protecting people with cameras, sensors, facial recognition, mobility, and more—things are not as rosy in the data center. Everyone wants access to critical, sensitive data through iPads, iPhones, SAAS apps, and more. All the while, outsiders are learning to exploit multiple avenues into mining others' sensitive data. This spreading infusion of technology throughout every part of an organization

increases the chance of a break-in from the outside, or a devastating theft of sensitive data from the inside (for instance, recall the DOD's situation with Wikileaks and the reputed theft from inside the organization simply by using blank CDs labeled with "Lady GaGa"). The best advice is to overinvest, protect the core, and use outsiders to help. Cloud computing, while still being largely shunned by enterprise computing gurus, has an unexplored opportunity: liability and deep pockets. If Amazon or another cloud provider allows negligent access to data, they have very deep pockets. Liability suits will be played out over the coming years. Unfortunately, it's likely an organization can't sue its own, internal staff for negligent security.

3. Competitive posture: Everybody is responsible for insuring their own organizations have the momentum, strategy, and execution necessary to prosper. If your company gets caught short by ignoring technology that could have been used to maintain or command more market share, the organization can perish despite all other efforts. That is not to say every marketing strategy (i.e. Facebook®, Twitter®, etc.) demands betting the company or making a huge investment. The CIO, if thoroughly integrated as a member of the company, should be a key driver of and collaborator in this area. He or she might take a great deal of input from the organization into account, but when we look at technology's capabilities of integration into the enterprise, success or failure usually depends on IT execution. Cloud computing may change this. For example, SalesForce. com allows entire sales departments to avoid IT if they so

desire, and if IT's response isn't good in other areas, this trend will continue.

4. Globalization: Your company, most likely, has data that is increasing in complexity and value moving around the globe. It's likely the company has to make that data available to an increasing number of partners, and to end customers, in real time. We have already covered securing the data, but maintaining, synchronizing, and improving usage is also very important. Organizations' members must watch for unanticipated problems—a store finder app posted on the company website may seem benign until someone realizes a competitor has procured a script or code that will vacuum up the entire list.

5. Cost position: Think about what the company paid for the last generation of technology and the capabilities contained therein. Moore's law is continuing, without pause, in terms of cost per unit of technology in almost every area. Unfortunately, that doesn't mean an automatic decrease in technology spending; lower unit costs make many more technology improvements possible, so spending can easily spiral out of control. Rogue IT projects are outside of the IT department's realm; they can be started with operating budget dollars while remaining unknown to almost all. Technology is great as a competitive weapon, but an organization needs someone to monitor its overall cost trajectory.

Many organizations' board members have found that a steering committee (composed of a cross-section of the organization's technology users) is a very valuable investment, and that such a committee can provide good input to oversight objectives. A balanced committee will ensure consideration of multiple strategies and allocation of resources across many areas, as well as ensuring that the CIO is receiving good organizational support in terms of meeting the most needs with given budget resources. If the CIO is part of the executive group making the top-level decisions, feedback may come from that level, either instead of or in addition to other sources.

CHANGING OF THE GUARD

The average tenure of a corporate CIO is very low compared to that of most executive positions, with some surveys putting average tenure at twenty-four to thirty months. Board members and directors can work to ensure that when a changes happens, these steps are taken, ensuring a better result:

1. Exit interview: Understand thoroughly why the current executive left, even if it was a non-performance based termination. If it was friendly, as in a retirement, a great amount of goodwill may remain. If the person is leaving or left because of the organization, it is important to find out why and what would have made a difference.

2. Organizational polling: Find out what was good under the last leadership and what could be vastly improved if all current restrictions were removed. There's a new chapter to write, so make it count.

3. Consider revamping responsibilities: The position may have been too narrow or too broad in scope; alternatively, it may be time to move to a centralized approach versus a decentralized, business-unit driven method.

4. Consider changing the reporting: If IT has been part of accounting for historical reasons, and board members feel

it should move up or down in the organization, defining that move before starting a search will improve the odds of a good replacement.

5. Look at the industry's best: When examining the universe of competitors, suppliers, customers, and other related organizations, which are admirable or envy provoking? What makes that approach superior?

6. Take inventory: How is the organization doing in terms of technology and business strategy? If the exiting executive had a critical mainframe or aging system built or maintained for years, finding someone with that expertise could be very difficult and put the organization either at risk or at an acceleration point for replacement.

7. Stem an exodus: There is risk of multiple key people leaving if this dismissal was highly charged, if people have strong loyalty to the executive leaving, or if individuals now perceive the organization as unprotected and vulnerable. While the economy's woes have locked many people into place, great people are still moving around, and some prevention of an exodus is recommended.

8. Identify the search committee: Most organizations employ a mix of executives who are technologically capable and who never had to understand much about technology's impact on the business or industry. Try to pick the people who are most capable of assessing potential new hires' technical skills, but also insist that the committee makes sure interviewees will fit in the organization. If you have to pick organizational chemistry over technical wizardry, we'd make that recommendation in most instances.

9. Consider board participation: Depending on circumstances and strategic importance, decide if a board committee should be included in the interview process. Doing so gives the organization a different perspective and underscores the importance of the position to those being interviewed. However, it's not always the right move.

EMPOWERING YOUR CIO

Whether the organization has a long-term CIO or is starting fresh, the board members need to oversee and empower technology efforts inside the organization, and ensure that a balance is created, monitored, and adjusted periodically. The below list includes a sampling of elements that must go into this balancing act:

- Control: While the "IT control-freak" stereotype is well known, and in many cases relevant, an organization really does need someone ensuring smart, well-thought-out controls are in place, managed, enforced, and continually updated. Areas like critical data, legacy systems, and access rules are all like icebergs; only the tip of the issue is visible, while its complexities are deep and entrenched.

- Innovation: The perennial "IT backlog" of twenty-four to forty-eight months immediately throws up an obstacle for many organizations, which are finding innovation very difficult. Rapid response teams work for some organizations, but "rogue IT" is becoming more prevalent. In rogue IT, operating units use cloud-based or locally acquired resources to build something to plug the tech gaps. As ex-CIOs, we have had multiple experiences with this problem—some great and others truly horrendous. In our increasingly global environment, scale is a tremendous problem for successful deployment.

- Protection: Despite fifty years of IT, companies are still losing data due to poor backups or other basic blocking and tackling activities. Many organizations have plans that don't work in the event of a catastrophe, such as a major flood, power outage, sabotage, workplace violence, criminal activity, or a multitude of other speed bumps that can destroy an organization's operating ability. The IT function must be a large part of the team that is continually readying the organization for such emergencies by planning, testing, and responding.

- Degree of uniformity: If an organization frequently moves people across its functions, the company could be losing large amounts of money and even more time if all the technology environments are allowed to be completely separate. We have a friend who recently moved from one internal Army department to another. She was amazed by the lack of uniformity, something the Department of Defense is famous for.

- Agility: The pace of change, even in our current recessive business environment, is still very strong. Some amazing savings are available to those who can execute effectively, and even more are available to those who can pressure the competition into mistakes or situations in which they try to respond and fail.

- Security: This is currently a wild card. The threats are high, the stakes are immense, and the tools are ineffective many times over—it's the equivalent of revolvers taking on automatic weapons in a firefight. Our best advice is to support the CIO; question him or her mercilessly in regards to other attacks; and bring in outside resources to validate, question, enhance, and monitor the company's cyber-security posture. Last year, one of us learned a lesson from nature out in Yellowstone: elk scatter when the wolves show up, and the weak end up as wolf appetizers and entrées. The buffalo make their herd circle, with the weaker and younger animals in the middle. A lot more elk get eaten than buffalo. So, team up with familiar organizations and build a network of trusted partners to help keep the cyber wolves at bay.

CONCLUSION

Like all board oversight tasks, the CIO and IT function is fraught with risk, creating demands that board members provide guidance and auditing. Working to build an acceptable risk scenario, funding the critical resources, and formally monitoring progress all make good sense. Like filling most executive positions, hiring a CIO with the right mix of drive, skill, and chemistry makes a marked difference. Maintaining the right balance between spending and results, current and future requirements, and speed and security are delicate acts, even in smooth seas.

ABOUT THE AUTHORS

PETE O'DELL is a technology executive based in Washington, D.C. He has been a CIO/IT Director for multiple companies (Autodesk, Microwarehouse), but transitioned to being a Division President, Chief Operating Officer, and board member, which allowed him to experience both sides of this critical equation. He has written multiple books, including *Silver Bullets: How Interoperable Data Will Transform Information Sharing in 2010*. In his free time, O'Dell is an avid fly fisherman, a reasonable runner, a voracious consumer of technology information, and a poor golfer. He can be reached at peterlodell@gmail.com.

NEIL EVANS is currently the Chief Information Officer at Microvision, Inc., in Kirkland, Washington. He was Microsoft's first IT Manager, and was with the company from 1983 through 1994, retiring as CIO. He hired the entire department and created systems, networks, and infrastructure worldwide through a period of incredible growth. Evans also developed some cutting-edge strategic initiatives at Bellevue Community College. He has an undergraduate degree in business and an M.B.A. from Northwestern.

CHAPTER 21

CORPORATE BOARDS AND UNDERSTANDING THE CFO

A Financial Lens, the CFO's Conscience, and the Gateway to Fiscal Understanding

By Frank J. Walker, Partner, Baker Tilly

INTRODUCTION

Over the last ten years, we have all read hundreds of news stories about companies facing financial challenges or regulatory investigations tied to "accounting irregularities," "misguided financing reporting," "a lack of internal controls," "illegal vendor payments or bribes," "flawed audits by outside accounting firms," and countless other financial and accounting problems, which have frustrated shareholders, embarrassed boards of directors, and destroyed market value. What steps can be taken to foster better quality, integrity, and transparency in accounting and financial reporting? In particular, what steps can board members, the audit committee, company leaders, members of the CFO's office, and outside accounting firms take to strengthen confidence in financial reports, budgets, forecasts, and internal controls?

Whether it's a case of public, private, early-stage growth, or mature business, the complexities of guiding companies appropriately require corporate directorship with a multidisciplinary approach. Many boards form special committees based on where specific skills and subject matter experts are focused, an action that sometimes leaves those outside the committee without a view across the entire business. An audit committee, for example, is usually comprised of trained accountants, finance professionals, and former or current officers with significant subject matter expertise. Former CEOs, CTOs, entrepreneurs, and professional investors alike are serving a variety of roles, from strategy and operations to corporate finance and risk management.

These are positive developments, certainly, when considering the wake of the well-publicized corporate scandals that have plagued the last decade and have shaken our confidence in the overall governance system. A great deal of effort has gone into restoring this confidence from legislation (e.g., the Sarbanes-Oxley Act and establishment of the PCAOB) to changes in boards' expectations in general. People have the higher expectation that board members will objectively and independently provide sage advice on strategy, governance, operations, finance, and risk. There is less "cow-tailing" to the CEO's desires and more board members operating in intended form.

Today's board members, especially those less experienced in directorship, need to understand the financial landscape in which they are operating. This need for understanding is heightened by the connections of global markets and the speed with which change can impact business. All directors, not just audit committee members, can better serve the companies they govern through a better understanding of transparency fundamentals and financial reporting accuracy, as well as through supporting day-to-day functions of the CFO office.

Knowledge of the key performance indicators of the CFO's team, the key strategic tasks of the CFO's office, and the different types of CFOs, along with knowing to ask the right questions at the right times, are critical parts of providing solid governance—regardless of your specific board role.

UNDERSTANDING THE CFO FRAMEWORK

First, having an appreciation for the CFO's role and functions (that are overseen by the board or audit committee) is important to understanding the CFO's perspective and views of the company. Many CFOs have a span of control or heavy influence not only over the traditional accounting, finance, and treasury functions, but also over mergers and acquisitions, partnerships, and company risk management. Moreover, they may also have responsibilities from human resources to technology, even though these areas are not traditionally associated with CFOs. Today's CFOs have evolved from individuals primarily engaged in strictly financial matters to individuals engaged in highly strategic company issues. They provide support for key decisions and are often trusted lieutenants of the CEOs.

To draw an analogy from sports, CFOs should be capable of playing both offense (that is, M&A, capital raising, and business advisory) and defense (that is, controls, compliance, and risk management). The CFO's multifaceted role provides him or her with a unique perspective, and that perspective can be a valuable barometer for both opportunities and risks within an enterprise. As such, properly understanding the lens through which the CFO is viewing the business, and the areas that the CFO has in his or her span of control can provide boards with valuable perspective.

Although the CFO is no longer expected to be the one viewing the business through green eyeshades, it is important for all members of the board to understand the CFO situation, along with the specific strengths and potential weaknesses of the person serving as finance chief; after all, different times may require different types of CFOs. Other than the general demands on the position, these inherent differences may be part of the reason CFOs have an average tenure of only five point one years.[1] As most significant issues in a business end up on the CFO's desk in one way or another, it is necessary the CFO have the right skills for the right times. The table below demonstrates the different skills required from the CFO during different stages in a company's life cycle.

CFO Type Matrix - Right Skills for Right Times?		
	Growth ⬆	**Stalled** ⬌	**Decline** ⬇
Strength	Capable of wearing multiple hats, running fast	Strategy minded	Taskmaster, decisive, Eisenhower Matrix
Qualities	Collaborative	Communicator	Autocrat
Personality	Right balance of speed and precision	Can operate in ambiguous environment, be creative, assist CEO	Force of personality, can make tough decisions quickly
Always	Trusted Advisor	Highest Integrity	Company First

---

1   David McCann, "CFOs by the Numbers" in CFO (CFO Publishing LLC, 13 Sep. 2011: accessed 21 Feb. 2012); see also Crist|Kolder Associates, "The Volatility Report 2011."

This general framework of desired leadership traits, according to different stages in a company's life cycle, provides perspective on whether an organization has the right CFO for right now.

For a company in a period of rapid growth, the skills and personality of the type of CFO required may be different than the type of CFO required by a company in a period of stalled growth or decline. A turnaround situation is different than that of a growth company. A turnaround generally requires relentless execution with a narrower focus. The anatomy of a turnaround requires a finance leader who is comfortable operating in a more autocratic leadership style (sometimes this is unpopular); in contrast, the growth company thrives on someone who participates in teamwork, wears multiple hats, and pushes forward on multiple fronts at once.

Generally, the most effective and proactive CFOs are highly adaptable and interested in continuous improvement. Thus, even if gaps in his or her role are identified, this identification doesn't necessarily mean a change is required. Rather, such identification may be directional in terms of pointing to areas where board members can provide additional support and feedback. In addition, the CFO is also the primary link to, or interface with, the company's external accounting firms, auditors, investment bankers, lenders, and financial advisors. The CFO needs to have dynamic and transparent agendas for and lines of communication with these key external relationships. Sharing important developments—both positive and negative—on a prompt and comprehensive basis will help curtail any problems down the road. These developments include vital challenges, trends, metrics, performance indicators, potentially jeopardized covenants, cash flow challenges, and so forth. All must be shared in order to create better, more accurate financial reports and audit reports, along with generally better-informed stakeholders and markets, especially for publicly owned companies.

A weak CFO represents substantial business risk, as well as potentially personal risk for board members. As the company, CEO, and board members are all so highly dependent on this position, the CFO's performance and overall fit within the organization should be assessed frequently. To do so, an understanding of "What" is needed to understand "How" the CFO is performing. The table below provides a summary of areas to which a skilled CFO should be contributing, along with indicators that he or she is performing at a high level. This table can be used as a guide to understand better the different areas of responsibility and best practices employed by high-performing finance chiefs.

CFO Best Practices - How are they doing?	
Area	**Best Practices Indicators**
Strategic	Forward looking. Key contributor to Board and Executive Committee on direction, focus, resources/needs to execute.
Transaction Support	Leading financing events, large purchases, M&A, divestitures, contratct negotiation/structuring, supply chain.
Business Advisory & Decision Support	Partner to business operators. Value-add contributions to decision making. Build v. Buy, expansion, new services offerings. At table for major decisions—not there just to say NO. Pricing & financial models.
Educator - Fiscal Understanding	Regular and meaningful communication with line managers. Assist operations in full understanding of financial picture.
Visibility of numbers	Well prepared insightful financial reports. Tell the story. Regular financial dashboard reporting. Open access to meaningful data. Frequent review of results.
Controls, Risk Management, Compliance	No surprises. Financial statements, internal controls, fraud tax, insurance, secure data and systems.
Financial Architect	Steward to capital structure, cash flow, tax minimization, rate structures.

The above should provide board members with perspective on the main ways an organization depends on its CFO, thereby putting directors in the best position to fulfill their leadership and governance roles by "seeking first to understand, then to be understood."[2]

RIGHT QUESTIONS AT THE RIGHT TIMES

The CFO is commonly the yin to the CEO's yang. If the CFO has the right personality and skills, his or her viewpoints will serve as a healthy counterbalance to the (often) aggressive force of that CEO's personality and views. For the board member, an understanding of this relationship is key to developing perspective on the organization. Developing such an understanding will best position you to view the organization through the proper lens and thereby enable you to ask the right questions at the right time.

Board meetings and interactions can be highly prescriptive if the company management is experienced at reporting to an independent board. Board packages including company strategy, investments, financial performance, and forecasts, should be well structured and concise. However, through the well-presented, polished presentations, board members should seek more insight by making sure they properly understand the situation and ask the right questions. When seeking a realistic view about the business, the CFO is often the best executive to whom questions should be posed.

Often, the CEO's presentations to the board are tilted away from the past, toward the company's future direction and strategic plans. Having the right strategy, leadership, and tone at the top are common denominators in most successful companies. However, strategy and vision are really just five percent.

---

2   Stephen R. Covey, *The Seven Habits of Highly Effective People* (New York: Free Press, 1989).

Execution is the remaining ninety-five percent. Listen carefully to the CFO. As a board member, it is seductive to think about spending the majority of time on strategy or the CEO's vision for the company. After all, thinking big thoughts and leaving the details to others is intellectually stimulating. However, board members can gain a healthy appreciation for how the business is really performing and is reasonably expected to perform (in the context of the current environment) through asking the CFO the right questions.

A CFO can address questions that are relevant to most stages of a business. The first practical time when a board member is able to formulate questions is when the board package arrives. A general guide to common questions, organized by area, is included in the following sections of this essay. Use these as a general guide for developing your own questions. Ask yourself, "Were these questions asked and answered in the materials, or is there another layer that would be appropriate to understand, from either the board package or the CFO presentation?"

The financial experience and savvy of each board member will vary—from veteran CPA/CFO to complete financial novice, and everything in between. However, it is critical each board member have the requisite skills to read and understand the financial reports, even if remedial training is necessary. Each board member should be in a position to read and understand financial statements, reports, budgets, and forecasts; in turn, all these documents should be footnoted thoroughly and include summaries of the company's performance, benchmarked against relevant industry ratios. Board members should be in a position to identify financial trends that may be a foreshadowing of problems down the road, such as: dependence on a particular revenue stream, increasingly aging accounts receivables, or overly aggressive forecasts during recessionary periods.

Board members should be looking for disconnects in the report, such as an uptick in projected revenues and a corresponding significant reduction in marketing expenses. In this day and age, the CFO's report cannot be the time that board members "zone out," check their e-mail or go get coffee. They must be engaged, informed, interactive and empowered to ask the right questions and insist on accurate answers. Here are some of the critical questions to be asked:

BUDGETING AND PLANNING

The board's oversight over the budgeting and planning process can tell you a lot about an organization and its management. Some companies fall into the trap of providing top-down plans that have little connection to the operating plan—other than the shared fact of the CEO dictating targets. The best example of this is when a company creates somewhat arbitrary growth goals expressed as a corporate mantra, such as the 20/20 plan: "We will grow the top and bottom line by 20 percent a year." If this type of tagline planning starts to drive business planning, board members should start asking questions. Often, these types of plans are unsustainable and they have little connection to actual operations or natural business cycles. These top-down plans may be dictated to operators, who in turn feel pressure to make short-term decisions at the expense of long-term value creation. All this is not to say that management shouldn't set big goals or challenge everyone to deliver; on the contrary, such ideas can serve to create healthy competition. Such ideas should not, however, take the place of realistic planning or the expression of a sound operating plan.

> **Budgeting and Planning Questions**
> » How much input into the final plan did the operating teams have?
> » Are the plans an expression of the operating plan or a top-down plan?
> » Were the plans adjusted to meet an overall corporate goal (e.g., a 20/20 plan)? If so, how much?

Some Additional Issues and Red Flags In a Board's Review of the Financial Statement

» Trends in margins (gross or operating) with significant variance to the plan (e.g., budget).

» Variances in key performance indicators (KPI) to industry benchmarks, especially when they have been in line during prior reporting periods.

» Realistic assessment of adequate reserves and allowances for various assets to ensure a realistic presentation of realizable value.

» Accruals of expenses for all known material liabilities. The company operators should know in which areas the amount could be reasonably estimated.

» A report by the CFO on the company's financials relative to covenants provided to lenders or investors.

» Non-financial trends that have significant financial consequences, such as high employee turnover rates, excessively long lead times prior to sales closings, high levels of customer dissatisfaction, excessive use of outside consultants, negative developments affecting the company's brand or social media reputation, or a particularly weak or shallow waterfall or backlog, etc.

MERGERS AND ACQUISITIONS

Mergers and acquisitions are corporate, once-in-a-lifetime events for many organizations and managers. Usually, they are not events with which management operators have had substantial prior experiences. The prospect of acquiring a company, forging new markets, and creating growth quickly excites both CEOs and their leadership teams. For a company, a merger or acquisition can represent tremendous opportunity to achieve plans; for managers, a merger can represent resume-building experiences and potentially greater jobs through growth. Mergers and acquisitions can be emotionally charged; they require the right balance of art and science to analyzing their prospects. The downside to getting this process wrong is monumental and will erase tremendous shareholder value for the acquirer. Most board members realize the risk in mergers and acquisitions, but may find that risk hard to assess while executives are presenting the investment case or the CEO is advocating the transaction. This instance is another place in which the CFO likely has some more valuable perspective board members should know, which may not be readily apparent in executives' presentations about the transaction. To be more informed about mergers and acquisitions, consider the following questions:

Mergers and Acquistions

» What are the key financial and strategic goals of this transaction? Will it be accretive or dilutive of shareholder value in the short and medium terms?

» Tell us, how has financial due diligence confirmed the thesis for the transaction?

» How high a risk is there for meeting the projections? How much are we counting on synergies in these projections?

» Were there any surprises in due diligence?

» What seller representatives are we relying on most heavily for the acquisition to work?

» What integration risks were identified? How do we plan to integrate corporate cultures?

CAPITAL STRUCTURE

As it relates to a business' financial operations, a profit-and-loss statement tells board members the actual story about how that business is performing. This is the moment in which the bottom-line results of a company's strategic efforts and challenges are often manifested. As a result, many board members will not focus as intently on the balance sheet and what story it is telling, assuming the business does not have a more immediate liquidity or solvency problem. However, since the balance sheet is akin to a foundation to a house, careful attention should be paid to both its strength and capacity. The CFO should be intimately aware of the balance sheet's details and its relevance to the business' ability to execute the plan. For example, every company has its own limits in terms of how much growth it can internally fund. Meaningful factors in this equation include items from the company's operating cash cycle, such as investments in inventory, accounts receivable, and other assets, all of which are offset by the amount of terms extended on payable items. As a result, the board members should understand how much every new dollar in sales requires from investing additional working capital. To understand the relationship of capital structure to a company's ability to deliver on future plans, the board should be asking the following questions:

Capital Structure
» How fast can our company afford to grow without requiring additional capital?
» To meet our growth plans, how much working capital will be consumed for the increases in revenue?
» How is our relationship with our senior leaders?
» Do we have any concerns that our plans may put us in a position of not meeting all of our financial covenants?
» If the business were down 20 percent this year, what would the impact be? Have we analyzed downside cases?

BUSINESS INTELLIGENCE AND SYSTEMS

All companies encounter problems—this is not a question of "if" but "when." It's of paramount importance to have the right systems and business process in place so that when there is a problem, the company has reasonable visibility and available information with which to make informed decisions. A business' size and complexity will usually dictate the types of systems needed (e.g., business intelligence) but even a smaller and less complex enterprise needs a process and reasonable system for analyzing information. For example, the advent of cloud computing solutions has produced systems that provide robust business analytic tools at a fraction of what these capabilities once cost. A lack of investment in adequately staffed accounting teams and adequate finance systems can turn into pervasive problems when something goes wrong. In today's business environment, the velocity of change is so high that people need to know the numbers on a real-time basis (i.e., not fifteen days after the month ends). A good CFO needs to know the numbers, but he or she cannot be attempting to do a twenty-first century job with twentieth century tools. This is not to suggest every company needs to be Wal-Mart in terms of ability to mine data and affect change; however, having visibility and early warning systems makes for a competitive advantage in any enterprise.

In order to understand how intelligent an organization's business systems and internal controls are, as well as the early warning systems available, board members should be asking the CFO the following:

Business Intelligence and Systems
- » How good are our management reporting systems?
- » Do we have strong internal controls in place to detect and prevent fraud, waste, and financial reource mismanagement? Do these controls also help facilitate prompt and accurate financial reporting, and is there a "dashboard" in place to manage key metrics?
- » Do our managers know how we are doing before they receive the P&L the following month?
- » How often are financial performance metrics discussed with management?

FINANCIAL REPORTING

Since the contexts of the organization's type, size, complexity, and capital structure are relevant to the above-mentioned areas, it's possible financial reporting issues can vary even more based upon specific facts and circumstances. A publicly traded, SEC-registered company will have different issues with and much more scrutiny on financial reporting than a private company that has no private investors or institutional capital will. The audit committees of publicly traded firms spend substantial resources to determine the adequacy of financial reporting and related disclosures. However, you don't necessarily have to be on a publicly traded firm's audit committee to get the benefit of understanding answers to certain basic questions about that firm's financial reporting. The saying, "The numbers don't lie," is not true in every context, even if no one had the intention of providing a misleading picture. To better understand the numbers presented, the board members must ask the CFO the following questions:

Financial Reporting

» What would you view as a difference in the firm's GAAP earnings versus its economic earnings?

» Has the company changed any significant estimates used in its accounting, or has it made elective changes to significant accounting policies?

» How involved are you in shaping customer/client contracts and fee arrangements? If you are not involved, does that lack of involvement create any issues regarding revenue recognition?

» Are there any differences between the company's accounting for revenue and cost in comparison to those of major competitors?

» Regarding significant differences in presentation of "pro forma" financial data and GAAP, ask why they are important and if there could be anything misleading to someone less sophisticated.

CONCLUSION

By understanding the CFO's role and the individual holding that position, and engaging him or her in appropriate dialogue, the board of directors will be in an infinitely better position to perform their duties, regardless of their backgrounds or financial experience. Although there is no "one-size-fits-all" in terms of the magic questions to ask, having a general framework to work from that helps board members ask the right questions at the right times is a tool that will help the board members, the company, and the CFO. Remember, the CFO can hold a great store of information and perspective and, by sharing it, can serve as the gateway to a sound understanding of the company.

ABOUT THE AUTHOR

FRANK WALKER is a partner in the Tysons Corner, Virginia, office of Baker Tilly, a global CPA and consulting firm. He began his career at the Big Four and has served as the CFO of several rapid-growth companies. Walker is a member of Baker Tilly's Consulting Group and leads its Transaction Advisory Services practice, which focuses on middle-market mergers and acquisitions, large financing events, post-deal advisory and integration, performance improvement, and turnaround advice. He has over fifteen years of public accounting and private industry experience in a variety of industries, including healthcare, government contracting, services, direct marketing, and technology. Walker is a frequent speaker and author of articles on corporate growth. He is a CPA and a graduate of The Catholic University of America.

CHAPTER 22

The Critical Importance of Evaluating and Testing Employees

By Joseph "Bud" Haney, CEO, Profiles International

Sound corporate governance practices dictate that organizational leaders should rely upon objective evidence to make sound decisions: these decisions affect the firm's well-being, its tangible valuation, and its intangible assets retained at large. Quantifiable information can serve as the foundation of a persuasive prospectus, an indicator of a company's recent performance, or a barometer of the firm's potential in the future. Hiring decisions can be some of the most critical moves an organization makes, and employment assessments provide a scientifically tested, quantifiable measure of the candidate's degree of fit.

Consider the original hiring of nefarious characters later involved in the recent collapses of some of the world's most well established financial institutions. At some point, someone said, "This is the type of individual we need on our team," and yet, such hiring resulted in bankrupting the entire organization and damaging the company's brand beyond repair. Industry experts agree that the costs of a hiring mistake do not only include additional recruiting costs and, on estimation, three to five times the mis-hire's annual salary; these costs also include the hiring manager's time and effort, damaged or even broken client relationships, and, eventually, the loss of hard-won consumer confidence in and respect for the company's reputation as a provider of quality products and services. Thus, the hiring decision's importance can hardly be understated, and yet, the selection of whom to hire is often an intuitive decision by the hiring manager conducting the talent search or candidate selection process, within the usual resource constraints.

Enter the role of effective employment and candidate evaluations and assessments, in particular, those providing job matching for candidates' full profiles of work-related behavioral tendencies, preferred areas of interest, and cognitive abilities. One way to objectify the hiring process and decrease the chance of hiring the wrong individual is to conduct pre-hire employment assessments that measure candidates' behavioral tendencies and cognitive abilities. These employment assessments, which provide invaluable insight into why an individual thinks and acts in a certain manner, go beyond the resume and personal statement to provide another measure of how likely a candidate is to fit in as a valuable and productive member of the organization. After all, organizational success relies heavily on key performers' ability to deliver their best, achieve organizational objectives, and contribute to corporate value, all of which is collectively referred to as employer branding.

Ensuring the right fit between candidate and job position is critical; it leads to increased engagement in the new hire's work and provides the company with value beyond the new hire's technical skill. Empirical evidence is mounting that employee engagement translates into reduced turnover and on-the-job accidents, as well as into increased job satisfaction, productivity, profits, and, most importantly, company growth, all of which is based on a solid foundation (itself built on employee investment of personal resources and utilization of job-provided resources). Personal resources include positive attributes, such as self-esteem, optimism, and emotional regulation: attributes that engaged employees exercise regularly while working toward both their organizational and personal job-related goals. For particular positions, these attributes are required to varying degrees. Using pre-hire assessments along with job percent-matching techniques can identify those qualities in candidates before they are brought aboard.

Job-provided resources include physical and social factors that assist employees in coping with the demands of a particular job; they can motivate employees both intrinsically and extrinsically. In the workplace, supervisor feedback, autonomy, and social support provide intrinsic motivation through learning and development opportunities, as well as fulfillment of social needs. Job resources provide extrinsic motivation by offering supervisors a productivity-assessing metric they can use to reward successful performance or to take steps for improving productivity, if necessary. All this has the serendipitous effect of increasing employees' roles as stakeholders in their own performance, since they value the job-provided resources that result from successful productivity. Thus, employees come to value personal and job resources; their engagement increases as they deploy personal and job-provided resources throughout the workday, toward various objectives; and their job performance and produc-tivity increases, resulting in organization-wide growth and increased market share.

However, employee turnover is an inevitable consequence of hiring the wrong individual for the wrong position. A host of workforce management studies have concurred that approximately 90 percent of managers believe people leave their jobs for more money;

yet, our research demonstrates 90 percent of employees leave their jobs for reasons *other* than money. This turnover can be prevented by placing the right individual in the right job—a placement facilitated, in part, by hiring assessments—drastically reducing the chances employees will leave positions because of job demands, management relations, or dissatisfaction.

Here is a case in point:

Not long ago, the board of directors of CashAmerica recognized the company was experiencing a serious employee turnover problem. Scores of new hires left the company in their first ninety days, and 53.3 percent of customer service personnel left within two years. The soaring hiring and training costs reached $2.3 million. The board members asked the company's newly hired Senior Vice President of Human Resources, Clint Jaynes, to develop a solution for reducing the company's turnover by targeting the hiring process itself. After assessing the alternatives, Jaynes chose to develop and implement a candidate selection procedure that included behavioral and cognitive assessments. His process resulted in increased store sales (by as much as $50,000); he saved the company $160,000 in new manager training costs and reduced customer service personnel turnover by almost 14 percent. In this case, and in countless others like it, hiring and employee performance assessments usage has produced returns on investment and significant savings on both hiring costs and labor expenses.

Boards of directors and executives understand that these types of returns and cost-saving opportunities can be scarce in a contracting economy and that high employee turnover rates can and will destroy the fabric of the company's culture. During a globally recessed economy's sputtering recovery, one of the best ways not only to survive, but also to thrive, is to protect stakeholders' interests, primarily by controlling the costs of doing business. Of course, one of the most costly areas of doing business involves human capital management—from hiring and retaining high-caliber talent to providing commensurate compensation and benefit packages—and the quickest and easiest ways for businesses to trim costs are by implementing hiring freezes and workforce reduction strategies. The long-lasting effects of economic contraction on hiring practices include the need to maximize recruiting efforts ROI (return on investment), the increased reliance on recruitment outsourcing, and the usage of assessments to assist in making better hiring decisions.

Board members should understand that the utility of existing employee performance appraisals can also be enhanced through the use of 360-degree feedback assessments (surveys), which include reviews from both those above and below the employee in the organizational structure. Ideally, such a tool is used for personal development and individual performance improvement. In 2002, 90 percent of Fortune 500 companies used 360-degree feedback assessments, which have multi-faced approaches that can incorporate a wide range of performance criteria and assessment perspectives, further supporting their effectiveness in determining the underlying reasons driving employee performance. Employee performance assessment tools, including 360-degree feedback systems, provide comprehensive and accurate pictures of employees' performance outcomes, behaviors, and competencies. The evaluation process provides a measure of objectivity when determining employees' performance that is otherwise vulnerable to performance raters' biases or perceptions when making hiring decisions.

Companies' board members and executives should work with in-house counsel and outside law firms to address the legality of human resources professionals using behavioral assessments, when the HR pros are operating in a climate where they fear repercussions of discrimination or favoritism, and their personal judgments and opinions must be kept at bay. The U.S. Department of Labor's Uniform Guidelines on Employee Selection Procedures, for example, includes a section on using assessment results to distinguish individuals amongst a pool of applicants. The document affirms that "evidence of the validity of a test or other selection procedure [should demonstrate] that the selection procedure is predictive of or significantly correlated with important elements of job performance." In other words, tests must assess candidates' behaviors and skills, as they are relevant to the job at hand. Furthermore, employment assessments based on scientifically sound principles of behavioral research should follow *Standards for Educational and Psychological Testing* (published collectively by the American Educational Research Association, the American Psychological Association, and the National Council on Measurement in Education). Pre-hire and employment performance tests conforming to these guidelines and standards provide organizations with information about job applicants that is valid for hiring assessment; fair to candidates; and reliable for hiring managers, who depend on these results to provide predictive information about the likelihood of new hires' success.

Board members can take the lead regarding the steps necessary for facilitating the HR department's transformation from administration, which primarily focuses on employee policies and cultural initiatives, to a key factor in and value-driver of strategic decisions, the latter strengthened by the acknowledgement that a company's most valuable—and, often, expensive—resource is the workforce it employs. Beyond information management and functional services, HR-related activities coordinate efforts that improve productivity and cultivate competitive advantages through effective talent management. Revenue can be generated through prudent HR practices, which include thorough vetting and assessment of new talent hires' organizational fit, and companies whose corporate leaders recognize the increasingly vital role of correct candidate selection will reap both the tangible and intangible benefits of a talented and engaged workforce for years to come. The optimum way to conduct hiring, then, is through scientifically developed, pre-hire behavioral assessments that discern those who could falter in a given position from those who are likely to shine and become sources of productivity and innovation for the company over time.

ABOUT THE AUTHOR

JOSEPH "BUD" HANEY is the co-founder and president of Profiles International, which is based in Waco, Texas. He has been the driving force behind the overseas expansion of Profiles International.

Haney was awarded a baseball scholarship to Sam Houston State University where he earned a degree in accounting and was a four-time All-American. Upon graduation, Haney signed a contract with the Kansas City Athletics. After his baseball career, he established a human resources development business of his own. In 2004, Haney was honored by his alma mater and named to the SHSU Hall of Fame. The following year, the SHSU Board of Directors and Alumni Association named him a Distinguished Alumnus. Haney has been honored by Sales & Marketing Executives International by being named to its Academy of Achievement Hall of Fame and receiving SMEI's Pinnacle Award in recognition of his high achievements. He is also a recipient of the Certified Emeritus in Marketing from SMEI and is a Miller Heiman Strategic Sales certified trainer.

Haney is a co-author of the best-selling business guide *40 Strategies for Winning in Business* and *Leadership Charisma*, which was written to help people harness their personal and professional charisma in order to improve their businesses and careers.

CHAPTER 23

HEALTHY GOVERNANCE

How to Build Healthy, Highly Effective Boards

By Robert H. Rosen, Ph.D., Founder/CEO, Healthy Companies International

In a world changing faster than at any time in its history, the context in which boards must govern is outpacing board leaders' capacity to feel secure and confident, making some board members reluctant to lead in an era when, paradoxically, board leadership is vital. Furthermore, the sustained stress of today's increasingly complex business landscape can erode individual and team effectiveness, leading the board to leave empty chairs for succession, stretch beyond prudent risk tolerance, overlook strategic misdirection, or rubberstamp questionable severance or incentive compensation plans.

Given the growing scrutiny of boards by institutional investors, shareholders and regulators, this is a critical moment. Companies have a compelling need for board members to refresh themselves. My belief is that by cultivating a new mindset, one grounded in the concept of "healthy governance," board members can become more resilient and adaptive in the face of rapid change and growing complexity; thus, they can contribute more tangibly to the sustenance of a healthy company that can stay ahead of the curve.

This chapter suggests six keys to healthy governance that board leaders can apply to build board effectiveness.

BEING A HEALTHY BOARD MEMBER

The most effective board members show up as complete human beings; they tap into their intrinsic, positive instincts and work as healthy leaders. My company's extensive research and work with great leaders worldwide has shown that healthy leaders manage themselves across six dimensions of health, listed below.

- Physical Health: sustain energy and stamina needed to tackle tough challenges; stay fully engaged; and achieve big goals.
- Emotional Health: adapt and respond wisely to the unexpected; embrace an uncertain future with practicality; lead others through change; and recover from setbacks.
- Intellectual Health: think critically and creatively; solve complex problems in exciting new ways; make well-informed choices; and take decisive actions.
- Social Health: bring your full self to the board; value diversity; build productive relationships and teams; and inspire collaboration, trust, and respect.
- Vocational Health: sustain peak performance; find fulfillment in the role; shape an environment that fosters success; and strive to stay ahead of global threats and opportunities.
- Spiritual Health: see the world through a lens of higher purpose and interconnectedness; have a humble

appreciation for life's lessons; lend perspective to change and uncertainty; and embrace diversity and global perspectives.

The healthy board member bravely faces questions others might fear, including any or all of the following: "How do I show up? Am I fully engaged? Can I keep my ego and self-interest separate from creating long-term, sustained company value? What legacy do I want to create as a unique, lasting contributor to this board and the company? Have I cultivated all the strengths required to be a good, and, ideally, great board member?"

Having high ethics, as well as respect for and trust of other board members and executive management, is, as always, essential. Other vital qualities include industry knowledge, technology insight, functional experience, and relevant geographical and cultural expertise. Yet, even for board members who possess all those strengths and more, learning remains a must, as does conscientious cultivation of healthy leadership's six dimensions.

BUILD A HEALTHY BOARD

Typically, a board is a gathering of strong individuals who work together only intermittently. As such, mature team behavior is critical. The board members' challenge of working as a team may be compounded by the need for diversity. Seldom does one individual bring to the table all the competencies needed for success. Greater diversity allows for a wider range of perspectives and real value creation; however, it may also test each member to maintain empathetic connection and extend the trust that brings the team its stability and continuity.

In personal interviews conducted with more than 300 CEOs from renowned companies worldwide, the team of interviewers at Healthy Companies repeatedly heard great communication is essential for engaging and aligning healthy companies. Similarly, a board's hallmarks are mutually respectful, professional interactions. The members of the best boards understand the complexity of human communication. These members carefully weigh not only what they wish to say, but also how their statements will be received. They are proactive and forthright, encouraging unfiltered insights while moving toward actions. Working as a team, they value self-awareness and forge trusting relationships using open communications—and they do all this even when their direct interactions are sporadic.

As importantly, every board member pursues the creation of sustainable value for shareholders and other stakeholders above all else, including personal interests and biases. A healthy board's members are open and inclusive in discussing how the board should operate. Guiding principles are clear, and goodwill, assumed. Every member is deeply and personally involved, yet he or she remains sufficiently detached in order to do what is best for the company and its shareholders.

HEALTHY, EFFECTIVE BOARD	UNHEALTHY, INEFFECTIVE BOARD
REALISTIC » Tackles tough questions readily » Probes for valuable information » Prioritizes strategy options	**REACTIVE** » Avoids controversy » Parses information » Recycles ideas, offers "kitchen cabinet" advice
COLLABORATIVE » Brings full humanity to inter-actions » Navigates balance of parts to drive decisions » Solicits honest feedback	**DIVISIVE** » Is ego-driven » Exhibits poor focus/agenda management » Puts personal agendas first
CONSTRUCTIVE » Creates strategic value (without creating strategy) » Tolerates productive failure » Is proactive and adaptive	**CONFRONTATIONAL** » Struggles to think/act strategically » Is prone to indecision and inaction » Listens passively
CONFIDENT AND HUMBLE » Continually revisits the question, "What business are we in; where should we be?" » Confirms sizable bets without betting the company » Embraces social responsiblity	**CONSERVATIVE AND CYNICAL** » Rubberstamps executive decisions » Has rigid mindset » Lacks higher purpose
OPEN-MINDED » Draws value from board's diversity of experience and roles » Effectively balances short-term and long-term imperatives » Confronts "hijacks" and blind spots	**NARROW-MINDED** » Lacks open, curious, or adaptive mindset » Reacts primarily to current noise » Fails to use anxiety positively

MENTOR THE CEO AND EXECUTIVES

In any company, actions of the CEO and executive team profoundly shape the organization's performance and sustainability. As such, the board members' ability to guide the CEO and top executive team productively can be a major contributor to shareholder value. The best boards are comprised of members chosen for their wisdom, experience, leadership expertise, and independence. Board members should bring their full selves to the task of mentoring and supporting the CEO and his or her team.

My company conducted research into what the best CEOs do, and found that the CEOs of high-performing companies tend to view what's known as "the human agenda" as *the* most fundamental contributor to performance. The human agenda makes or breaks the company's success in terms of finance, marketing, and operations. As such, the best boards' members encourage the CEO to focus proactively on the human agenda, while actively supporting his or her efforts to shape and execute strategic talent management. Members of good boards focus on building a strong succession pipeline for the company's top 10 percent and on identifying leadership gaps connected to the current strategy's execution. Members of a healthy board take an even broader view, looking at the connections between business, leadership, and culture strategies.

At minimum, the chairman or lead director should actively work with the CEO to explore questions, such as the following: "What is your legacy?" "Which positions are most crucial to building shareholder value?" "What are we doing to attract and retain the best talent in the industry at all levels?" Discussion of these questions should be approached with a spirit of mutual respect, trust, and professionalism, under clearly defined rules of engagement.

MAKE BOLD CONTRIBUTIONS

With the increasing complexity of decisions about strategic direction, risk management, succession planning, and compensation, members of healthy boards govern for both today and tomorrow. Certainly, both the ongoing pressure for quarterly results and the need for dealing with crises as they arise require the board members' immediate attention. Yet, a healthy board's members maintain a long-term view, articulating a bold vision for the company, along with the CEO, and working as one toward vision fulfillment. In this way, members of the board steadily guide the company toward its long-term goals, even as the business continually adjusts to changes in the market and adapts strategically to new competition.

To be bold yet pragmatic, the healthy board's members exhibit both constructive impatience and realistic optimism. While a healthy diverse board may experience pulls from many different directions, every member finds his or her own ways to be supportive while constructively challenging assumptions. All board members should be willing to explore every side of a strategic issue.

The best boards become a truly strategic resource for management, helping the company's executives choose the right people, craft an effective organization, sustain superior business processes, and take decisive steps (as needed) to safeguard the company in changing circumstances. In a global economy, understanding the constantly changing needs of customers in different geographies is also vitally important, and direct interaction with key customers is generally advisable.

The executive team shapes and manages short- and long-term business strategies, but a healthy board's members understand well and closely monitor those strategies.

MAKE JUDICIOUS EXECUTIVE COMPENSATION CHOICES

Today, executive compensation has both a business and a social aspect. Given heightened societal sensitivity to the gaps between a CEO's salary and average pay, the social repercussions of compensation decisions, if overlooked, can create a ticking time bomb. The healthy board's members recognize this and engage in difficult conversations, as needed, to achieve an empathetic view of gaps in compensation; anticipate the possible repercussions of compensation choices; and find prudent, sustainable paths forward.

The essence of the challenge is balancing what it takes to attract or keep a great CEO and rewarding performance while honoring the company's values and meeting the board's solemn obligation to optimize shareholder value. Compensation choices must be backed by consistent performance assessment of both the CEO and the board members. Ideally, these assessments will be keyed to relevant, objectively selected, comparative benchmarks.

In the end, a healthy Board is made up of members courageous enough to do the "right thing," which in general means making reasoned, defensible decisions that are consistent with the company's business, values, and shareholder goals, as well as backed by appropriate performance linkages.

ADOPT A HOLISTIC NOMINATING APPROACH

Traditionally, nominating committees have focused on what potential board members do and have done; committee members take inventory of nominees' achievements and experiences, while also considering candidates' value-adding expertise, competencies, and skills. My view is that as the global context demands increasingly bold board contributions, nominating criteria must become more holistic. That is, when weighing what individuals might add to your board, consider them as full human beings—not just what they do, but also who they are. Systematically assess each candidate across the six dimensions of health cited above: physical, intellectual, emotional, social, vocational, and spiritual.

Just as you want your board members to exhibit a sound balance of business expertise and experience, strengthening the board's comprehensive health will increase its resilience and adaptability when it is, inevitably, tested by adverse conditions in a rapidly changing marketplace. Adopting a holistic mindset allows current board members to look more comprehensively at who they are, and, more accurately, identify whom to add to the Board, thus successfully navigating the twists and turns of the marketplace, while awakening hope and creating fresh possibilities for the company.

CONCLUSION

Much has been written about board members' responsibilities and ways to improve board effectiveness, yet the idea of healthy governance reveals truly new ground that holds profoundly important potential. Healthy governance is a concept suited to a time in which relentlessly rapid change and compounding complexity are fast overwhelming narrow notions of what makes board members fully fit to serve. In today's dynamic environment, capable corporate governance is every bit as much about superior leadership and people as it is about sound judgment and inviolable ethics.

Healthy board members lead to healthy leaders, who in turn will foster and maintain a healthy culture and workforce. In these turbulent times, there is no alternative to ensuring these objectives remain a top strategic priority. Board leaders who are determined to deliver superior, sustained value creation to shareholders will embrace the holistic concept of a healthy board and act decisively to build a board composed of healthy directors, while recognizing that healthy governance is a critical part of the evolving equation for taking a company to the next level.

ABOUT THE AUTHOR

ROBERT H. ROSEN, Ph.D., is an internationally renowned psychologist and senior advisor to boards, CEOs, and their executive teams around the world. As Founder and CEO of Healthy Companies International (HCI), he has worked with hundreds of CEOs in over forty countries. HCI is a global leadership company that provides strategic advice to top executives on how they can develop better leaders and drive positive organizational change. He has published several books, including his most recent, *Just Enough Anxiety: The Hidden Driver of Business Success*, in 2008.

CHAPTER 24

CORPORATE INNOVATION

Measuring Readiness and Results

By Dr. Donald F. Kuratko, Indiana University

"Innovation distinguishes between a leader and a follower."

—Steve Jobs

"Corporate innovation" (sometimes known as "corporate entrepreneurship") refers to the entrepreneurial actions and initiatives that transform organizations through strategic renewal processes, and/or extends the firm's scope of operations into new domains (i.e., new product-market segments or technological arenas); such innovation must serve at the heart of a governance agenda. People typically view firms that exhibit corporate innovation as dynamic entities prepared to take advantage of new business opportunities when they arise; these firms' employees seem willing to deviate from prior routines, strategies, business models, and operating environments in order to embrace new resource combinations, which in turn hold promise for new innovations.

In general, corporate innovation or entrepreneurship flourishes at established firms when individuals are free to pursue novel actions and initiatives. Innovation initiatives are not limited to private enterprise: the board members of non-profits, universities, and NGOs—even government leaders—must embrace principles of what many call "intrapreneurship." As Steven Brandt of Stanford once said, "Ideas come from people. Innovation is a capability of the many."[1] However, as pointed out by Michael H. Morris, Donald F. Kuratko, and Jeffrey G. Covin in their latest book, *Corporate Entrepreneurship and Innovation*,[2] entrepreneurial activity must be carefully integrated into the organization's overall strategies in order for it to be successful.

Over the years, people have written numerous articles and books advocating the importance of "unleashing the entrepreneurial potential" of individuals by removing constraints on entrepreneurial behavior (see, for example, Gary Hamel's *Leading the Revolution*, Gifford Pinchott's *Intrapreneuring*, or Andrew J. Sherman's *Harvesting Intangible Assets*[3]). Employees engaging in entrepreneurial behavior make the foundation for organizational innovation; so, in order to develop "corporate innovation," organizations must establish a process through which individuals in an established firm can pursue entrepreneurial opportunities to innovate without regard to the level or nature of currently available resources. However, keep in mind that in the absence of proper control mechanisms, firms that manifest corporate innovative activity may "tend to generate an incoherent mass of interesting but unrelated opportunities that may have profit potential, but that don't move [those] firms toward a desirable future."[4] Therefore, those factors that drive corporate entrepreneurial activity to produce high levels of innovation performance are, most

1   Steven C. Brandt, *Entrepreneuring in Established Companies* (Homewood, IL: Dow-Jones-Irwin, 1986), 54.

2   Michael H. Morris, Donald F. Kuratko, and Jeffrey G. Covin, *Corporate Entrepreneurship and Innovation*, Third Edition, (Cengage/South-Western, 2011).

3   Gary Hamel, *Leading the Revolution* (Boston: Harvard Business School Press, 2000); Gifford Pinchott, Intrapreneuring (Book, 2000).

4   G. Getz and E.G. Tuttle, "A Comprehensive Approach to Corporate Venturing," in *The Handbook of Business Strategy*, Vol. 2 (#1), pp. 277-279.

likely, contingent upon a firm's ability to use control mechanisms judiciously for the proper selection of and effective guidance on entrepreneurial actions and initiatives.[5]

In spite of the potential for corporate innovation to create value by contributing to improved organizational performance, many established companies do not encourage entrepreneurial behavior because executives worry about innovation being portrayed in chaotic images. In addition, structural impediments are often in place to stifle or prevent innovation from occurring: most of these impediments are the products of bureaucratic routines that have outlived their usefulness. Developing an internal work environment capable of cultivating employees' interest in and commitment to effective entrepreneurial behavior, and the innovation that can result from it, is produced by all levels of managers' effective efforts.

CREATING A PROPER ENVIRONMENT FOR SUPPORTING CORPORATE INNOVATION

Board members must take responsibility for directing their executives, in turn, to inspire and cajole top-level managers into creating a work environment highly conducive to innovation and entrepreneurial behaviors. Within such an environment, each employee has the opportunity to step up to the plate. Willingness and ability to act upon one's innate entrepreneurial potential is based on a calculated assessment. Conditions in a company's internal culture and ecosystem dictate the perceived costs, benefits, and incentives

---

5   J.C. Goodale, D.F. Kuratko, J.S. Hornsby, and J.G. Covin, "Operations Management and Corporate Entrepreneurship: The Moderating Effect of Operations Control on the Antecedents of Corporate Entrepreneurial Activity in Relation to Innovation Performance" (Journal of Operations Management, 29.2 [2011]), pp. 116-127.

associated with taking personal risks, challenging current practices, devoting time to unproven approaches, persevering in the face of organizational resistance, and enduring the ambiguity and stress that entrepreneurial behavior can create. Therefore, credible innovation is more likely in companies in which all individuals' entrepreneurial potential is sought and nurtured, and those in which organizational knowledge is widely shared. The managerial challenge then becomes using workplace design elements to develop an "innovation-friendly" internal environment.

As research on corporate entrepreneurial activity has evolved, numerous researchers have acknowledged the importance of internal organizational dimensions for promoting and supporting an innovative environment. This research has identified five specific dimensions that are important determinants of an environment conducive to entrepreneurial behavior: top management support, work discretion and/or autonomy, rewards and/or reinforcement, time availability, and organizational boundaries. In order for individuals to perceive an innovation-friendly environment, these underlying organizational dimensions are required.[6] Let's briefly examine each one from the perspective of the organization's employees.

1. Top management support: the extent to which one perceives that top managers support, facilitate, and promote entrepreneurial behavior, including the championing of innovative ideas or provision of the resources people require to take entrepreneurial actions. Top management support has

---

6   J.S. Hornsby, D.F. Kuratko, D.A. Shepherd, and J.P. Bott, "Managers' Corporate Entrepreneurial Actions: Examining Perception and Position" (Journal of Business Venturing 24.3 [2009]), pp. 236-247; J.S. Hornsby, D.F. Kuratko, and S.A. Zahra, "Middle Managers' Perception of the Internal Environment for Corporate Entrepreneurship: Assessing a Measurement Scale" (Journal of Business Venturing 17.3 [2002]), pp. 253-273.

been found to have a direct positive relationship with an organization's innovative outcomes.

2. Work discretion: the extent to which one perceives that the organization tolerates failure, provides decision-making latitude and freedom from excessive oversight, and delegates authority and responsibility to lower-level managers and workers. Research suggests those with discretion over how to perform their work are often best at recognizing entrepreneurial opportunities, along with those encouraged to engage in experimentation.

3. Rewards and reinforcement: the extent to which one perceives that the organization uses systems that develop rewards according to entrepreneurial activity and success. Reward systems that encourage risk-taking and innovation have been shown to have a strong effect on individuals' tendencies to behave in entrepreneurial ways. Numerous studies have identified "reward and resource availability" as a principal factor in entrepreneurial behavior by middle- and first-level managers.

4. Time availability: the extent to which one perceives that workloads ensure extra time for individuals and groups to pursue innovation, with jobs structured to support such efforts and the achievement of short- and long-term organizational goals. Research suggests that managers' time availability is an important resource for generating entrepreneurialism. For example, the availability of unstructured or free time can enable would-be corporate innovators to consider opportunities for innovation that might otherwise be impossible because of their required work schedules.

5. Organizational boundaries: the extent to which one perceives there are flexible organizational boundaries that may be useful in promoting entrepreneurial activity because they enhance the flow of information between the external environment and the organization, as well as between organizational departments or divisions. However, innovative outcomes emerge most predictably when innovation is treated as a structured and purposeful (versus a chaotic) process. Consistent with this point, organization theorists have long recognized that productive outcomes are most readily accomplished in organizational systems when uncertainty is kept at manageable levels. This can be achieved through setting boundaries that induce, direct, and encourage coordinated innovative behavior across the organization. In short, organizational boundaries can ensure the productive use of innovation-enabling resources.

MEASURING READINESS: DIAGNOSING
THE INTERNAL ENVIRONMENT

A firm's internal entrepreneurial climate should be assessed to evaluate in what manner it supports the existence of entrepreneurial behavior and how managers perceive that support. When attempting to take inventory of a firm's current situation regarding innovation readiness, managers need to identify the parts of the firm (its structure, control systems, human resource management systems, and culture) that inhibit and the parts that facilitate entrepreneurial behavior. Such identification will contribute to the foundation for successfully implementing corporate innovation.

One example of such an assessment instrument is the CECI (Corporate Entrepreneurship Climate Instrument),[7] which was developed around the five dimensions to corporate entrepreneurship discussed earlier (management support, work discretion and/ or autonomy, reinforcement, time availability, and organizational boundaries). In addition, this instrument measures the degree to which a firm's culture supports entrepreneurial activity. An instrument like the CECI can be used to develop a firm's profile across the five internal climate dimensions. Low CECI scores in one specific dimension suggest the need for the company to focus on that particular dimension for improvement, thus enhancing its readiness for entrepreneurial behavior and, eventually, success in corporate innovation. This testing can significantly benefit organizations by providing a likely indication of a firm's being able to use a corporate innovation process successfully. This test highlights which specific dimensions of the internal work environment should be the focus of ongoing design and development efforts. Furthermore, the CECI can be used as an assessment tool for evaluating corporate training needs with respect to entrepreneurship and innovation. Determining these training needs sets the stage for improving managers' skills, as well as increasing their sensitivity to the challenges of eliciting and then supporting entrepreneurial behavior.

Managers and employees, across a firm, are most likely to engage in entrepreneurial behavior when the organizational dimensions for that behavior are well perceived, widely known, and universally

---

7   R.D. Ireland, D.F. Kuratko, and M.H. Morris, "A Health Audit for Corporate Entrepreneurship: Innovation at All Levels" (Journal of Business Strategy 27.2 [2006]), pp. 21-30. See also Michael H. Morris, Donald F. Kuratko, and Jeffrey G. Covin, Corporate Entrepreneurship & Innovation, Third Edition (Cengage/South-Western, 2011).

accepted. Remember, individuals assess their entrepreneurial capacities in reference to what they perceive to be organizational resources, opportunities, and obstacles related to entrepreneurial activity. Once an organization's executives have determined that the value of an environment that encourages entrepreneurial behavior exceeds that which encourages all other organizational behaviors, managers will continuously champion, facilitate, and nurture that innovation-friendly environment.

MEASURING RESULTS: ASSESSING YOUR FIRM'S ENTREPRENEURIAL INTENSITY

Organizations differ with respect to the levels of entrepreneurial activity they are capable of achieving; board members should monitor the enterprise's capability of and access to resources in these areas. Extending this thought a bit, we can say that organizations have different levels of "entrepreneurial intensity" (EI), and the levels are derived from two basic questions: First, how many entrepreneurial initiatives is the company pursuing (measuring the frequency of entrepreneurship)? Second, to what extent do those initiatives represent incremental or modest steps versus bold breakthroughs (measuring the degree of entrepreneurship)? The latter, the degree of entrepreneurship, indicates the extent to which an organization's efforts are innovative, risky, and proactive. This measurement helps assess the actual results from innovative efforts.

To assess an organization's EI, its frequency and degree of entrepreneurship should be considered together with any number of possible frequency and degree combinations being possible. Thus, a firm may be engaging in numerous entrepreneurial initiatives (high on frequency), but none of them may be especially innovative, risky, or proactive (low on degree). Another company may pursue a path that emphasizes breakthrough developments (high degree), which are only initiated every two or three years (low frequency). Yet another firm might achieve a balance of moderately high levels of both degree and frequency.

To assess a firm's degree of entrepreneurship, assessors must establish definitions of "innovativeness," "risk-taking," and "pro-activeness." "Innovativeness" refers to seeking creative, unusual, or novel solutions to problems and needs. Commonly, these solutions take the form of new processes as well as new products (goods and/ or services). "Risk-taking" involves the willingness to commit significant resources to opportunities that have a reasonable chance of failure as well as success. However, these risks should be carefully calculated based on potential gains and losses associated with the decisions. "Proactiveness" is concerned with anticipating and then acting in light of a recognized entrepreneurial opportunity. Proactiveness demands that firms tolerate failure and that employees be encouraged to persevere in their efforts to exploit opportunities that can be innovation sources

When developing measures for EI scores, know that norms for entrepreneurial intensity differ across industries. For example, the computer and information technology industry tends to be quite entrepreneurially intense, while the consumer foods industry is much less so. Regardless of the industry's norms, however, EI scores generally tend to be associated with higher levels of company performance (using both financial and non-financial performance measures), and this association appears to be the strongest for firms competing in highly turbulent industries. However, this is not meant to suggest that ever-increasing amounts of EI will always result in superior firm performance. Experience leads me to believe that firms should view EI pursuit in relative, not absolute terms, in that there is no absolute EI standard.

PREPARING THE ORGANIZATION

Executive leaders must create an understanding of the innovation process for their employees. Having assessed whether the firm's internal work environment supports innovative activity, as well as the entrepreneurial intensity of potential outcomes, senior managers should also determine if the firms' employees understand corporate innovation and entrepreneurial behavior. Key decision-makers must find ways to explain the purpose of using the corporate innovation process to those from whom entrepreneurial behaviors are expected.

Understanding and supporting a corporate innovation process should not be left to chance. My experience suggests that executives need to develop programs with the purpose of helping all parties who will be affected by corporate innovation understand the value of the entrepreneurial behavior that the firm is requesting of them (as the foundation for successful innovation). Here, I provide a sample outline of this type of program.

A Corporate Innovation Development Program

1. *Introduction to Corporate Innovation and Entrepreneurship*: This session includes an examination of the concept of corporate entrepreneurship and corporate innovation strategy, examination of more well-known innovations in established companies, and review of several corporate innovation cases.

2. *Innovative Thinking*: This session challenges participants to think innovatively, emphasizing the need for innovative leadership in today's organizations. It reviews the misconceptions about thinking innovatively, followed by a discussion of the most common inhibitors. After completing a personal innovation inventory, managers should engage in several exercises designed to facilitate their own innovative thinking.

3. *Innovation Acceleration Process*: In this session, managers explore how specific ideas are developed within the corporation, including structural barriers and facilitators; examine the concepts behind "idea stoppers"; and use video clips to illustrate some examples of entrepreneurial thinking.

4. *Barriers and Facilitators to Innovative Thinking*: This session focuses on a discussion of the most common barriers to innovative behavior. This effort includes examining a number of the firm's cultural aspects. Participants complete exercises that help them deal with barriers in their internal work environments and see video case histories that describe innovators' entrepreneurial behaviors (in the participants' firm) that have contributed positively to implementing innovation.

5. *Assessing the Innovative Culture*: The major thrust of this session is learning how to assess an organization's innovative culture. Managers must understand the methods they can apply to comprehend their organization's "readiness" for innovative strategies. The session introduces some unique methods managers participate in, in order to gain experience. It also provides a unique assessment instrument

that assesses the organization's internal level of innovative culture. Participants complete the assessment and discuss the areas for improvement based on their "perceptual" results.

Finally, my experiences suggest that this type of program should be ongoing. As new innovative opportunities surface in a firm's external environment, as the internal work environment changes, and as new employees join the organization, it is appropriate for those from whom entrepreneurial behavior is expected to work together in finding the best ways to proceed when implementing a corporate innovation process. In this sense, successful efforts to engage in corporate innovation must themselves be innovative, changing in response to the ever-changing conditions in the firm's internal and external environments.

RELEVANT ISSUES TO CONSIDER

As I have discussed, corporate innovation provides the context in an established firm within which innovation takes place. Here are the six most relevant issues that boards of directors and corporate executives need to consider when designing a corporate innovation process for their organization:

- Where do they want the firm to be in terms of its level of entrepreneurial intensity? Do they seek a condition of high frequency and low degree, high degree and low frequency, or some other combination?
- To what extent are the firm's entrepreneurial efforts oriented to growing new businesses and starting new ventures outside the current portfolio, versus oriented to transforming existing businesses with the objective of

developing new products and/or serving markets that are new to the firm?

- In what areas do they want the firm want to be an innovation leader versus an innovation follower vis-à-vis the industry? In what market spaces do they want the firm to be a first mover? In what market spaces do they want the firm to be a fast second mover?

- In what areas of the firm are managers seeking higher versus lower levels of entrepreneurial behaviors? Which business units or product areas are expected to be the most innovative or to serve as a model for the remainder of the firm?

- What is the relative importance over the next three or so years of product innovation (introducing new goods or services in the marketplace) versus process innovation (developing more efficient and effective ways to produce the firm's goods and services)? What is the relative importance of new versus existing markets?

- Finally, to what extent are innovation stimuli expected from top-, middle-, or first-level managers? Are all managers clear about what the firm expects from them in terms of stimulating entrepreneurial behavior as part of the path to creating product, process, and/or administrative innovations?

Dealing with these decision issues is important: innovation experience shows entrepreneurial behaviors are more likely to become the norm in firms using a corporate innovation process produced by developing answers to the decision issues listed above. Moreover, firms that have a carefully designed process tend to elicit more tightly integrated entrepreneurial behaviors, which, in turn, lead to better operational efficiency. Without such a process, managers and employees can waste significant resources on initiatives that make little sense for the firm or that have little likelihood of long-term success. Another benefit of a carefully designed and executed corporate innovation process is that regularly using such a process allows organizational knowledge to be shared across the firm. Creatively developing and using organizational knowledge is a critical source of competitive advantage for today's firms.

CONCLUSION: LESSONS LEARNED

This chapter has several important implications. First, boards and executives who are too hasty to "unleash the entrepreneurial hostages" in their organizations by simply removing constraints on their innovative behaviors are likely to ignore the innovation-related importance of encouraging, directing, restricting, or prohibiting innovative behaviors and initiatives, according to alignments with the organization's interests. Not all corporate entrepreneurial behavior is good for the organization; even innovation must have boundaries. People running all initiatives and projects must be accountable to defined performance metrics and internal gates, screens, and filters. Yet, research about the corporate innovation area tends implicitly to regard such behavior as inherently virtuous.

As noted by Donald F. Kuratko and Michael G. Goldsby,[8] the encouragement of corporate entrepreneurship can and often does result in counterproductive, rogue behavior by organizational members. Thus, it's critical to deliberately design and develop orga-

---

8   D.F. Kuratko & M.G. Goldsby, "Corporate Entrepreneurs or Rogue Middle Managers? A Framework for Ethical Corporate Entrepreneurship" (Journal of Business Ethics 55.1 [2004]), pp. 13-30.

nizational systems that reflect the corresponding dimensions for an environment conducive to corporate innovation. As a result, a senior manager's task is not simply to build an organization in which core qualities are conducive to innovation; rather, the task is to design and develop innovation-facilitating and control-facilitating mechanisms that complement one another. In fact, such complementariness should ensure that the innovative potential residing within the organization is leveraged for the highest and best organizational purposes.

Second, and on a related note, exhibiting certain controls is not adversarial to corporate innovation's interests; instead, it is an inherent part of those interests. As such, policies written to the effect that control is the enemy of successful innovation are naïve. Boards of directors and corporate leaders should understand innovation is a process, and a process that is amenable to application of structured, disciplined oversight. The successful pursuit of innovation demands managers approach their innovation challenges with the understanding that they can provide ways of creating desirable innovation outcomes that are clearly understood and deliberately constructed. Rules, methods, and general process knowledge can all be brought in as resources to help facilitate successful innovation efforts. Often, it's not the absence of rules or well-understood procedures that results in successful innovation; instead, it's their presence. Managers would do well to recognize this.

Finally, keep in mind that boards of directors have the obligation to ensure every senior manager proactively seeks promotion of an innovation-friendly environment: this both encourages the best entrepreneurial behavior in individuals and helps design the most effective procedures, decision processes, and actions necessary for pursuing innovations. Firms in which board members and executive leaders focus on developing "innovative mindsets" also have senior leaders who are continually assessing the degree to which employees are prepared to engage in entrepreneurial behavior.

To summarize, this essay recommends three steps. First, the board members should assess the company's internal work environment. Through such assessment, they will be able to understand the factors that account for perceptions employees have regarding the key dimensions needed for an innovation-friendly environment. Second, the firm's level of entrepreneurial intensity can be determined by measuring of the results experienced within the organization. Third, board members and senior leaders must be committed to helping managers and employees form an understanding of the innovation process and how an entrepreneurial mindset can be the source of the entrepreneurial behavior needed for chosen corporate innovation projects.

While entrepreneurial actions are a phenomenon that have captivated the interest of board members and executives in many corporate strategic planning sessions, there is a danger that managers can get too caught up in the excitement of innovation, as a concept, or by inspiring stories about individual corporate innovators. It is easy to become enamored with the idea of innovation, but its true value lies in the extent to which director and executive leaders are committed to making innovation a part of overall corporate strategy, thereby creating sustainable competitive advantage.

ABOUT THE AUTHOR

DR. DONALD F. KURATKO (known as "Dr. K") is the Jack M. Gill Chair of Entrepreneurship, Professor of Entrepreneurship, and

Executive Director of the Johnson Center for Entrepreneurship and Innovation at the Kelley School of Business, Indiana University Bloomington. He has been named one of the Top 50 Entrepreneurship Scholars in the World, having written over 180 articles on aspects of entrepreneurship and corporate innovation, which were published in major journals. He has also written 28 books, including one of the leading entrepreneurship books in the world, *Entrepreneurship: Theory, Process, Practice* (8th ed., 2009). His other books include *Corporate Entrepreneurship and Innovation* (3rd ed., 2011), and *Innovation Acceleration* (2012).

Dr. Kuratko was named the #1 Entrepreneurship Program Director (*Entrepreneur* magazine); selected as one of the Top Entrepreneurship Professors in the United States (*Fortune* magazine); honored as the inaugural recipient of the Karl Vesper Entrepreneurship Pioneer Award; and granted the Academy of Management's prestigious Entrepreneurship Advocate Award for his contributions to the development and advancement of the discipline of entrepreneurship. Under Dr. Kuratko's leadership, Indiana University has continually achieved the rank of the #1 Business School for Entrepreneurship Research, granted by the *World Rankings for Entrepreneurship Productivity*; and the rank of both the #1 Graduate Business School for Entrepreneurship and the #1 Undergraduate Business School for Entrepreneurship (Public Institutions), granted by *U.S. News & World Report* and *Fortune* Magazine. Dr. Kuratko has consulted on corporate innovation for a number of major Fortune 500 corporations.

CHAPTER 25

THE BOARD'S ROLE IN DRIVING A CULTURE OF "INTRAPRENEURSHIP"

Board members and company leaders are the stewards of an organization's assets, both tangible and intangible. Cultivating, harvesting, and protecting those assets (particularly the intangible ones), is more important than ever, as companies are operating in an increasingly competitive and global business environment, during an era of employee mobility and start-up dreams. Board members who do not take their responsibility to develop or manage the company's intangible assets of the company—and simply leave this critical strategic issue to managers who might lack the authority, budget, visibility, or ability to advance strategy—may miss out on key market opportunities or strategies to increase shareholder value. Depending on the nature and extent of that oversight failure, boards may lose favor with Wall Street, draw institutional and activist investors' attention and scrutiny, or subject themselves to shareholder suits by aggressive, creative plaintiffs asserting breaches of fiduciary duty.

The leadership of a company or organization must be committed to establishing, maintaining, and supporting (with both tangible and intangible resources) a genuine culture committed to all types of innovation. Once this culture has been put firmly in place and the seeds of innovation have been planted, caring for those seeds begins with the irrigation process: a commitment to building an organizational foundation on pillars of "intrapreneurship."

"Intrapreneurship" has been defined in many ways, but for the purposes of this chapter, it is a person or team within a large corporation that takes direct responsibility for turning an idea into a profitable, finished product. Such a product is created through assertive risk-taking, gathering of internal resources, support, and innovation. This process is not merely invention, which may create something new, but does not typically—by itself—create value to customers or drive shareholder value.

When this process is applied inside the four walls of a growing company committed to a culture of innovation, great things begin to happen. People feel empowered, directed, rewarded, appreciated, invigorated, and reconnected to the reasons they chose this career path—and this company as a place where they spend ten to twelve hours a day. They feel like they are part of something much larger than themselves and realize that their rewards for work far transcend their individual corporations, as they became true drivers of and contributors to maximization of shareholder value. These happier and more challenged employees are not only considerably more productive; they are also more loyal and tend to stay at the company for much longer periods, which significantly reduces costly employee-turnover expenses.

Within a company, the board of directors and executive team must set the tone and initially write the playbook for the intrapreneurship parameters. Such a playbook will detail rules for success and failure, resource allocation, inventors' ownership, rewards and incentives, and strategies and structures for intrapreneurship. Innovation and intrapreneurship can both be central parts of a company's mission, values, and branding (such is the case with IBM, Proctor & Gamble, and DuPont), or they can be much lower strategic priorities. If there is too wide a gap or disconnect between the company's intrapreneurial playbook and its potential entrepreneurs' skill sets and desires, then all innovation efforts will be derailed. If traditional-thinking corporate managers surround visionary board members and CEOs, such surroundings will make innovation virtually impossible. We could compare this to trying to drive a sports car with no engine around a racetrack. Conversely, creative and forward-thinking employees whose projects are constantly being shut down or mired in red tape will either leave the company or, worse, give up and fall back into their risk-free, daily patterns. Alignment and shared values are critical; all employees should have crystal-clear pictures of *how* and *where* they fit into the intrapreneurship process and *why* intrapreneurship's mission is critical to both the organization and its stakeholders. For example, some companies, such as Google, have adopted policies, such as "20 percent time," that expressly permit employees to set aside time to pursue pet projects and ideas. These types of top-down policies encourage and give employees a path to follow when pursuing bottom-up experimentation and innovation.

Successful intrapreneurship ventures within companies can lead to huge rewards. That's what happened when Sony's Ken Kutaragi helped his company enter into the video game market; by 1998, this move was providing 40 percent of Sony's operating profits. The combination of Kutaragi's forward thinking and Sony's backing and support led to the PlayStation's astronomical success. Initially, Kutaragi had worked on a CD-ROM-based gaming system for Nintendo as an outside consultant, in a position that nearly cost him his job at Sony. After Nintendo decided to forego the new CD-

ROM-based system, Kutaragi convinced Sony, after much delibera-tion, to enter the gaming industry. Sony invested $2.5 billion in the intrapreneurship venture; ultimately, this investment resulted in the benefit of a huge financial success. Although Sony had hesitancy at first about investing in Kutaragi's vision, the company's openness to the possibility of entering new markets and willingness to take on the associated risks paid off.[1]

Sometimes, drawing connections between two very different yet simple concepts can serve as a catalyst for intrapreneurship. The story of the Post-it®, for example, reminds us to keep the lines of communi-cation open and to maintain forums where employees can share ideas across divisions. Three employees at 3M worked together to create the Post-it®. In one department, an employee invented some not-so-sticky glue; in another, a colleague experienced frustration with disheveled papers and falling notes. (The quirky marketing efforts of a third employee resulted in the completed invention's financial success). The frustrated colleague remembered a series of discussions led by the inventor of the not-so-sticky glue and realized he had the perfect application for the product. As this story shows, large corporations have a huge advantage: they have many really talented employees with different skill sets and interests. Sometimes, great ideas require cooperative learning and discovery for inventions to reach the point of becoming viable market solutions. In addition, just because the good application of an idea is a mystery today, does not mean it will be a mystery tomorrow. Holding this philosophy, coupled with employees who are allowed to spend 15 percent of their time working on new ideas, positions companies like 3M well to be market pioneers and to succeed at intrapreneurship.

---

1   See http://www.intrapreneurshipconference.com/2011/10/12/the-sony-playstation-an-intrapreneurship-story/.

Typically, the person who is both the bridge over, the glue cementing, and the catalyst responsible for this internal organizational alignment is the Chief Innovation Officer (CIO). The position of CIO is a relatively new one in global companies, and its precise job description is still evolving as of 2012. Companies from diverse industries, such as Coca-Cola, Humana, Owens Corning, AMD, and Citigroup, are all including CIOs among top leadership positions as the pressure to innovate and harvest intellectual capital rises to the top of corporate agendas. However, only a handful of companies have made this commitment, compared to the tens of thousands of organizations that have no senior person or team accountable for managing innovation and fostering intrapreneurship.

In building the position descriptions for the CIO, some common themes have emerged, including the following:

- **Developing a common and consistent set of innovation values and policies**: The CIO needs to develop company-wide values and policies, so that everyone is singing from the same hymnal, and communicate these policies through training, shared success stories, and best practices.

- **Determining intrapreneurship strategies and structures**: Intrapreneurship can take many forms. Larger, traditional companies tend to gather everything and everyone together under a research and development (R&D) department that may service multiple divisions within the conglomerate. However, more nimble and progressive companies are turning to a variety of tactics in order to foster intrapreneurship, such as *ad hoc* venture teams, new venture divisions and groups, innovation centers, internal venture capital (VC) funds or research growth, offsite "skunk works" operations, and even innovation sabbaticals. External strategies include outsourcing, teaming or partnering with university research projects, cross-licensing, and embarking on M&A or joint ventures to achieve intrapreneurship objectives.

- **Attracting and retaining intrapreneurial talent:** A CIO must work closely with the HR department to ensure innovative workers are recruited, rewarded, and retained. Policies must be put in place to recognize creative teams' accomplishments (and failures/efforts), both financially and otherwise. There must be flexibility for rewarding people who help drive genuine shareholder value and keep those people connected to the energy level and culture that initially attracted them to the company. This is not as easy as it seems, even with the highest-profile, rapid-growth companies. Early employees of Facebook® have already begun leaving to start their own companies, as the excitement of the start-up has morphed into the potential dullness of a larger, more established environment. Recently, Google® has also struggled to hold on to some of its most creative people as the attractiveness of smaller, high-growth companies (such as LinkedIn®, Zynga®, Twitter®, Asana®, and Jumo®,) offer the ability to replicate the innovation-birthing process. A CIO must ensure that the company's best and brightest stay loyal and stay put, or at least know how and where to find replacements if the best and brightest depart for greener pastures.

- **Executing high-level innovation priorities and evaluating bottom-up proposals:** Innovation and intrapreneurship are both top-down and bottom-up when the systems that support them are working properly. The CIO must develop screens and filters for evaluating ideas, assigning resources, establishing teams, providing capital, and ensuring organization-wide innovative goals are met. Greenhouses and safe-places must be established: there, new ideas can be vetted and prototypes and working models tested. The selection and management of test markets, early customer adopters, advocacy groups, market influencers, and early-stage channel partners are all within the CIO's domain. The CIO must also share the knowledge and best practices gathered when these assumptions are tested across company lines and, where and when appropriate, with external partners and stakeholders.

- **Collaboration and innovation management**: The CIO must develop, implement, maintain, and improve the company's Intellectual Asset Management (IAM) programs, policies, and systems in order to facilitate collaboration and cooperation with all internal and external stakeholders, as well as to foster harvesting strategies for unlocking and driving shareholder value.

- **Serve as the chief steward for the company's brands**: The CIO must work closely with marketing, branding, and sales executives to protect and enhance the company's brands, slogans, designs, reputation, and Web 2.0 campaigns and communities. Every day, these intangible assets increase in strategic importance as sources of potential revenues and profits. From a budget-management perspective, their beauty lies within the fact that they often already exist; however, an effort must be made to uncover them enough to begin extracting of shareholder value.

- **Serve as the gatekeeper and taxi dispatcher for company-wide innovation initiatives:** In a company dedicated to intrapreneurship, somebody needs to be responsible for "herding the cats" and for ensuring that everything is running on time. The CIO is the cat herder, train conductor, and taxi dispatcher who helps ensure that intrapreneurial projects are coming in on time and on budget. He or she must be in the loop and have a full understanding of the variables that will influence the costs, the timetable, and the metrics used for both determining success versus failure and targeting returns on investment.

- **Serve as liaison to outside advisors and stakeholders (lawyers, technical support, co-investors, partners, etc.):** Working together with more traditional company leaders, such as the CFO and General Counsel, the CIO must be a critical point of contact for outside advisors, consultants, partners, and investors who influence innovation results. He or she is the "face" of the company's innovation progress to the outside world.

Board members and leaders who are committed to supporting intrapreneurship, either as an implementing tool for achieving innovation or as an irrigation method for growing strong inventories of intellectual capital, view employees as resources, not expenses. They assemble teams for the purposes of creating, not maintaining. In such circumstances, people receive rewards for breaking the status quo, not for protecting it. Some degree of failure is a given and can be embraced, as long as it becomes part of a learning experience. Micromanagement is tossed out the window in favor of a hands-off approach, which fosters a creative culture that smaller-company entrepreneurs might enjoy within a larger mothership. The rewards for creating new products and services can include significant bonuses, equity awards, internal and external recognition, or even spun-off into newly created, partially-owned subsidiaries.[2]

---

2   These subsidiaries can be created in lieu of management buy out (MBO), restructuring, or a divestiture.

CHAPTER 26

BUILDING INTELLECTUAL ASSET MANAGEMENT (IAM) SYSTEMS

As the stewards of a company's tangible and intangible assets, boards of directors and leaders must put intellectual asset management systems in place in the same ways they would put systems in place to manage tangible and physical assets. Failure to do so is not only a breach of fiduciary duty to shareholders but it also may even rise to the level of board liability in being too complacent when harvesting the company's intangible assets. These issues are in fact part of the board's domain and must be embraced at the board level. Shareholder derivative and activist groups are expecting and even demanding that the board properly manage and harvest the intangible assets and intellectual property of the company.

When I speak at business conferences around the world, and to companies of all sizes in all industries, and ask whether the listeners' companies' have an intellectual asset management (IAM) system in place, I am typically greeted with blank stares. After a few feeble hands go up, I then ask whether the IAM systems in place have been effective and yielded profitable opportunities, and even fewer hands remain. When I ask whether their companies' organizational charts have been altered to reflect a transformational shift toward an economy driven by intangible assets, they look at me as if I have just arrived from Mars. Finally, when I ask them to name the person in the company who serves as the CHIPPLE (that is, the Chief Intellectual Property Protection and Leveraging Executive), people look at me as if I were from Venus. (I am not aware of any extraterrestrial family roots, so I am pretty sure that at such points I am not the one in the room who is clueless.)

Such reactions raise important questions: How can we, as leaders of companies and as fiduciary guardians of an entity's assets (on the stakeholders' behalf), continue completely ignoring the management and leveraging of our most important strategic assets? How long will it take, and how many more lawsuits will be filed against board members and company leaders for the "gross undermanagement and underleveraging" of the company's most important assets, before we finally make this management and leveraging top priorities?

Now is the moment for companies of all sizes, and in all industries, around the globe to commit time and resources to deploying effective, multidisciplinary IAM systems that will help them properly cultivate, manage, and harvest intellectual assets. As stewards, guardians, and fiduciaries of companies' assets, managers have a basic duty and obligation to maximize those assets' value, especially in a post-Sarbanes-Oxley regulatory environment. (For more on this topic, see my 2011 book, published by AMACOM, entitled, *Harvesting Intellectual Assets: Uncover Hidden Revenue in Your Company's Intellectual Property*.)

WHAT IS INTELLECTUAL ASSET MANAGEMENT?

Intellectual asset management (IAM) is a system for creating, organizing, prioritizing, and extracting value from a company's various sets of intellectual property assets. While a company's intellectual capital and technical know-how are among its most valuable assets—they provide its greatest competitive advantages and are principal drivers of shareholder value—rarely do companies have adequate personnel, resources, or systems in place to manage and leverage these assets properly. IAM, as a matter of strategy and competitive intelligence gathering, also involves monitoring certain developments in the company's marketplace, through elements such as:

- Gathering intelligence on direct, indirect, and potential competitors
- Monitoring developments abroad
- Keeping one step ahead of a constantly changing landscape (over 20,000 new patents are issued per month in the United States alone)
- Maintaining license agreements and streams of royalty payments on both an inbound and outbound basis (e.g., royalty audits to ensure against underreporting (outbound) and overpayments (inbound).

IAM also helps company representatives answer the following questions: Are you getting paid? Is there anyone you are paying that you shouldn't be paying? Are performance standards being met? Are you in relationships with the right parties? What could be done to strengthen existing relationships or distribution channels?

Intellectual capital consists of many different types of human capital, intellectual property, and relationship capital. These are key assets for driving growth and maximizing shareholder value in all types of economic conditions. To evaluate such assets properly, IAM also involves understanding how and where intellectual assets sit in the company's strategic parameters and food chain. Over the past three decades, three strategic views about the use of intellectual capital have evolved in the boardroom.

First, under the *traditional view*, intangible assets enhance the company's competitive advantage and strengthen its ability to defend a competitive position in the marketplace. Intellectual properties are seen as barriers to entry or as shields with which to protect market share. In today's rapidly moving and highly competitive marketplace, this approach may be too passive and archaic.

Second, under the *current view*, intangible assets should not be used merely for defensive purposes; they should also be viewed as important strategic assets and profit centers, capable of being monetized and generating value through licensing fees or other channels and strategies. Such monetization exists only if time and resources are devoted to uncovering these opportunities—especially those related to dormant, intangible assets that do not presently serve the company's current core competencies or focus (this is also known as the "proactive/systemic approach").

Third, under the *future view*, intangible assets are the premier drivers of business strategy within the company: they encompass human capital, structural and/or organizational capital, and customer and/or relationship capital. IAM systems must be built and then continuously improved to ensure that such assets are used in two ways: one, to protect and defend the company's strategic position in domestic and global markets; and two, to create new markets, distribution channels, and revenue streams in a capital-efficient manner that maximizes shareholder value (this is also known as the "core focus/strategic approach").

Board members and executives from companies of all sizes, in all types of industries, are often guilty of committing a serious strategic sin: failure to properly protect, mine, and harvest the company's intangible assets. This is especially true at many technology-driven and consumer-driven companies. During the dot.com and Web 1.0 Internet boom from 1997 to 2001, billions of dollars went into venture capital and private equity markets; entrepreneurs primarily used these proceeds for creation of intellectual property or other intangible assets. Ten years later, however, emerging growth and middle-market companies have failed, in many cases, to leverage this intellectual capital into new revenue streams, profit centers, and market opportunities. Often, this failure is because of a singular focus on the company's core business or a lack of the strategic vision or expertise needed to uncover (or otherwise identify) other applications or distribution channels.

Entrepreneurs and leaders of growing companies may also lack the proper tools for understanding or analyzing the value of the company's intellectual assets. For example, as Baruch Lev, a finance professor at the Stern School of Business, New York University, has observed, the financial statements of Standard & Poor's 500 stock index companies captured only 15 percent of their "true intrinsic value." Given the resources of an S&P 500 company, it is likely that smaller companies have even more deeply embedded intangible assets; the corresponding number for privately held companies might be as low as 5 percent. Imagine the consequences or opportunity cost if you were preparing to sell your business eventually (or structure an investment) and 95 percent of your company's inherent value got left on the table! The gap in capturing and reflecting this hidden value points out the critical need for a legal and strategic analysis of any emerging company's intellectual property portfolio.

Leaders and boards of directors must understand that the inversion of the tangible to intangible assets ratio, as a percentage of total company value, has been dramatic. In 1978, tangible assets (e.g., property, plants, equipment, and/or inventory) made up approximately 80 percent of a typical S&P 500 company's total value. By 2002, this number had been reduced to 20 percent, and the numbers continue to drop, especially in this web-centric, virtual-focused world. Today, for many emerging small- to mid-size enterprises (SMEs), the ratio of intangible to tangible assets can be as high as 8 (or 10) to 1.

Harvesting intellectual capital is a strategic process that must begin with the company's management team, along with qualified outside advisers, taking inventory in order to develop a comprehensive understanding of the scope, breadth, and depth of the company's intangible assets. In these times of shareholders' distrust with and disappointment in management teams and boards of directors (that is, of publicly held companies), corporate leaders have an especial obligation to uncover hidden value and make the most of assets developed with corporate resources. Company leaders will never know whether they have a Picasso in the basement, so to speak, unless they both take the time to make an inventory of what's hiding in the basement and have a qualified intellectual capital inventory team (in this comparison, a team capable of distinguishing between a Picasso and a child's art project) to make that inventory). Once the team has properly identified the assets, company leaders should develop an intellectual asset management system in order to ensure open communication about and strategic management of the assets. At that point, the company is ready to engage in strategic planning, and to determine how to convert these assets into profitable revenue streams or new opportunities that will enhance and protect shareholder value.

IAM helps leaders of growing companies ensure they recognize and capture strategic growth opportunities, and then harvest them into new revenue streams and markets. Board members and company leaders should conduct periodic reviews of their IAM practices, and they should be asking the following questions:

- What IAM systems, procedures, and teams are currently in place?
- How and when were these systems developed?
- Who is responsible or accountable for managing these systems within the company?
- To what degree are adequate systems for internal and external communication and collaboration now in place?
- What ideas and/or technology-harvesting filters and procedures for making decisions about and analyzing innovation (e.g., deciding whether to move forward, allocating a budget, and creating a timetable) are currently in place?
- Are the strategy and process for harvesting and leveraging intellectual assets reactive or proactive?
- What are the real or perceived hurdles, both internal (i.e., politics, red tape, budgeting processes, and organizational structure) and external (i.e., market conditions, rapid changes in the state of the art, and competitors' strategies), which presently obstruct better IAM practices and procedures?
- Finally, what can be done to remove or reduce those barriers?

CHAPTER 27

The Critical Importance of Diversity in Board Composition

(with Linda Bolliger, Chairwoman, Boardroom Bound and former Chairwoman, National Association of Women Business Owners [NAWBO])

As a nation, we have more than acknowledged the critical role of embracing, appreciating, and celebrating diversity in both society and the workplace. Enabling diversity is not only the right thing to do; it is the smart thing to do, especially when a company is serving a diverse set of customers and markets. A diverse work team leads to better decision-making, better results, and a greater level of innovation and creativity. (See www.innoversity.com for additional resources on the intersections between diversity and innovation.)

However, in terms of diversity in our nation's boardrooms, *we still have a lot of work to do.*

As a report by the Alliance for Board Diversity (ABD) recently showed, women and minorities remain grossly under-represented in U.S. corporate boardrooms, which crimps companies' potential to lead in the global economy. According to the ABD, which advocates the inclusion of women and minorities on corporate boards, white men held 73 percent of board seats at Fortune 100 companies in 2010; the number had risen from 71 percent in 2004. In 2010, white women accounted for 15 percent, compared with 14 percent in 2004; in contrast, minorities made up 13 percent in 2010, down from 15 percent in 2004. So, in Fortune 100 companies, between 2004 and 2010, white men gained thirty-two seats on boards and white women gained nine. Minorities lost twenty-five seats overall: African-American men, specifically, lost forty-two. Overall, Fortune 100 companies also added sixteen seats to their boards during the period.

Last year, only fifteen Fortune 500 companies—including Citigroup, Inc.; International Business Machines Corp.; and Procter & Gamble—had boards that included representation from each of the U.S. Census Bureau's major groups: men, women, Whites, African Americans, Asian Pacific Islanders, and Hispanics. In our view, companies can't truly drive shareholder value until their boards reflect the markets they serve or hope to serve, which means having leaders from different backgrounds, ethnicities, and genders.

In 2011, new legislation passed in several countries—Norway, Spain, France, the Netherlands, Iceland, Italy, and Belgium—designating a required number of women in each boardroom, which resulted in dramatic increases in the number of board seats held by women in Europe.[1] In both Europe and Australia, corporate governance codes, which themselves require the inclusion of gender-diversity language, have driven increases in the percentage of women in board seats. Worldwide, the United States lags behind the pact—the country has only increased the number of women on boards by 3.3

---

1   See http://www.globewomen.org/cwdi/cwdi_2011_Fortune%20Global%20200%20
Press%20Release.html.

percent since 2004, a figure surpassing only that of Japan, which had a 1.1 percent increase.

In the United States, however, we are moving slowly into a realm where diversity considerations are a top priority in board composition. In 2009, the SEC adopted "The Governance Disclosure Rule," which requires companies to disclose how diversity has influenced their consideration of candidates for directors. The SEC adopted this rule because commentators believed disclosure of diversity considerations would help inform investors about corporate culture and governance practices; commentators also saw a demonstrated correlation between diversity and improved corporate financial performance. However, the SEC did not define what "diversity" meant for the purposes of this rule, which leaves companies to decide upon the appropriate definition.

A lack of gender diversity has subjected companies like Facebook®, which had no women on its board, to public criticism. While preparing for the biggest IPO to date, stakeholders questioned the ethical implications of the oversight; potential investors were left to wonder if Facebook® was leaving money on the table. This wonder became so great that the corporate governance director Anne Sheehan, who works for CalSTRS, the second-largest pension fund in the United States, wrote a letter urging Zuckerberg to increase the board's size and diversity of the board, prior to the IPO.[2] These concerns had good cause: according to an Ernst and Young report, even less-qualified, gender-diverse groups outperform more qualified, homogenous groups. Ultimately, gender-diverse boards have a positive effect on shareholder value.[3]

---

2   See http://www.reuters.com/article/2012/02/08
us-facebook-calstrs-idUSTRE81703H20120208.

3   See http://www.txwsw.com/pdf/board_brief.pdf.

A joint McKinsey & Company and Amazone Euro Fund study showed that companies with gender-diverse boards are more effective; between 2005 and 2007, gender-diverse boards outperformed their homogenous counterparts in three categories: on equity return, they outperformed by 1.1 percent; on operating results, they outperformed by 5.3 percent; and on stock price growth, they outperformed by 17 percent.[4] According to 2020 Women on Boards, a national campaign working to increase the number of women involved with boards, many Fortune 1000 companies have board compositions that include less than 20 percent women: in fact, 71 percent of the companies fall into this category. However, of the top ten Dow companies, ten have board compositions that include over 23 percent women.[5]

WHAT IS GENUINE DIVERSITY?

Diversity is not about quotas, affirmative action, or doing what is "politically correct." Instead, diversity is a commitment to embrace all viewpoints and perspectives at the board level for the selfish purpose of driving shareholder value. The business case for diversity reminds us that diversity of thought at the board level helps to ensure productivity, creativity, and a better understanding of all markets the company serves. Diversity objectives cannot be merely gender-based or racially driven; rather, they must include diversity of religious beliefs, backgrounds, training, global experiences, politics, and philosophical perspectives. Diversity drives debate and debate drives effective decision-making, which, in turn, will drive share-

---

4   See http://www.txwsw.com/pdf/board_brief.pdf.
5   See http://www.2020wob.com/learn.

holder value. Such a convergence of different perspectives leads to effective leadership and decision-making.

Some companies craft diversity objectives and policies around principles of tolerance. When did "tolerance" become the acceptable standard? Toleration-based phrases, such as, "I will tolerate you," do not create a warm and fuzzy feeling likely to drive true understanding and integration of beliefs that will foster effective governance. For example, in 2009, the Council for Institutional Investors amended its board diversity best practices and recommendations to clarify that its support for board diversity was based on its belief that a diverse board can "enhance corporate financial performance," and the National Association of Corporate Directors (NACD) has made diversity education and programming among its top priorities for 2012 and beyond. In several studies, researchers have demonstrated empirical evidence to support the positive relationship between the percentages of common and ethnic minorities on a board and returns on assets and equity. However, in these cases, people saw diversity as a philosophy that drove good governance, not a quota or designated number of board slots to be filled, irrespective of the actual experience or value to be added. In recruitment and selection processes, the board's nominations committee must embrace and understand principles of true diversity beyond the simple moral and social reasons that often justify diversity goals and objectives.

THE WORK OF BOARDROOM BOUND®

In addition to the ABD's great work, firms such as Boardroom Bound® founded by Linda Bolliger are helping qualified candidates from diverse backgrounds get truly ready for board service.

One of Boardroom Bound®'s featured programs is The Boardology Institute™, which is a director-candidate training program held within an intensive, multiple-day framework. It requires prospective candidates complete pre- and post-seminar work to learn governance, best practices, legal compliance, and risk management, as well as to better understand the time, commitment, risks, liabilities, and protocols for-profit board service requires.

The Boardology™ program goals and agenda include:

1. Attain an in-depth understanding of for-profit board service requirements;

2. Identify areas of needed development in order to establish board service credentials;

3. Create a "Strategy and Action Plan" to address identified needs;

4. Learn to use Boardroom Bound® as a resource for implementing strategies;

5. Create an on-going peer and professional support network. Specific topics covered include:

   • Board Requirements + Directors' Roles and Responsibilities

   • Corporate Governance: Implications of the Sarbanes-Oxley Act (2002) + Recent SEC Legislation

   • The Priorities and Expectations CEOs, Board Chairs, and Secretaries have of Board Members

   • Directors' Fiduciary Responsibility:

     » Types of scenarios directors encounter

     » What financial skills are required

   • Board Dynamics: Balancing Fitting In with Effecting Change

- Straight Talk About Board Principles *(hear directly from directors about personal board selection and service experience)*
- Strategies for Getting Appointed to a Corporate Board
- Positioning Yourself with an Executive Search and Board Placement Firm

Programs like these help ensure that shareholders are being served by well-trained, highly informed, and truly diverse boards of directors. If your company does not have a board orientation and training program, or lacks the effort to improve diversity of board composition, now is the time to develop an initiative.

THE FUTURE IS NOW

Boards that fail to embrace and appreciate the value of a commitment to genuine diversity will be left behind, struggling to fend for themselves (just like dinosaurs struggling to keep up with an evolving ecosystem), as other companies and competitors evolve in the right strategic direction. Women and minorities represent different voices and different points of view—thus, in conjunction with the rest of the board, they offer a better understanding of markets the company serves. The pipeline of future directors can and will be more diverse. In 2001, women made up only 21 percent of the students in M.B.A. programs. Today, that number is well over 30 percent and growing: in some of the nation's top programs, such as Wharton's, the number is just under 50 percent. At the executive level, companies are creating new positions, such as that of the Chief Diversity Officer (CDO), in which individuals are tasked with creating an environment and a culture in which genuine diversity principles can truly flourish; this flourishing drives employee satisfaction, loyalty, and productivity, as well as, ultimately, shareholder value. Over 50 percent of Fortune 500 companies have a CDO (or someone in an equivalent position), providing an example that smaller and middle-market companies ought to follow. The most effective CDOs have executive-level positions and report directly to their CEOs. Others may be part of administrative or HR functions, and thus are typically less effective in achieving true diversity principles.

Remember, these are not times to have your head in the sand regarding critical strategic, leadership and governance issues. Competing in global markets can only be achieved with the help of a diverse leadership group made up of individuals who have the experience, knowledge, and varying perspectives that can lead the way to sustainable business growth.

About the Contributor

Linda K. Bolliger is Founder and Board Chair of Boardroom Bound®, a national program fostering quality corporate governance. The program's Boardology™ Institute is a leader in the board candidate development space with the nation's largest database of inclusive, pre-qualified director-candidates for private business and publicly traded company board service. Bolliger, an accomplished entrepreneur and executive, is the former Chairwoman of the National Association of Women Business Owners (NAWBO) and other professional groups.

CHAPTER 28

Inspiring a Culture of Creativity and Passion in the Workplace

with Dr. Alaina Love

While our politicians and policy-makers fret and debate about how to solve our nation's nearly 9 percent unemployment rate, a much broader problem is standing in the way of our country's advancement and ability to compete, innovate, and grow: the *under*employment rate, which is over 25 percent! Almost one-fourth of the nation's workers are under-challenged, under-appreciated, under-motivated, and under-paid; these factors do not exactly create ideal workplace conditions and cultures inside companies across America. Leaders and board members need to be acutely aware of this disturbing trend, and develop strategies and systems to empower their teams.

Recently, a multitude of sobering reports have emerged about the state of employee engagement around the globe. In late 2011, a study by Mercer, which covered nearly 30,000 workers in seventeen countries (including 2,400 U.S. workers), indicated that one out of every two employees is either planning to leave his or her organization or is "mentally missing in action" on the job. The report mirrors a Gallup study in 2011, which demonstrated that a whopping 71 percent of America's employees are disengaged, often actively so, at work. As if that's not disturbing enough, the economic impact of the "actively disengaged" worker segment alone—the workers who are ready to leave and making their current places of employment disagreeable while they wait—costs the United States over $500 billion per year in lost productivity. Add these facts to the numerous studies that relate worker disengagement to the markedly increased frequency of physical and emotional illness (from stress-related diseases to depression) and the significant impact on company healthcare costs is evident. Happiness at work is not a "soft" issue; it has implications both inside and outside of the organization.

If you are reading this essay in your capacity as a board member or leader of any type of organization, then we hope you're taking note of this crisis of passion-less culture. More importantly, we hope that you'll accept accountability for conditions that have led to a massive disengagement of the nation's workforce. That's because the lack of engagement among American workers is not just affecting your business: it's impacting the growth and quality of our domestic (and overseas) economy. Every disengaged employee has a cache of untapped potential that could contribute to the country's productivity. Engaged workers deliver more to their organizations: they work beyond the job's requirements and demonstrate the level of discretionary effort our economy so sorely needs. So, we've got more than a dearth-of-jobs issue in this nation—we have a staggering human potential gap in existing jobs, which we must address in order to get the American economy back on its feet.

If you want to build engagement within your organization, begin by creating a culture that ignites people's passions. Recent data from an international study on the topic of employee purpose and passion proves that one of the most essential factors for igniting the energy, motivation, and engagement that drives our economy is capturing the human spirit. Research conducted by Alaina Love's firm, Purpose Linked Consulting—which surveyed over 1,300 professionals, managers, and leaders—identified direct connections between employees' motivation, their sense of affinity to the organization's mission, and their sense of personal fulfillment at work from over 80 percent of respondents. Even more respondents (86.3 percent) correlated fulfillment with their ability to "translate [their] purpose in life to tangible work contributions." Thus, employees are offering up a much-needed elixir for productivity and economic recovery by telling leaders, in essence, "If you want the best from me, give me work that aligns with my purpose and passions."

Love's book, *The Purpose Linked Organization*, identifies and discusses eight passion archetypes in order to find the right character traits that can make up a framework for effective governance, leadership, culture creation, and teambuilding. The archetypes are: the Builder, the Connector, the Creator, the Transformer, the Altruist, the Teacher, the Processor, the Discoverer, the Conceiver, and the Healer. To implement this framework, leaders are put through a proprietary evaluation process, the Passion Profiler™ Analysis, to help them understand their core skills and tendencies; this understanding serves as the basis for developing the Passion Linked Action Plan. One of the keys to this plan is to link a leader's objectives and core responsibilities with his or her underlying skills, passions, and values—the strength and alignment of that link will directly and indirectly impact that leader's effectiveness. Strong links between tasks that lie ahead and the degree and type of passion within will yield the best results. To determine these links, organizations' charts and position descriptions can be broken down and then rebuilt (the way that muscle is torn and then strengthened after a good workout) to create more effective leaders, as well as more profitable, high-performing organizations.

Once we understand people's true passions, it is easier to identify the tools, training, and resources they will need to make the greatest impact on an organization. Once we understand people's true passions, we can better uncover any "alignments and disconnects" that may be affecting their performance. Thus, once we understand people's true passions, we can finally, and genuinely, chip away at our nation's underemployment rate.

Beyond aligning passions with roles, leaders must understand how to lead in a knowledge-driven economy. This new economy has created a paradigm shift in organizational effectiveness, a fact that has escaped the notice of companies still operating under antiquated models of leadership or employee engagement. Under these new models, companies can view the establishment of robust operational systems as the primary (and sometimes only) foundation for business success. These are systems underpinned by effective strategies, strong internal communication networks, and a keen focus on efficiency and execution to produce reliable results. On paper, it sounds great. In action, such a system often overlooks critical elements of organizational effectiveness that have become even more essential in today's market, in which "innovate or die" has become the mantra.

What are the characteristics of leaders who build effective organizations that generate groundbreaking ideas? These leaders focus on people, not just systems. More importantly, they work to understand individuals' rational sides and emotional composition, nurturing culture and purpose as vigorously as they craft strategy. These effective knowledge economy leaders engage in conversation with employees, rather than dictating one-way communications; they favor relationships over processes. These savvy leaders focus on igniting energy, innovation, and creativity as much as they do on harnessing efficiencies, executing business plans, and delivering predictable results. In short, they measure, reward, and support those who brave the chaotic, risk-laden, and, often, tortuous path to sustainability and success.

In this new economy, organizational growth and innovation will not progress in a linear way. They will grow through a culture of creative chaos, a culture in which people, purpose, and passions are all catalysts for "breakthrough" thinking—the kind of thinking that can't easily be "systemized" into being. As a result, leadership in the new economy must support this essential creative tension, while also, at the same time, adopting models of governance that can uphold an innovation culture.

Leading with good governance means understanding your role as a fiduciary to company stakeholders, a group that includes the entire workforce. Governance means acting, truly, as a steward to protect the company's key assets, which include human capital. When those assets are underperforming at a rate of 25 percent or higher, you must immediately adopt strategies to bring passion back into the workplace. Then, with passion deeply embedded in your culture, we are confident that innovation, productivity, and profitability will soon follow.

About the Contributor

Alaina Love is a nationally recognized leadership expert and speaker, and the president of Purpose Linked Consulting (www.thepurposelink.com). She is co-author of *The Purpose Linked Orga-*

nization: How Passionate Leaders Inspire Winning Teams and Great Results (McGraw-Hill, 2009), a book that identifies and explores the power of aligning individual employee passions with work roles to increase productivity and fulfillment. Love is a frequent contributor to *BloombergBusinessweek.com* and is a leadership panelist for *WashingtonPost.com*. She can be reached at (540) 631-0215 or at alove@ thepurposelink.com.

CHAPTER 29

CORPORATE SOCIAL RESPONSIBILITY

From Being Best in the World to Being Best for the World

By Dr. Mrim Boutla, Co-Founder and Managing Partner, More Than Money Careers, LLC

Are traditional capitalism and our notions about corporate governance (as policy centered on businesses maximizing short-term shareholder value), responsible for the worsening of current social and environmental challenges? Many believe so. As shown through the efforts of the multi-faceted Occupy Movement, many believe that companies (and their investors) are prospering at the expense of the environment and communities in which they are operating. The Chicago Booth/Kellogg School Financial Trust Index survey's latest results confirm the erosion of trust between Americans and their financial system. Of respondents surveyed in spring 2011, only 13 percent indicated that they trusted big corporations. Only 12 percent trusted the stock market, and only 32 percent trusted banks.

So, are business and the quest for profitability really inherently bad for society and the environment? Is it possible that sound governance practices can help business leaders drive economic growth without increasing the social and environmental challenges we face?

Like all human-designed systems, capitalism and the governance principles we derive from it are only tools. Leaders leverage these tools to maximize the results they are expected to deliver. Traditionally, business leaders have long been leveraging governance and management principles to maximize short-term shareholder value. In the process of doing so, unfortunately, many business leaders have been contributing to social and environmental challenges. However, for some time now, more and more innovative business leaders (of both sustainable businesses and social enterprises) have been successfully leveraging sound governance principles to maximize long-term stakeholder value. These leaders have been working diligently over the past twenty-five years—even more so since the start of the global recession in 2008—to make the business case for social and environmental sustainability.

Meanwhile, consumers and investors have been learning about these mission-driven businesses. As a result, on an increasing basis, consumers and investors have been demanding more transparency, as well as environmental and social performance metrics, from the traditional firms they buy from or invest in. In this chapter, I discuss current trends and models of scalable sustainable businesses and social enterprises. I also address trends in governance approaches and new legal forms of business entities, which leverage market-driven governance approaches to maximize long-term value for shareholders and other stakeholders.

THE GREAT NEWS ABOUT THE GREAT RECESSION

The Great Recession has refueled that old debate centered on a business' role and goals. It encourages us to consider whether it is possible for private entities to be profitable while doing the right thing (i.e. producing goods and services without harming the environment or exploiting workers). A number of recent studies' results seem to suggest that the answer is yes. For example, a study by the Mega Trends Group at Boston Consulting Group showed that, despite the recession, the proportion of consumers willing to pay a premium for green products has grown. Furthermore, professionally-managed, socially responsible investing has grown 13 percent in the past few years. Both the growth of sustainable businesses and that of socially responsible investing are contributing to increase the visibility of business models that integrate economic, social, and environmental value creation into their very beings. These models are somewhat akin to the corporate social responsibility (CSR) efforts implemented by most global companies. As Jeffrey Hollender elegantly puts it, most global companies "confine their sustainability and responsible business initiatives to a limited number of highly compartmentalized efforts." The models focused on in this chapter are business models that operate with economic, social, and environmental value creation embedded in their governance DNA.

CORPORATE SOCIAL RESPONSIBILITY (CSR) INITIATIVES: A GOOD START, BUT OFTEN NOT GOOD ENOUGH

Over the past few years, people have seen a tremendous increase in CSR initiatives from traditional businesses. At most big companies that operate globally, though, social and environmental responsibility usually remains a type of strategy used to mitigate brand equity risks. True, these CSR initiatives can lead to tremendous positive impact when measured on an absolute scale. However, in most cases, they remain limited efforts, compared to the size of the overall negative impact generated by these same companies. Most global companies now issue an annual corporate social responsibility report. Indeed, the 2008 KPMG International Survey of Corporate Responsibility Reporting showed that while only about 35 percent of companies listed in the Global Fortune 250 issued a CSR report in 1999, 80 percent of them issued an annual CSR report by 2008.

However, a major challenge remains: to integrate each company's social and environmental performance into its annual core business report. Fortunately, a number of new standards enable companies to undertake this integration. For instance, the method recommended by the Global Reporting Initiative (GRI) has been gaining momentum as a way for any business in any industry to report social, environmental, and financial value creation. While the adoption of GRI reporting has been increasing in Europe and the Asian Pacific, attitudes to its adoption among companies headquartered in the United States have been, at best, tepid. Consulting firms such as KPMG and Deloitte now offer specialized advisory services and training programs that assist companies seeking to integrate environmental and social performance metrics into their annual core business reports.

HOW SHOULD WE DEFINE CSR?

CSR can be defined in many ways, including the following:

- As a form of citizenship or conscience that shapes how a corporation will interact with its community and its constituents (top-down versus bottom-up);
- As reporting undertaken for several reasons (on a voluntary/self-regulating basis; through encouragement from competitive peer pressure; because of government interaction/influence; because of government fine/penalty; or due to a crisis/scandal);
- As something that can serve all stakeholders in the ecosystem(s) in which the company operates;
- As a form of marketing and branding *versus* as a reflection of moral and ethical responsibilities to the community.

These initiatives can be manifested in a wide variety of programs and initiatives, such as:

- Cash support of various community initiatives/charities (philanthropy);
- "Do no (or minimal) harm" mindset and values;
- In-kind donations;
- Standalone general or specific purpose foundations;
- Corporate legal department pro bono work;
- Direct support/staffing of educational centers and initiatives;
- Ethics training programs and adoption/enforcement of a clearly defined code of conduct;
- Workforce health and wellness programs, in which coverage extends to employees' families;
- Resource management, efficiency programs, and recycling programs;
- Safe and responsible working conditions and respect for L&E laws;

- Enforcement of CSR through supply chain, channel partners, and strategic alliance partners;
- Idea of a "triple" bottom line (profit/people/planet).

SUSTAINABLE BUSINESSES: THE GAME CHANGERS

In contrast with the more typical, frequently compartmentalized CSR initiatives championed by global corporations (as discussed above), sustainable businesses take these ideas to the next level and integrate social, environmental, and economic value creation into their organizational DNA. There are examples of successful sustainable businesses in a number of industries. For example, in the retail industry, Whole Foods and Trader Joe's have emerged as leaders in maximizing profitability while focusing on socially and environmentally responsible product lines. In the food industry, pioneers such as Organic Valley, Newman's Own, and Stonyfield Farm have shown that high profitability can be achieved through sustainable governance practices that both help local famers and ensure long-term environmental sustainability. In the clothing industry, companies such as REI, Patagonia, and Eileen Fisher have demonstrated that sustainable sourcing practices and governance principles focused on long-term value creation for all stakeholders can lead to healthy profits, higher consumer loyalty, and lower employee turnover costs.

Many leaders and board members who oversee sustainable businesses committed to corporate citizenship have been working diligently to create a business entity that would enable managers to gain a new kind of legal protection against their investors: this protection is in case of the possible event that investors' financial return would be lower because of managerial decisions that maximized social or environmental value creation. These conversations led to the creation of the Benefit Corporation (B Corps) Certification process. Becoming a B-Corp is akin to becoming a sort of hybrid between a for-profit and non-profit organization. As of January of 2012, the United States was home to 517 certified B Corporations operating in a variety of industries, including energy, consumer-packaged goods, transportation, and environmental services. As a general matter, these companies' characters allow social objectives to be placed ahead of profits on their strategic priority lists; governance and leadership best practices and strategies are adjusted accordingly.

Furthermore, the B Corps certification model is at the core of a movement aimed at passing B Corp legislations in each state. Maryland first passed the B Corps as a new legal business entity in April 2010. As of January 2012, B Corps legislation had passed in six states (Maryland, Vermont, California, New Jersey, Hawaii, and Virginia), while Philadelphia-based sustainable businesses can receive a tax credit. B Corps legislation has been introduced or discussed in five other states (Michigan, Colorado, Pennsylvania, North Carolina, and New York), and future studies are needed to determine the possible contributions of B Corps to the growth (and strengthening) of state economies.

SOCIAL ENTERPRISES: THE CROSS-SECTOR PIONEERS

Sustainable entrepreneurs and leaders develop businesses that have economic, social, and environmental value creation integrated into their governance DNA; in contrast, social entrepreneurs use market-driven approaches to eradicate a social or environmental challenge. One of the most well-known social enterprise models is microfinance. By lending money to the poorest of the poor, micro-finance institutions (e.g., Grameen Bank, SKS Microfinance, and

Project Enterprise) have developed profitable entities while enabling clients to lift themselves out of poverty. Yet social enterprises operate in all industries. For instance, Harbor City Services (in Baltimore, MD) is a nonprofit that offers warehousing, shredding, and moving services to customers, while creating vocational opportunities, treatment programs, and support systems for workers, who are recovering from mental illness or substance abuse.

Several examples come to mind. Another is Berrett-Koehler, a company that publishes books that create a better world. The books Berrett-Koehler publish introduce new thinking that challenges the status quo, fostering positive change at the individual, organizational, and societal level. An example in the apparel and shoe industry is TOMS® Shoes, which started out with the mission of providing each child with a good-fitting pair of shoes. To achieve its mission, TOMS® developed a "One for One" model. For each pair of shoes sold, the company gives a pair of shoes to a needy child. In the hypothetical scenario that all kids have shoes that fit them, TOMS® will need to reinvent its mission (and business model). The company is mitigating this unlikely risk to business survival by broadening its product line: to eyewear.

Coca-Cola®: A Case In Point

Corporate social responsibility (CSR) has become an integral way for companies to keep stakeholders engaged while building or maintaining trust in the company. A case in point is Coca-Cola®.

At Coca-Cola®, the notion of shared value (a CSR value proposition developed by Michael Porter) takes on a specific resonance. Coca-Cola® is, of course, one of the most famous and iconic of global brands. At the same time, through local bottlers, Coca-Cola® is involved in communities around the world. Concerning the issue of future or current access to arable water, sustainability takes on a double meaning, signifying environmental responsibility as well as discovering sustainable sources for the main ingredient in the company's product. Coca-Cola® has taken its global involvement with water seriously for some time, working with NGOs to find solutions and making commitments to replenish water the company uses. It also protects sources of water, by using treatment plants, to ensure water the company uses is treated to a high standard before being returned to communities.

Employees, as well as leaders, of Coca-Cola® relate that CSR has become a substantive part of the company's way of thinking about its business, not a separate activity. CSR is a way to engage consumers and other stakeholders; it is also a way to build shared value and even a way for employees to act as advocates. Boards should note that CSR can often only be sustainable when it is directly related to a company's core business. Through the lens of business strategy, management practices such as communicating with stakeholders, ethical behavior, and building brands that stand for organizational values, can also be seen as central to the exterior business' long-term sustainability.

Over the past twenty-five years, social incubators, such as Echoing Green, Ashoka, Endeavor, and the Draper Richards Foundation, have provided seed and growth capital to social entrepreneurs (along with advisory services). Furthermore, impact investors (such as Investor's Circle, Calvert Foundation, RSF Social Finance, and Opportunity Finance Network) have allowed social entrepreneurs to scale and drive social change across different ecosystems. Social enterprises are not all businesses; indeed, many are hybrid organizations, which can be formed as either businesses or nonprofits. Many social enterprises combine revenue generation schemes with grants or Program-Related Investments (PRI) to achieve their social missions.

Most social enterprises aim, primarily, at creating social or environmental value while also still creating some financial return for their investors. One current debate among individuals working on social enterprise and impact investing is on the topic of measuring social impact: debaters are interested in being able to compare social investment opportunities across countries and social or environmental issues. Leading impact-investing groups have created several valuation metrics. Currently, the Impact Reporting and Investment Standard (IRIS, which is spearheaded by the Global Impact Investing Network) and the Global Impact Investing Reporting System (based on B Corp certification) are both gaining momentum as primary social, environmental and financial valuation metric systems. As the field of social entrepreneurship and impact investing continue to grow, its systems are likely to converge in a standard adopted by social entrepreneurs and investors across issues and geographical locations.

U.S.-based social entrepreneurs have been burdened in their missions by the lack of legislation enabling them to operate as business-nonprofit hybrids. To respond to this need, pioneer social entrepreneurs have advocated for creating a new legal form of business entity in the United States. The low-profit limited liability company (L3C) is an entity that can receive for-profit and nonprofit investments to achieve its social mission. L3C legislation has also proven useful in simplifying compliance requirements related to Internal Revenue Services rules about principles for responsible investment (PRIs) in social businesses. As of January 2012, L3C legislations had been passed in eight states (Illinois, Louisiana, Maine, Michigan, North Carolina, Utah, Vermont, and Wyoming), as well as in two federal jurisdictions: The Crow Indian Nation of Montana and The Oglala Sioux Tribe. As of the time this essay was written, L3C legislation was being discussed, with the possibility of being introduced, in at least ten other states (California, Florida, Georgia, Iowa, Minnesota, Nebraska, Ohio, Texas, Washington, and Wisconsin). According to InterSector Partners' latest survey, over 540 L3Cs were operating in the United States in January 2012.

As Justmeans co-founder and 3BL Media Chairman Martin Smith points out, "Capitalism worked because people couldn't see into the kitchen." Technology has enabled business stakeholders (consumers, investors, and employees) to demand higher transparency as they make purchasing, investing, and employment decisions. To remain competitive, traditional global businesses feel increasingly compelled to report their social and environmental performance along with their financial performance. To attract new consumers and investors, sustainable business leaders and social entrepreneurs have been driving new legislations that enables them to manage sustainably while gaining market share and providing a "good enough" return on investment. How much these new models will enable the U.S. economy to create growth through higher transparency and sustainable governance remains to be seen. However, the momentum gained by new acts of legislation, such as B Corps and L3Cs, along with the growing number of emerging sustainable business leaders and patient investors, might be a winning combination, increasing the proportion of businesses that blend traditional business approaches with social and environmental value creation to maximize long-term stakeholder value.

ABOUT THE AUTHOR

MRIM BOUTLA is a brain scientist turned career coach turned social entrepreneur. Both at Brown University and at the Kelley School of Business, Indiana University, Boutla has successfully coached hundreds of liberal arts graduates, M.B.A. students, and Ph.D. candidates interested in pursuing careers that successfully blend financial return with social impact and environmental responsibility. By combining her ten years of studying the brain's inner workings with her in-depth knowledge of career planning, career-switching strategies, and job-search techniques, Boutla has developed proprietary career management and job search systems to generate both financial and emotional rewards over the long term.

CHAPTER 30

THE "INNOVENTION" OF GLOBAL GOVERNANCE

By Jack Hughes, Principal, PHOENIX Financial and Advisory Services, LLC

The world and the global economy have certainly changed over the past few years; some would say for the better and some would say for the worse. Nevertheless, companies that wish to continue to operate successfully on a global basis must have leaders with passion for their cause and the courage to be consistent in their approach to doing business, even when their colleagues may see things differently. Since most companies that operate globally, by necessity, have far-flung operations in many parts of the world, they are effectively virtual companies. Teams of employees are often spread across the globe, in places ranging from different offices to different cultures, and they must find ways to operate effectively across time, space, and organizational boundaries. There is no water cooler in a global, virtual environment; a company's people are generally spatially decentralized, geographically dispersed, and technologically harnessed.

There are, however, some benefits to a global, virtual environment:

- People are more productive—there's less time traveling and commuting;

- There is more flexibility and more responsiveness—people are not tethered to the traditional workday;
- Companies are better able to address the world's increasing globalization;
- Employees tend to be higher caliber and have international experience;
- There are more critical and insightful contributions from people who might not otherwise be able to work together;
- Onsite employees are better able to adapt to local cultures and customs;
- It's less expensive—there are fewer brick and mortar infrastructure costs;
- And, generally, there is better employment of communications and information technologies, out of necessity.

There are also some serious challenges to operating in a global, virtual environment:

- There is more difficulty in managing team performance;
- Communications misunderstandings are more rampant;
- Challenges in contacting and/or connecting with other team members in a timely manner are the norm;
- Time zone differences are real;
- Limited face-to-face contact prevails;
- Trust building is a bigger hurdle;
- The meaning of text-based messages is harder to comprehend fully;
- And, there is reduced project visibility present in the real-world workspace.

Thus, in environments where the global meets the virtual, I believe the "innovention" of global governance must occur. Governance for large entities operating on the world stage must be innova-tive: it must be tailored to each company's particular circumstances and culture. In addition, it must be inventive: it must be adapted to be effective, exceptionally so, in a virtual environment. The key tenets of the "innovention" of global governance are this essay's topic, and there are four of them, as shown in the diagram below: uncompromising leadership, imbedded core ideology, enlightened governing principles, and effective communications. All four must come together for proper governance to occur.

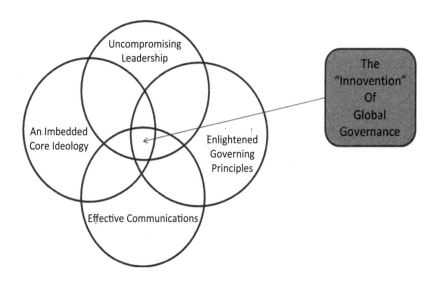

UNCOMPROMISING LEADERSHIP

What does uncompromising leadership mean in today's world? I define it as follows: it is the process of influencing others through service to them that turns vision into action, all supported by courage, conviction, and integrity. How does one do that? The answer is by taking responsibility: move from the sidelines to the playing field, and prove that one has the vision, resourcefulness, ability, endurance, and character to get things done the right way, the first time.

Let's take a deeper look at what this level of leadership and its specific attributes look like in action. The below list provides definitions of the key attributes.

- Vision: ask where your heart-of-hearts is leading you; what it is about the future that you are passionate about today
- Wisdom: be continuously learning and open to new ideas; to stop learning means to stop growing
- Courage: when the going gets tough . . .
- Perseverance: never, never, never give up; and always play to win
- Servanthood: service to others is job one
- Integrity: always do the right thing, even when it's hard
- Humility: don't let your ego cloud your vision; practice self-control
- Justice: be fair in all things
- Gratitude: you didn't get there by yourself; also, when you lose, do so graciously
- Endurance: out-think, out-gun and out-last your opponents
- Generosity: give back; and then give some more
- Composure: take risks and bear strife with equal equanimity
- Decisiveness: ready, aim, fire
- Communication: talk the walk and walk the talk
- Team-building: no single one of us is as effective as all of us

You might ask, "So what?" I like the following statement, because I think it sums up the "so what?" nicely. Leadership is definitely not what you do to your team; it's what you do with and for your team.

AN IMBEDDED CORE IDEOLOGY

When I talk about an imbedded core ideology, what exactly do I mean? Try this as a working definition: it's a combination of a higher purpose and a set of core values that permeates an organization. It's both the culture upon which the company is built and the behavior expected of every single employee in the organization, with no exceptions. Every leader needs to set a vision for his or her company. That vision communicates a compelling picture of the future. It answers the question, "What are you passionate about?" (If you are passionate about something, you will most likely accomplish it!) It also presents a set of discriminators that set your company apart from the rest.

However, let's go a few steps deeper into the cultural aspects of a company. A business needs sales, earnings, and cash flow like a healthy body needs blood and water; these needs are essential for life, but they are not the essential point of life. There must be a higher purpose for why your company exists, beyond just making money. What is it that inspires the drive and passion to accomplish your company's strategic objectives? For example, is your company customer-centric? Is your company, first and foremost, focused on providing the best products and services to your customers, solving customer problems with immediacy, being responsive, operating on time and within budget, and striving for 100 percent customer satisfaction? If not, perhaps your company is people-centric, focused on hiring the best and brightest personnel, training them, incentivizing them, and providing them with the best tools and most enhanced processes in order to serve clients with passion and innovation. Or, maybe your company is focused on a third platform and is community- or society-centric, creating best-value products and services that make important and lasting contributions to humanity's improvement and well-being. Before you sell your "what" to the customer, you need to understand your "why."

The second absolutely necessary set of elements within your company's core ideology is its core values. They are essential and enduring guiding principles that are not to be compromised for financial gain or short-term expediency: they represent the company's highest priorities and deeply held driving forces, forming the framework for management style, business decisions, and overall culture. When it comes to core values, many companies have very similar items (the usual suspects) on the list; honesty, integrity, truth, respect, collaboration, customer satisfaction, and so on. What about some others to consider? For example, your company's values could include prudent risk taking, empowering key employees, developing future leaders, protecting interests of all stakeholders, being profitable, or acting as a good corporate citizen.

Defining your core values is critical to your success; if your employees do not completely understand the behavior that is expected from them, you can't expect them to act right.

All this is not to say that defining your core ideology, and thus the culture of your company, is easy. This takes hours of thought, contemplation, collaboration, and, ultimately, buy-in by the entire corporate team. Some of the obvious issues might include:

- Identifying the organization's true purpose;
- Enumerating core values in a concise manner;
- Implementing the core purpose and values throughout the organization in such a way that all employees know them and live them;
- And, creating quantitative and qualitative metrics with which to measure the usage and effectiveness of the company's core values.

So, then what? I like the following quotation from one of Ken Blanchard's books: "Managing only for profit is like playing tennis with your eye on the scoreboard and not on the ball."

ENLIGHTENED GOVERNING PRINCIPLES

So, what might a set of enlightened governing principles look like? Perhaps the following: an internal set of processes, customs, policies, laws, and institutions affecting the way a corporation or company is directed, administered, and controlled through the application of good business savvy, objectivity, accountability, and integrity. In essence, this set is a multi-faceted process designed to ensure the accountability of certain individuals in an organization. Accountability is ensured through mechanisms that try to reduce or eliminate self-interest and misalignment of interests, while driving economic efficiency with a strong emphasis on shareholders' welfare.

The players on the stage of responsibility for appropriate governance include the shareholders, management, and the board of directors. Many people want to level this responsibility squarely and only on the board's shoulders; I beg to differ. Let's define each player's role. The shareholders' responsibility is to ensure that the board of directors is carrying out its duties to protect stakeholders' rights and interests. Management's responsibility is to run the day-to-day financial, administrative, and operational aspects of the organization in accordance with the strategy and policies established by the board of directors. Finally, the board of directors' responsibility is to endorse the organization's strategy; develop directional policy; promote the right culture; appoint, supervise, and remunerate senior executives; ensure accountability of the organization to its owners and authorities; and correct failures in a rapid and effective manner.

A number of outside players may intersect with the governance role (such as lawyers, bankers, auditors, insurance brokers, etc.), but, from my perspective, this outside group is tangential to the main players on the stage noted above. Documentation and application of the necessary internal controls is the underpinning for defining an effective set of enlightened governing principles. Some of the key considerations are as follows:

- Monitoring by the board of directors: The board of directors, with its legal authority to hire, fire, and compensate top management, safeguards invested capital. Regular board meetings allow potential problems to be identified, discussed, and avoided. While non-executive directors may seem more independent, they may not always provide results of more effective corporate governance and may not increase performance. Different board structures are optimal for different firms. Moreover, the board of directors' ability to monitor the firm's executives is a function of its access to information. Executive directors possess superior knowledge about the decision-making process; therefore, they evaluate top management on the basis of the quality of decisions that lead to financial performance outcomes and can also look beyond the financial criteria.

- Internal Control Procedures and Internal Auditors: Internal control procedures are policies that are directly related to reliable financial reporting, operating efficiency, and compliance with laws and regulations. An organization's board of directors, audit committee, management, and other personnel implement these policies in order to provide reasonable assurance that the organization is achieving its objectives. Internal auditors are organizational personnel who test the design and implementation of the organization's internal control procedures and its financial reporting reliability.

- Balance of Power: The simplest balance of power is very common; require that the president be a different person from the treasurer. Such a simple application of power separation is developed further in companies that have separate divisions to check and balance each other's actions. One group may propose company-wide administrative changes, another group review and can veto the changes, and a third group can check that the interests of people outside the three groups (such as customers, shareholders, or employees) are being met.

- Remuneration: Performance-based remuneration is designed to relate some proportion of salary to individual performance. This may be in the form of cash, shares, share options, superannuation, or other benefits. Such incentive plans, however, are reactive in the sense that they provide no mechanism for preventing mistakes or opportunistic behavior, and can elicit myopic behavior.

In addition to the considerations above, there are some basic concepts that provide a foundation for the consistent application of enlightened governing principles. These include:

- Rights and Equitable Treatment of Shareholders: Organizations should respect the rights of shareholders and help shareholders to exercise those rights. Company representatives can help shareholders exercise their rights by communicating information, which is understandable and accessible, effectively and by encouraging shareholders to participate in general meetings.

- Interests of Other Stakeholders: Organizations should recognize that they have legal and other obligations to all legitimate stakeholders.
- Role and Responsibilities of the Board: The board needs members with a range of skills and understanding who can deal with various business issues and have the ability to review and challenge management performance. The board needs to be of sufficient size and its members must have the appropriate level of commitment to fulfill responsibilities and duties. Its makeup should be an appropriate mix of executive and non-executive directors.
- Integrity and Ethical Behavior: Ethical and responsible decision-making is not only important for public relations; it is also a necessary element of risk management and lawsuit avoidance. Organizations should develop a code of conduct for their directors and executives promoting ethical and responsible decision-making. Understand, though, that reliance by a company on the integrity and ethics of individuals is bound to fail eventually. Because of this, many organizations establish compliance and ethics programs to minimize the risk that the firm may step outside of ethical and legal boundaries.
- Disclosure and Transparency: Organizations should clarify and make publicly known the roles and responsibilities of board members and management in order to provide shareholders with a level of accountability. They should also implement procedures to verify and safeguard the integrity of the company's financial reporting independently. Disclosure of material matters concerning the organization

should be timely and balanced to ensure that all investors have access to clear, factual information.

Before I leave this topic, I want to outline, as I did above, some of the issues a company may face in establishing appropriate and effective enlightened governing principles. These may include:

- The lack of internal controls and internal auditors;
- The independence of the organization's external auditors and the quality of their audits;
- Oversight and management of risk;
- Preparation oversight of the organization's financial statements;
- Review of compensation arrangements for the chief executive officer and other senior executives;
- Diversity on the board of directors and throughout the organization;
- The supply of adequate accounting and financial information;
- The resources made available to directors in carrying out their duties;
- And, finally, the way(s) in which individuals are nominated for board positions.

Why does a corporation need enlightened governing principles? Think about the following statement: "The mighty Mississippi without levees is just water everywhere."

EFFECTIVE COMMUNICATIONS

The fourth and final area I want to talk about with respect to the "innovention" of global governance in a global, virtual environment is effective communications. I would like to define "effective communications" as the sharing of information between two or more individuals or groups to reach a clear and common understanding. Conceptually, effective communications needs to be a series of two-way streets, places where information is exchanged through a variety of mediums (both internally, between management and employees, and externally, between the company's staff and clients, suppliers, and vendors). In this global, virtual environment, I have a few suggestions about how to facilitate improved effective communications:

- Create regular quarterly opportunities for face-to-face meetings;
- Have more extensive use of webcams and video teleconferencing;
- Use weekly conference calls to provide updates on project statuses and where projects are heading;
- Have calendars for every employee so everyone's schedule can be seen by each team member;
- Create a communications code of conduct to establish ground rules, avoid delays in responses, and diminish misunderstandings;
- Store data and information where all team members can readily and easily access them;
- Implement standardized collaborative software to ease communications, as well as for task and document organization;
- Assume nothing, and spell out everything in detail in communications;
- Conduct training on email use to put all team members on the same playing field;
- Encourage text messaging and IM-ing to facilitate ease and rapidity of informal and offline communications;

- Establish a viable Intranet and keep it current;
- Consider creating a newsletter to keep team members and their families up to date on what's happening across the company;
- And, finally, immediately publicize and celebrate all successes throughout the company.

Several key participants are involved in ensuring effective communications: the CEO/president, business unit managers, and administrative managers.

The CEO/president also needs to be the chief communicator. The company's vision, strategy, and core ideology all need to come from the top. This is not to say that all key players shouldn't participate in the preparation of each of these elements, in order to achieve across-the-board commitment, but the CEO/president needs to spearhead the passion for each. If this type of leadership does not come from the highest level in the company, don't expect anyone to follow.

However, the CEO/President can't be everywhere, all of the time. Accordingly, the business unit managers, who are regularly interfacing with employees, suppliers, and customers, need to reinforce communications from the CEO/President continuously and consistently. Every employee should understand where the company is headed and how management plans to get the company there. If not, chaos will soon rear its ugly head. The business unit managers must beat the drum daily to make sure the entire company team remains on the same page.

Again, the CEO/President can't be everywhere all of the time. Accordingly, the administrative managers, much like the business unit managers, must regularly interface with their respective employees, suppliers, and vendors, and, perhaps to a more limited extent, customers. They also need to reinforce communications from the CEO/President continuously and consistently. Like the business unit managers, the administrative managers must also reinforce the CEO/president's message daily to make sure their team members remain on the same page.

I would be remiss here if I didn't also mention the downside: the lack of effective communications may lead to misunderstandings, a lack of information, decreases in employees' performance, increases in employee turnover, employee frustration, and conflict between parties.

So what's the big deal about effective communications? As the saying goes, "We have two ears, but only one month; use them wisely." The "innovention" of global governance in a global, virtual company is not for the faint of heart.

About the Author

Jack Hughes is currently the Co-Founder and Principal of *PHOENIX* Financial and Advisory Services, LLC, a company that provides management consulting services to small and emerging companies in the government and in the commercial technology, media, and entertainment industries. Hughes is also a Principal Consultant with Altus Associates, which specializes in buy-side merger and acquisition services.

Hughes has a proven record of progressive leadership and management experience in fast-growth organizations. Prior to co-founding *PHOENIX* Financial and Advisory Services, he served as Executive Vice President and CFO of Alion Science and Technology Corporation. Along with his daily responsibilities of Alion's financial and accounting functions, he contributed to the strategic vision for the future expansion of the corporation, directed the implementation of financial and accounting policy, and participated directly in the execution of multiple mergers and acquisitions and associated financings, growing the company from $200 million to $750 million, with over 3,000 employees, in five years. Previously, Hughes was the Senior Vice President and CFO of BTG, Inc., accountable for business and operations management, as well as for creating winning proposal strategies, mergers and acquisitions, and growth financing, taking BTG from a $50 million to a $600 million business, with 1,650 employees, in five years. While at BTG, Hughes also executed the first successful IPO in the government technology services industry in over twelve years. Preceding his work at BTG, Mr. Hughes was the Senior Vice President and Corporate Treasurer of ManTech International Corporation, growing the company to $200 million in business, with nearly 3,000 employees in seventy locations worldwide. He played a key leadership role in the development of industry positions on major issues, resulting in new legislation, government policy, and regulations on uncompensated overtime, profit policy, contract awards without discussions, and best value contracting.

Hughes has a B.S. in Economics and Business and a minor in Political Science from Frostburg State University, and has performed graduate coursework in contract law/formation, government procurement, mergers and acquisitions, and financial management. He also serves on several corporate and non-profit boards. Hughes is a frequent speaker on the topics of mergers and acquisitions, financing, and strategic planning.

CHAPTER 31

The Six Gut-Wrenching Questions Every Non-Profit Board Must Ask

Saving the Ship by Rocking the Boat

By Mario Morino, Chairman, Venture Philanthropy Partners (VPP)

In my career and in my personal life, I have built and sold several very successful companies, launched many non-profit organizations, and served on dozens of boards. I have learned over the years that effective governance is paramount for success, whether the enterprise's aim is to make a profit or make an impact. No matter what the company's underlying mission, board members are ultimately responsible to the stakeholders for the organization's success or failure in accomplishing its mission: they serve as the guardians of the organization's values and culture. Although my focus (and that of this guest essay) in recent years has been on effective governance and structure of non-profits, I am confident that board members from all types of organizations will benefit by taking heed of the thoughts below.

Ever since the launch of Venture Philanthropy Partners, I have implored those who serve on nonprofit boards to "summon the courage to face the music and prepare for the future, even if things are going swimmingly today." In this guest essay, I will arm you with the six questions I believe every nonprofit board and executive team must ask to prepare for the rough financial straits and the unpredictable market conditions for fundraising and growth that lie ahead.

Fair warning: The questions below are not a tame, staid checklist. Wrestling with these questions will require you to challenge long-held assumptions, stir conflict within yourself, and venture far from your comfort zone.

Before I share the questions, allow me to share a good example of the bold thinking that our times require. Shockingly, this story comes from academia's ivory tower, a sector that is notoriously tradition-bound and change-averse.

Smith College, in Northampton, MA, has recently launched a "Futures Initiative" to take a hard look at some of the basic assumptions that have guided the college for well over a century. Under the leadership of its president, Carol Christ, the college is "reconsidering not only the financial model of the institution, but also the types of students the women's college attracts, ways it can move beyond the residential campus model, and how it goes about delivering instruction," according to *Inside Higher Ed*.

The fact that an institution like Smith is undertaking this initiative is an important harbinger. Smith has faced budget cuts, but it's under no imminent threat. It's a thriving, highly selective college with a billion-dollar endowment. Smith's initiative is a great example of the proactive planning we all need to do in this disruptive new era.

THE CRITICAL SIX

The tricky part is posing these important, tough questions in order to prepare for change ahead while you also stay focused on the here and now: the management and day-to-day execution of your organization. Here's one approach to consider: create an *ad hoc* group made up of key board members, executives or managers, and outside advisors (six to nine people total) to answer these future-focused questions. The rest of the leadership team can maintain its focus on ensuring the organization continues to run well.

Question 1: What conditions could change precipitously, endangering our mission and those we serve?

In high school I played left field for a gifted baseball coach who taught us to be prepared for anything. He demanded that each of us "live the play before it happens." Given that I was the only kid on the team whose IQ was higher than his batting average (and my IQ wasn't that high!), I paid very close attention to anything that would improve my game. Between every pitch, I would see in my mind's eye the batter "singling" (getting ready to hit a single) to the right; I'd imagine running in to backup a throw to second. Then I'd "see" the batter grounding to the shortstop; I imagined hustling in to be there in case of an error. And this went on and on.

In my professional life I drive folks crazy, because I'm constantly asking, "If this happens, then what?" All I'm doing is trying to see the play before it unfolds.

The "play" that so many of us are watching develop is the decline in public funding. For organizations that are highly dependent on public dollars, these cuts can mean drastic cutbacks, or even shutting their doors. If I work at a charter or parochial school and discover our scholarships (read: vouchers) are cut, what percentage of tuition revenue is hit? Are there alternative revenues to offset this loss? Can we continue?

Even if you're not the direct beneficiary of public funding, please don't assume that you don't need to think about public funding cuts. The competition for foundation grants, major gifts, and fee-based contracts will skyrocket as those whose public monies are cut look to other funding sources—like yours.

The loss of public funding is far from the only adverse thing to find at the doorstep one day. For instance, suppose you run an independent school. What would you do if a securely endowed, proprietary, competing school opened for business in your locale with a lower tuition? What if you work to reduce gang violence and your local government cuts the number of police officers, inadvertently placing a greater strain on the services you provide? What are the implications of these adverse conditions?

If you have outstanding debt, what protections have you put in place to guard against higher interest rates once inflation raises its ugly head? Could you withstand the increase in debt servicing costs? Should you consider doing something to "collar" the rate? Alternatively, better yet, should you try to clear or reduce the debt to lessen your vulnerability?

Finally, can your endowment withstand a severe market hit, and, if so, at what cost in programs and services? If not, what is your board and organization's plan B?

Question 2: Within current constraints, what can we do to improve the outcomes of our programs?

This sounds so basic, yet the board members and leaders of too many organizations give this subject little more than lip service. They dwell in long discussions about "process" and never actualize big, non-incremental improvements that can save more lives, enable more youth to graduate from college, or help more unemployed workers get living-wage jobs.

Some years back I was in a board retreat where my colleagues and I were trying to prioritize a set of strategic initiatives. I stressed that we needed to focus first and foremost on financing, because I was worried that the organization was in a precarious financial state. Another board member, the CEO of a major firm, respectfully but assertively took issue with my position. "I disagree with Mario on this," he said. "The quality of our product is number one. Not finances. If we don't get the quality right, finances won't matter." He was absolutely right.

I can't guarantee that quality will pull an organization through a crisis. However, an organization doing great work and making a discernable difference will certainly have a better chance than others do to compete for scarce resources and capitalize on disruptions in its space. So please don't curtail your creative thinking with the excuse "we don't have the money." You have a staff and advisors with a lot of knowledge. So, tap them: free their thinking. Try creating "improvement circles," where folks come together to brainstorm. Explore, together, how to increase quality, lower cost, and improve outcomes. Do the same with those you serve; you might be pleasantly surprised.

However, most of all, I urge you to consider undertaking a rigorous "theory of change" effort (not to be confused with strategic planning). David Hunter, the former director of evaluation and knowledge development at the Edna McConnell Clark Foundation, describes the approach very well in his essay from *Leap of Reason* (published by Venture Philanthropy Partners May 2011).

I've long believed that this kind of thoughtful (and emotionally challenging) review of programs and services, conducted by experts with deep domain expertise, is an essential practice, not a luxury.

Done well, it leads to clearer focus, improved program alignment, pruning of programs with incremental or tangential value, and tangible improvements in how the company members deliver on the mission. I've seen this with my company's VPP's, investment partners who have gone through this process. I've also seen it on recent site visits to organizations outside VPP's portfolio, including Congreso de Latinos Unidos and ROCA. Their redesigned, high-quality, high-performance efforts are a direct result of investment in their theory of change. As one leader said, "Doing this helps save more lives."

The bottom line is, in times of crisis, improving quality is a way through. It's not a locked guarantee for success. However, if you're not doing your job, you risk being toast when things really get tough.

Question 3: What is our organization's baseline budget for providing the minimum acceptable level of service to clients?

You don't want to be caught like a deer in the headlights should your organization incur a big cut in revenue (e.g., loss of funding from a patron funder), experience an unexpected disruption (e.g., an embezzlement or other scandal), and/or see your costs soar (e.g., the financial crisis-induced fee spikes on credit default swaps held by nonprofits and municipalities). These crises tend to come with little or no notice. Most organizations are forced to take extreme corrective action quickly, without the benefit of thoughtful planning and deliberation that would ensure "smart actions."

Yet there is a way to prepare yourself for such unforeseen hits: use zero-based budgeting as a way of analyzing the minimum funding you need to provide your core service with acceptable quality.

I'll explain. In the spring of 1988, my software and services firm recruited a young, talented businessman to join us as president. He had sped along the managerial fast track at GE and gone on to work as a senior executive at a major software firm. He brought strong business analytical skills into our rather loose managerial world. One of the valuable tools in his arsenal was the zero-based budget, which, after much initial reluctance, I eventually came to appreciate as an excellent method for looking at activities and costs.

Unlike a traditional budget, which uses the existing expense structure as its baseline, a zero-based budget assumes no history and starts with a baseline of zero: no activity, no costs. My firm used zero-based budgeting as a one-time exercise to find the critical set of activities we absolutely had to do to keep our doors open for business; then, we also determined the costs associated with this baseline. The results made us evaluate each major component of our operation on its relative merit and cost. As you can guess, it was emotionally trying to do this. It was very hard, but necessary, to be highly objective and to keep history and allegiances from coloring our decisions.

With zero-based budgeting, organizations can create a dooms-day-scenario plan for eliminating all the programs except those that are absolutely necessary for survival. For example, in the case of a multi-facility organization, the first action might be to consolidate operations in one of the facilities and shut down or sell the others. A multi-service organization might cut back on programs that are not absolutely essential to its primary intervention model. A school might have to make the hard call of eliminating library services or the school nurse's position, or it might face higher student-to-teacher ratios.

The leader of a private school shared his experience of this approach with me: "I was guided through the process by one of our trustees, who was a retired CEO. We incorrectly started with the assumption that we would have all the same staff, which of course defeats the purpose of starting from scratch and trying to align staffing with mission. Having to justify each member of our team and program was an eye-opening process for me and the leadership staff at the school."

While the idea of bringing your expenses down to zero may be horrifying, there is tremendous value in this exercise. If your organization is able to clarify its priorities through a zero-based budgeting exercise, your organization will do a better job of allocating resources according to its core mission and knowing when to say no to less important efforts and projects. Then, when you hit those turbulent storms, your board, leadership, and key staff will already be mentally there and ready to move.

Question 4: Who would be our "knight in shining armor," so to speak, if we needed one? In other words, who could we turn to if we were at risk of having to close down?

In my corporate life, my business partners and I have strategically thought through to which companies we would turn if we had to sell the business (for whatever reason). Please understand this was not something we wanted to do, but we felt preparing for it was necessary and prudent. When you engage in this kind of thinking, you take purposeful steps to get to know the potential "knights" who could step in to help your company, to understand their leadership and culture, and even to do partnerships or joint ventures with them. Then if you find yourself in a situation in which you need to sell the firm to protect your shareholders, staff, and customers, you can approach one of your "knights." This is far better than starting out cold with someone you don't know at all or, worse, sitting prey to a hostile takeover.

I'm sure this thinking sounds brutally corporate, but it is absolutely applicable to the world of nonprofits, too.

Ask these questions: What organization or organizations would be your logical collaborators or merger partners? What synergies would exist? What value would you bring to them and they to you? In addition, what would be the cost in dollars and mission?

How real is this thinking? This discussion is already underway in the world of private, independent schools, as demographic shifts are leading to lower student enrollment. It has unfortunately been the bane of many Catholic dioceses and independent Catholic schools, which have a mandate to liquidate assets and decrease expenses, especially in older, poorer communities. It has been at play in an aggressive way in healthcare, as a result of a wave of hospital consolidations. Municipalities that have long protected their fiefdoms are looking, increasingly, to consolidate services across jurisdictions and, in extreme cases, even merge the jurisdictions—actions forced in most cases by declining revenues. And the beat goes on.

Thus, identify those organizations and leaders to which you could turn if you were faced with saving your organization by consolidation or some form of collaboration. Develop relationships with each organization. Enter into pilot collaborations to get to know them. Then, develop scenarios for both what you would propose and what the rationale to support it would be.

Question 5: What are "one-step-away" opportunities? In other words, how can we change our prospects by building on what we already know?

In the '80s I had the chance to work with some top thinkers from McKinsey & Company, and my exposure to that line of thinking helped me better understand two related concepts: one, the importance of exploring new opportunities that are directly tied to your mission, yet are not more than one step away from your core competency; and two, the value in exploring whether your core products and services might be relevant in other areas (secondary markets), without the need of material revamping.

For example, if you run an independent or charter elementary school, you might improve your organization's outcomes and generate additional revenue by establishing an early childhood development program. Similarly, if you run a high school, your organization might offer an additional preparatory year to help students gain a better foundation for college, both developmentally and academically.

Take this thinking further. Encourage (and incentivize) your staff and board to constantly be on the lookout for new ideas: these ideas could open up new opportunities to improve on current programs or expand and grow based on the "one-step away" principle. However, don't look only at the organization's own niche and geography (e.g., healthcare in the United States). Keep open to ideas from other sectors, industries, and, especially, innovation occurring beyond our shores. I like futurist Faith Popcorn's idea of reading a trade magazine or journal in a field other than your own in search of ideas and developments that may have transfer value.

Question 6: What can we do to strengthen our revenue base?

In these times, it is imperative that board members and leadership teams do all they can to protect the revenue sources they have while starting the arduous process of finding new ones. The first, and the logical, step is taking an in-depth look at the organization's attitude toward fund development and the capacity it has to deliver the required dollars.

First of all, break down the myth that raising money is the fundraising team's responsibility. Everyone can and should play a role. We need to accept the brutal reality that higher education came to grips with years ago: the president is the chief fundraiser for the organization, with all hands at the ready to help. Next to ensuring the quality and integrity of organizational programs, this is the most important priority. Michael Worth, a colleague and respected thought leader in the National Capital region, does a nice job of laying out the key fundraising issues organizations should consider in threatening economic times in his column, "It's the Economy."

Rather than just focusing on increasing an organization's current funding base, ask how you are considering new sources of funding, perhaps tying the question back to one-step-away opportunities. However, please be careful not to launch new revenue-generating ventures without serious consideration. The highway to these ventures is littered with roadkill. Instead of bringing in significant revenues, they often lead to a loss of mission focus and a dilution of scarce internal resources.

That said, some nonprofits with strong leadership, mission focus, planning, and staff resources can do the above well. My good friend Bob Templin, president of Northern Virginia Community College, has had good experiences. "I look for new lines of business that can be profitable for us," Templin explains. "For example, NOVA has been teaching immigrants and the children of embassy officials for more than forty years. We've gotten to be very good at working with people from many different cultures, so it was not a big step from our core competency to launch a program to recruit international students. International students pay nearly two and one-half times the tuition that 'in-state' students do, and they enrich our collegiate environment by being here. In the last five years, our international student enrollment has grown by more than 70 percent, and these students now generate a 'surplus' of more than $1 million annually after all expenses are paid."

THE UNTHINKABLE ISN'T

In my pieces written over the years directed at leaders of non-profits, I have outlined a number of "unthinkable" events that have come to pass over the last decade—from 9/11 to the financial collapse. In the past twelve months since 2011, the Occupy Wall Street protest has grown rapidly, across the country, and become a magnet for deep frustration and anxiety about what the future holds. MF Global, a huge securities firm run by former Goldman Sachs CEO and former New Jersey Governor Jon Corzine, collapsed when a potential "knight" found accounting irregularities and backed out of rescuing the company. The city of Harrisburg, PA, filed for bankruptcy. Only a week after euro zone leaders sparked euphoria in financial markets around the world with their announcement of a massive deal to reduce Greece's debt, the crisis once again threatened the global economy, and the Greek government teetered on the edge of collapse.

I hope that the parade of unthinkable events shakes us up. If we look at the kind of questions I've posed in this guest essay through a purely intellectual lens, it's too easy to keep them at arm's length. As a good friend told me recently, "We in the social and educational sector need to get a sharp punch to our solar plexus, [be] forced into a skunk works, and kept there until we start coming up with some new ideas." I'm afraid he's right.

We need, desperately, to get past nice discussions. We need to be ready to rock the boat during board meetings and leadership sessions, and we also need to be prepared to deal with the consequences of uncovering the truth. This resolution is not about self-reflection and introspection as a touchy-feely New Age exercise. It's about ensuring our organizations' continued ability to make a material difference in the lives of those we serve. That's why these tough questions are worth asking.

ABOUT THE AUTHOR

MARIO MORINO is co-founder and chairman of Venture Philanthropy Partners and chairman of the Morino Institute. His career spans more than forty years as entrepreneur, technologist, and civic and business leader. He also has a long history of civic engagement and philanthropy in the National Capital Region and more recently in northeast Ohio.

In the early 1970s, Morino co-founded and helped build the Legent Corporation, a software and services firm that became a market leader and one of the industry's ten largest firms by the early 1990s. He retired from the private sector in 1992 and, since then, his focus has been almost exclusively on the nonprofit sector.

Morino founded the Morino Institute in 1994 to stimulate innovation and entrepreneurship, advance a more effective philanthropy, close social divides, and understand the relationship with and impact of the Internet on our society. In 2000, Morino co-founded Venture Philanthropy Partners, a philanthropic investment organization that concentrates investments of money, expertise, and contacts to improve the lives and boost the opportunities of children of low-income families in the National Capital Region.

In addition to his roles with Venture Philanthropy Partners and the Morino Institute, Morino serves on a number of nonprofit and for-profit boards, including the Cleveland Clinic Foundation and Brookings Institution. Morino's current private sector work is limited to his affiliation with General Atlantic LLC, one of the leading global growth-equity firms providing capital for companies in markets with high-growth potential that are typically driven by globalization, industry consolidation, technology, demographics, liberalized markets, and other transformative factors. He has been associated with the firm for more than twenty years, initially as its second investment in 1983, later as a Special Advisor, and now as a member of its Executive Advisory Board.

CHAPTER 32

THE ESSENCE OF
ENTREPRENEURIAL
LEADERSHIP

Listening to the Council

By Verne Harnish, "The Growth Guy," CEO and Founder, Gazelles International

It's lonely at the top—especially for entrepreneurs.

That's why the three most important pages ever written in business are pages 114—116 in Jim Collins' landmark book, *Good to Great*. This is a bold statement, but I've seen the transformational impact on entrepreneurs and their growth companies that takes place when they implement the concepts described in these three pages of Collins' book.

This concept was key to putting $160 million in Richard Kay's pocket; it's been critical in helping Brian Scudamore manage the growth of one of North America's top franchises; it repaired Lance Pederson's executive team; it aided Lee Prosenjak in designing a new dance studio and Scott Mesh in solving a major staffing problem; and it's already brought Nick Arrigan closer to his children. This simple concept, which even underpinned one of the most successful college football seasons for a rookie coach in 2006, was something that drove the success of John D. Rockefeller, the wealthiest entrepreneur of all time. What Collins outlines on these three pages are the eleven characteristics of what he calls "the Council."

Unlike the standard executive or management team meeting that's a weekly staple at most companies (or should be) or the less frequent board of directors or advisory board meeting, the formation of a Council as an additional governance tool is aimed solely at providing objective and un-biased advice to company leadership on a weekly basis. The Council is not concerned with consensus building; it generates "talk time" in an era when leaders have been driven to silence by technology and left to solve problems via email and text messages.

This concept generates conversations on what's genuinely vital to a business' success and helping the entrepreneur discover and face "the brutal facts" that Jim Collins so aptly describes as critical to greatness.

STRUCTURING SUCCESS

"Players that shoot foul shots the same each time make a lot of shots," notes Richard Kay, co-owner of the NBA Washington Wizards and founder of OTG Software. "The same in business. I felt my most important job was creating a consistent structure for being successful."

And successful his organizations were. Launched in 1992, Kay's data management software firm, OTG, grew to 450 employees with 12,000 customers, including more than 1,000 credit unions and over 500 hospitals. After going public in 2000, Legato acquired OTG two years later for $403 million, of which Kay received 40 percent. EMC then acquired Legato for $1.3 billion while Kay was on the board of directors.

Underpinning this success was a simple meeting and accountability process that started with a 7:00 a.m. breakfast every Monday morning (including most Monday holidays), at the Bethesda Marriott Suites across from OTG's offices in Maryland. From the day Kay started OTG until the day it sold, he and his executive team stuck to this routine. "The reason we met so early on Monday was we knew we were up against a lot of smart, well-prepared competitors," recalls Kay. "This early start to the week motivated us to prepare and helped us generate excitement as the company grew. And some of the best conversations occurred on the walks over and back from these meetings."

Following Kay's "council" breakfast came a standard set of management, sales and marketing, software development, and finance/accounting meetings that often took the executive team (and department heads, as the company grew) through to lunch. The key is that they had this additional, more open-ended breakfast meeting, which gave the top team a chance to talk through challenges facing the company every week. I sat in on some of these meetings and observed, as Kay's team would debate, laugh, discuss, decide, and, most importantly, talk openly and candidly with no set agenda. People handled the more tactical issues during the following functional meetings.

THE STORM

1-800-GOT-Junk? is one of the fastest-growing franchisors in North America. Key to driving and managing this growth is a weekly three-and-a-half hour STORM (Strategic Operational Review Meeting) attended by a nine-member leadership team (made up of the CEO, the COO, the CFO, the VP of Information Technology, the VP of Strategy, the VP of Operations, the VP of the Call Center, and the Director of People).

We meet to engage in dialogue and debate focused on our strategic plan," explains founder and CEO Brian Scudamore. "We'll discuss and debate opportunities six months to three years out, a lifetime when your business is growing rapidly. We really try not to argue to be right but debate to really ensure we all get our fears and worries out on the table.

Sometimes the discussions just continue to align us further in our goals and [in the] strategic opportunities facing the company. We have a set of norms that we try to follow and respect to make the meeting as productive, focused, and respectfully contentious [as possible]. Considering the level of debate, there is a ton of respect too.

The cool part about this STORM meeting is that we never get into any other issues. It's always strategic. If we have more tactical or urgent issues to discuss they are always held at other times," concludes Scudamore.

What Scudamore and his team understand is that if you want the company to move faster you have to increase its pulse. Whereas members of most teams moving as fast as Scudamore's would exclaim there is no way they could take this much time each week to meet, Scudamore knows that the strategic issues must stay at his team's "top of mind" and continuously be tweaked.

EXECUTIVE TEAM HEALTH

Pat Lencioni, author of the bestseller *Five Dysfunctions of a Team*, emphasizes the importance of a team being both smart and healthy, defining "healthy" as having a level of trust and understanding that allows conflicts to surface among team members.

"The state of our relationship as a management team wasn't very good," recalls Lance Pederson, CEO of the Oregon-based organization Convergence Networks. "I think secretly each of us had issues with one another in more ways than one."

So, in January of 2012, Pederson, his business partner, and the VP of Sales and Marketing started meeting every Thursday morning at 6:00 a.m. at Sheri's, a local breakfast joint near their offices (they've recently switched to Friday mornings).

"At first I would say that our conversations weren't the greatest, but we kept showing up each week," explains Pederson. "Eventually what started to happen was that we began to talk more and more about the future of the company and the things that we would like to see happen."

One recurring topic was how they would be able to bring on five new employers a day. "This is when I finally understood the term 'blue sky.' Some of the things you come up with are pretty wild but if you could pull them off they would totally work," recalls Pederson.

The team then started to spend more time just talking about themselves when they were younger and the crazy things they did. (Lencioni has emphasized the importance of team members doing just this to develop a deeper level of understanding and trust.) "We would talk about our families and stuff like that," notes Pederson. "Now, for most, that probably doesn't sound like a big deal, but I just happen to be one of those guys who is pretty much dead serious all day long at work." The informal breakfast setting worked out better for Pederson because he didn't feel pressure to discuss strictly business topics: he knew his team would have time to cover the tactical issues of running the company in a more formal meeting later in the day.

"I could go on and on at how beneficial it has been for us, but the bottom line is that we are more connected as a management team in every facet. We no longer spend countless hours debating the semantics of a point. We accept each other for who we are because we know each other at a deeper level than we previously did," explains Pederson. "As we all know running a great company starts at the top. If your management team isn't on the same page, then the rest of the organization doesn't stand a chance."

MAJOR DECISIONS

Lee Prosenjak, founder of the Colorado-based troupe Cherry Creek Dance, hosts his council meeting Friday mornings at 7:45 a.m., rotating breakfast places so the group doesn't get bored with the menu. Often, they'll bring in an expert to help facilitate the discussion.

"We invited in a real estate broker one morning when we knew we were going to talk about where to move our location," explains Prosenjak. "The whole team was then a part of the planning process, engaging in a blue-sky conversation to design the perfect new space. In speaking with the broker afterwards, [I learned] he walked away from the discussion with as much as we did from him."

Scott Mesh, co-founder of Los Ninos, a New York-based provider of early childhood services, has tackled similar big issues at his company's regular Friday lunch meeting. Separate from the company's Monday morning management meeting, though the same management team attends both, the purpose of these Friday meetings is to dig into one topic deeply and a bit more informally.

"The goal is to get to the bottom of big, hairy problems," notes Mesh. "For instance, one summer we lost five case managers over a change in their service coordination (SC) Plan and compensation plans. That got our attention!" Mesh used these Friday lunches to talk through and reexamine every aspect of the compensation plans, core values, and staff management. Then, he decided to create a new Senior SC position. This new position provided an additional salary step with added responsibilities, allowing Los Ninos to "hire up" and provide a career path for current SCs.

"Morale turned around 180 degrees," beams Mesh. "And we're growing significantly again. Many of the issues facing our firm need significant talk time, which you have to schedule, or else it just doesn't happen."

A LONG WALK

For Nick Arrigan, Senior Account Manager at New Jersey-based Vega Consulting Solutions, the idea of the leadership "council" spurred him to start taking weekly walks with each of his children. Recalling his first week, Arrigan shares, "It was like a typical sappy Broadway review. We laughed, we cried; it was amazing."

Another weekly walk was behind a successful first season for Bret Bielema, coach of the Capitol One Bowl Champion Wisconsin Badgers college football team. Since he was following in the footsteps of the legendary Barry Alvarez, who took the Badgers to eight bowl wins in sixteen seasons, that season all eyes were on Bielema, the second-youngest coach in U.S. college football.

Though Alvarez and Bielema talked frequently, every Thursday Alvarez and Bielema took a scheduled hour-and-a-half walk. Bielema, in a *Wisconsin State Journal* interview, noted, "During the season, it was about games that weekend, match-ups. I'll usually go in there with a couple thoughts, questions to bounce off him about the direction of the program. We've really become good friends, more than anything else."

When Alvarez asked if it was okay if he missed the Capitol One Bowl game, since he was doing commentary for the Fiesta Bowl the same day, Bielema responded affirmatively, so long as they could still do their Thursday walk—which was actually scheduled on a Saturday, in order to keep it two days before the game (just like in the regular season).

Now that's sticking to a routine!

I hope the pattern of success is apparent. Like John D. Rockefeller's daily luncheon with his directors or the late Steve Jobs' regular "walk and talk" sessions with Bill Campbell, getting regularly scheduled talk time is crucial to your company's success and your own as an entrepreneur.

About the Author

VERNE HARNISH is the founder of two world-renowned entrepreneurship organizations, the Young Entrepreneurs' Organization (YEO) and the Association of Collegiate Entrepreneurs (ACE). Harnish is presently the founder and CEO of Gazelles, Inc., which serves as an outsourced corporate university for mid-size firms and hosts a faculty of well-known business experts, including Jim Collins, Geoff Smart, Jack Stack, Neil Rackham, Seth Godin, and Pat Lencioni, and sponsors best-practices trips to GE, Southwest Airlines, Microsoft, and Dell.

The "Growth Guy" columnist for several publications and a contributing editor for *Fortune Small Business* magazine, Harnish is the author of *Mastering the Rockefeller Habits: What You Must Do to Increase the Value of Your Fast-Growth Firm*, which has been translated into Spanish, Chinese, Japanese, and Korean. Named one of the "Top 10 Minds in Small Business" by *Fortune Small Business* magazine, he appeared on the cover of the December/January 2002 issue of the magazine.

Harnish chaired the renowned "Birthing of Giants" entrepreneurship leadership program at MIT (for fifteen years) and the MIT/WEO "Advanced Business Program." For many years, he also chaired the leadership program of Canada's prestigious "Top 40 Under 40" program and is going into his seventh year leading an executive program in Malaysia called, "Taipan: The Making of Asian Giants."

Harnish has a B.S. in Mechanical Engineering and an M.B.A. from Wichita State University. His hobbies include piano, tennis, and magic; he is a member of the International Brotherhood of Magicians. His honors include National Leader of the Year from Omicron Delta Kappa (an honorary leadership organization) and being one of the first two recipients of the National Laureate Award for Leadership by Tau Beta Pi (an honorary engineering organization).

Harnish can be reached at vharnish@gazelles.com.

CHAPTER 33

BUILDING THE RIGHT
FOUNDATION FOR GROWTH

Who is responsible and accountable for the growth and future direction of any enterprise? By this point in the book I hope you don't have to think too long or too hard about the answer: clearly, it's the company's board of directors. The board members must have a clear grasp of the organization's general growth plans and strategies, as well as of the security and effectiveness of the foundation upon which growth plans will be laid. This essay provides board members with the guidance they need to ask the right questions and provide direction to company officers, who are responsible for implementing and managing the company's growth strategies.

Growth for growth's sake is a waste of time and resources. Each growth strategy should be implemented with a set of specific objectives, which can be monitored and measured, in mind. Boards of directors and leaders of rapid-growth companies must have tools, screens, and filters with which they can evaluate various growth strategies properly and provide general guidance to those exactly responsible for meeting growth objectives and performance matters. At the heart of all growth strategies should be four primary motivators: optimization of shareholders' value, employee motivation and retention, competitive forces, and strategic relationships' management and growth.

Business growth is truly a double-edged sword. When it is controlled and well managed, it has the potential of providing tremendous rewards to enterprise stakeholders. When growth is poorly planned and uncontrolled, it often leads to financial distress and failure. What this means is that the company's need to grow must be tempered by the need to understand that meaningful, long-term, and profitable growth is the byproduct of effective management and planning. Failure to create this balance will result in vulnerability to attack by competitors, creditors, hostile employees, and creative takeover specialists.

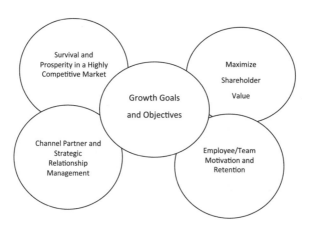

I have spent the better part of my professional life and nearly thirty years of practicing corporate law in order to help companies of all sizes in many different industries develop strategies for building their businesses. During that time, I've observed that companies of all types and sizes want to grow in one way or another, whether that growth is in terms of revenue, profit, number of employees or customers, market share, or number of locations.

However, given the rapidly moving changes in our marketplace, the key challenge and subject of strategic debate is how and when to grow. At multiple points in a company's evolution, the board members will need to define the pace and breadth of growth. The board members and company leaders will need to stare into the chasm and either step forward, and assume risk, or step backward, into safety. This realization leads to other key questions that can be difficult for board members to answer:

- What strategies should be used to facilitate growth?
- How do you know whether these strategies will be effective for your company?
- Does your business structure have problems that need resolving before you can implement the selected growth strategy?
- How can you build on your strengths and compensate for your weaknesses?
- How might the selected growth strategy present new risks or make you vulnerable? If so, to whom?
- Is this the right time to grow? That is, have you put a proper foundation for growth in place?
- Are the necessary capital and other resources (strategic, relationship, human, and intellectual, etc.) available to fuel growth?
- Are market conditions ripe for growth opportunities?

The wide variety of strategic issues inherent in business growth that must be determined presents different management, legal, and financial challenges. Growth means that new employees will be hired, and they will be looking to top management for leadership. Growth means the company's management will become increasingly decentralized, which may create greater levels of internal politics, protectionism, and dissension over company goals and projects. Growth means that market share will expand: the company will have to prepare new strategies for dealing with larger competitors. Growth also means that additional capital will be required, creating new responsibilities to shareholders, investors, and institutional lenders. Thus, growth brings with it a variety of changes in an enterprise's structure, needs, and objectives, which can be a great deal to digest all at once.

Momentum is a critical component in executing an overall growth plan. The board members and the leadership team must ensure that resources and systems are in place to enable forward progress toward stated objectives. Every day, week, month, quarter, and year, management must establish benchmarks and milestones, and measure company progress against these goals; then, these measurements should be presented to board members for analysis and feedback. An extended loss of momentum can be detrimental. It will also stand in the way of the company's ability to raise additional rounds of capital or receive access to other resources necessary for continued business growth. It will also make attracting and retaining talented employees, who will be needed to execute the growth plan, more difficult. Measuring performance against these benchmarks, combined with leaders who are focused on maintaining high employee motivation and strong customer relationships, means the company will rarely lose momentum.

SETTING THE STAGE FOR GROWTH: INTERNAL FACTORS

When laying out a game plan to grow a company, first, it is critical to establish an understanding of the foundation that must be put in place in order to allow a company to begin its growth path. Before you can prepare a company for growth, you need to analyze its strengths and weaknesses. Looking for what's working well serves to concentrate your efforts where you have the best chance of success. Looking for strengths enables you to also spot the weaknesses. Start with these internal areas:

Costs and revenue. Examine every part of your business. Is revenue rising or falling? How about profit margin? Which divisions or departments stand out? Why? Do you enjoy a strong, positive cash flow?

Personnel. Do certain employees show exceptional skills or produce outstanding results? Where in the company is the strongest management, organization, and planning? Do you have the talent on staff to handle anticipated growth, or would you have to hire new personnel?

Operations. Are the areas that seem to be trouble-free functioning with little supervision and always delivering results? How do the managers in these areas achieve such consistent results?

Philosophy or mission. Do you have a written statement describing your company's philosophy or mission? If so, does it define the essence of your business exactly, so that you know which kinds of activities fit your company's goals and which don't? Is the company diluting resources by engaging in any activities outside its mission? Have you developed a set of company core values, and have your employees embraced those values?

SETTING THE STAGE FOR GROWTH: EXTERNAL FACTORS

Once you've sized up your business internally, take a long and careful look at the external factors that should reveal whether the business is in a position to take advantage of current business trends and cycles. These include the following:

Market. Is the company's market share—its percentage of estimated total business available—increasing or decreasing? Is the marketing strategy based on careful research or on instinct and hunches? Is the customer or client base shrinking?

Competition. Do you know exactly who the company's competitors are, and where they pose the largest threat(s)? Which part of your business is most vulnerable to competition, and which is least vulnerable? Are some parts of the market becoming crowded with competitors?

Economic climate. Are changes in economic conditions—interest rates, inflation, housing developments, or industry earnings—likely to affect the company? Do you or your colleagues make efforts to stay on top of things so that the company can anticipate changes in the marketplace, or are you often surprised by developments that affect your company?

The answers to these questions will provide the board members with the guidance they need to determine where the company is strong and where it could improve, as well as which type of growth strategy would be best to articulate to the organization's executives. Consider the questions carefully and respond as if the company's future growth depends upon answering them thoughtfully—because it does. These steps will help you and your company to define growth objectives, allowing you and company representatives to keep these objectives in proper perspective and monitor the success of each strategy.

The board members' focus must be on profitability and enterprise value, not on merely capturing market share. Being the first to the market and the biggest player in the market is of marginal value if it yields a mediocre bottom line. Remember that not all dollars of revenue are created equally: some revenue streams are much more profitable than others.

UNDERSTANDING THE DNA OF GROWTH COMPANIES

What factors drive a company to fast-track business growth? What is the genealogy that motivates an entrepreneurial growth company to get bigger or faster, diversify, enter new markets, and develop new products?

1. **The Edison Syndrome:** Some companies develop a culture of creativity and innovation that drives their employees to new product development and technological breakthroughs. In such cases, the pride of inventiveness is combined with skillful management to provide the fuel for growth. Cisco® Systems®, Apple®, 3M®, and Johnson & Johnson® are examples of modern success stories about companies driven by innovation, both internally and via acquisition of developing companies and technologies.

2. **Fear:** Some companies are driven by fear of competition, the fear of missing an opportunity, or the fear of not being the market leader. Andy Grove, the founder of Intel, wrote, "only the paranoid survive," and certainly the fear of failure or the insecurity of the company's leadership can, if harassed properly, be a strong motivator for growth.

3. **Boredom:** One entrepreneur I met recently told me that he and his team decided to triple the size of their building supplies conglomerate through recapitalization, establishment of new offices, and acquisition of existing businesses, primarily because they got bored. When everything is going smoothly, the entrepreneurial challenge can be significantly diminished. Many companies remain stagnant (and often begin to deteriorate slowly) because ownership and management has become "fat, dumb, and happy" with the EBITA (earnings before interest, taxes, and amortization) and cash flow. They transform from gazelles to elephants, unless company leadership determines to develop new challenges. The failure of many companies to continue to evolve may also eventually lead to the loss of key employees, key customers, and other key strategic relationships. Never ever take business growth for granted: getting bored relatively easily and always striving for new challenges can be strong characteristics for a growth company.

4. **Publish or Perish:** Some industries, particularly those that are technology-driven, mimic the old "publish or perish" culture of academic tenure. They must continue to be productive and innovative or the markets and their customers will punish and abandon them. The misjudgment of a market or the mistiming of a new product winds up being very costly.

5. **First Mover Advantage/The Land Grab:** Many emerging industries are driven by who has the first "over advantage": that is, seeing which company can get its product or service out the fastest, and begin building brand equity with its targeted group of customers. This "1890s gold rush" style

of market dynamic becomes a market and business growth motivator: companies must put strategies in place in order to be first to market, first to build brand, etc. The theory here is that the company that grabs the most market share the fastest wins the battle and the war. In other words, the view never gets any better for the second dog pulling the sled. This type of business growth motivator came under attack after the market crash in 2000, when a "best beats first" mentality crept into the marketplace. Being the first to market in the dot.com arena didn't guarantee that the company would be around twelve months later.

6. **Ego:** The stereotypical public image of CEO or founder at the helm of a growth company is that he or she has an ego the size of New Jersey. This is often, but not always, the case. It is often true that entrepreneurs have very large egos, and their self-confidence or pride becomes a motivator for continued business growth. However, a successful company cannot be built on the basis of ego alone. If a founder views the company as, basically, a monument to himself, then that company will at some point surely fail. Similarly, if selfish greed is at the heart of the compensation and ownership structure, then the company will often fail or lose momentum. The better entrepreneurs, like Sam Walton and Bill Gates, take great pride in helping thousands of employees and shareholders build wealth, knowing that their rewards would be even greater if they could have everyone around them prosper. A balance between ego and greed must be struck. The words of Rabbi Hillel are particularly insightful here: "If I am not for myself, then who shall be for me? But if I am only for myself, then who

am I?" The entrepreneur or management team focused on the enrichment of employees, customers' satisfaction, and a steady increase in shareholder value will build wealth by helping, instead of hurting, others along the way.

7. **The "Chip on My Shoulder" Phenomenon:** Many entrepreneurs at the helms of rapid growth companies have some external motivating factors that drive them to succeed day in and day out. They may have been kids that never got picked in schoolyard basketball, produced by broken homes, or raised under difficult economic or social conditions. This "something to prove" syndrome becomes part of the corporate culture: employees who shared similar backgrounds are attracted to cultures in which "geeks rule," "David beats Goliath," or, "the nice guy gets the girl." The United States is a nation that often cheers for and rewards the underdog. Many companies have grown and flourished because resources were made available to them in hopes that they could overcome past and present hurdles.

IMPORTANCE OF MOMENTUM

Isaac Newton's second law of motion states that the time rate of change in momentum is proportional to the force acting on the particle (the object). From Newton's second law, it follows that, if a constant force acts on a particle for a given time, the product of force and the time interval (the impulse) is equal to the change in its momentum. Conversely, a particle's momentum is a measure of the time required for a constant force to bring it to rest.

Momentum is a critical component of all seven key motivators for growth discussed above. Company leadership must ensure that resources and systems are in place to enable forward progress toward stated objectives. Every day, week, month, quarter, and year, the management must establish benchmarks and milestones, and measure its progress against these goals. A loss of momentum for an extended period of time can be detrimental. It will also stand in the way of the company's ability to raise additional rounds of capital or access other resources needed for continued business growth. By measuring performance against these benchmarks, together with fostering leadership focused on maintaining high employee motivation and strong customer relationships, companies will rarely lose momentum. The "Big Mo," as entrepreneurs and venture capitalists often refer to it, is critical to continued success.

Common Traits and Best Practices of Successful Rapid-Growth Companies

» Beyond Seed Capital—They have already received early rounds of capital: the challenge shifts from "How do we get start-up capital?" to "We've been seeded but now how do we grow?"

» Proven Team—The team has demonstrated an ability to work together and proven an ability to execute. Their peers and their employees view team members as leaders. Are they committed to reinvesting resources into the company?

» Scalable Business Model—The founders of the company have developed a business model and infrastructure that fits with current customer demand patterns, but that can also evolve profitability as needed, as future demand patterns increase when the market embraces the company's products and services.

» Recognizable Innovation—Many of today's rapid-growth companies are truly innovative pioneers. They are focused on the creation of products and services that are ten times faster, cheaper, or more convenient for the user than those the competition creates. Rapid-growth companies often aim for improvement ten times over as the goal because they realize and understand that by the time the product or service hits the marketplace, it will only be three times better. The rapid-growth company must demonstrate that its products and services are several orders of magnitude better, and more valuable for targeted customers, or it will be virtually impossible to get them to switch to the solution.

» Intellectual Vision and an Ability to Evolve—The company's founders have created a vision and a culture devoted to the intellectual challenge of developing a great idea into a great product or service that customers will line up to get. The founders have anticipated change, stayed ahead of the curve, and ensured that the company's plans were nimble enough that the company could change directions when circumstances dictated. In such situations, a continuing commitment to the development of new initiatives is critical.

» Loyal Customer Base—Real customers who have paid real dollars (and are happy they did so) for products and services help to demonstrate that the company's solutions work and that somebody wants what is being offered. These customers are initially attracted to the differentiation of the product or service, and the company's ability to deliver both creates mindshare and builds brand loyalty.

» Competitive Analysis—The fast-growth company's leaders have a strong sense of where it is currently set in the marketplace and have demonstrated some sustainable competitive advantage. They have done so either by being first to the marketplace in building brand or by developing a portfolio of intellectual property that creates barriers to entry for others. They find an initial niche to exploit and then begin building a company around that opening in the market.

» Financial Performance—The company's leaders have developed a stream of durable revenues and profits built on a foundation of defensible accounting and revenue recognition practices.

» A Healthy Attitude to Future and Risk—Leaders of rapid-growth companies understand how to put risk into proper perspective. They understand that entrepreneurial companies need to be prepared to fail in order to succeed. They view some degree of failure as inevitable, and their company culture of resiliency helps them quickly rebound without getting overly discouraged. These companies' leaders know how to learn from their mistakes (and when and where possible, to avoid making them twice). Acceptance and encouragement of risk is part of the culture that drives ongoing innovation.

» Commitment to Empowerment—Company leadership practices are committed to empowering team members at all levels with the resources and the decisional authority to do their jobs effectively, without excessive red tape or internal politics. The company leaders continuously set goals and milestones, communicate these goals to employees at all levels, and regularly measure the company's performance against these benchmarks. The company's compensation and reward systems revolve around the accomplishment of (and the ability to exceed) these benchmarks.

» Always Monitoring Competitive Trends—Leaders of more successful rapid-growth companies are never caught with their heads in the sand. They devote capital and resources to developing market information systems, as well as to gathering and analyzing market intelligence. They carefully monitor key market trends and indicators, and the moves made by their competitors.

» The Art of Spin Control—Rapid-growth company leaders quickly learn how to manage the rumor mill. Along the growth path, these companies are especially vulnerable to attack by jealous competitors, disgruntled employees, and Wall Street analysts. The smarter companies stay ahead of this information and control the flow of data effectively. When bad news does hit, they deal with each problem in a direct and straightforward manner that will often prevent employees and customers from running for the hills.

CHAPTER 34

BEST PRACTICES IN STRATEGIC PLANNING AND IN FORMULATING STRATEGIC GROWTH PLANS

Board members should demand that executives lead the company through periodic strategic audits: these are often effective precursors for the company's overall strategic planning processes. The results of these periodic audits will also help a board of directors assess the strength of the current management and advisory team; define the key sections of the business growth strategic plan, which needs to be drafted; examine the current systems, distribution channels, and financial resources available to determine whether plans for growth can be supported; and look at industry trends and macroeconomic factors that will either support and expedite growth plans or serve as an implementation barrier. Board members should benchmark the company's performance to date and plans for growth against those of other direct or indirect competitors that are similarly situated, in order to see how the company is performing by comparison.

The strategic audit may reveal the organization's initial set of growth objectives were misdirected, overly conservative, too aggressive, or just plain inconsistent with current market trends. It will serve as a reality check and an opportunity to refine objectives, before resources are expended to implement the wrong set of objectives. The business growth strategic plan can be adjusted accordingly, or missing resources can be put in place to help achieve the original plan.

CATEGORIES OF GROWTH

The strategic audit should also help the company define which specific categories or aspects of the business it intends to grow. For example, the business plan might revolve around a desire to grow profits while holding the number of employees steady; alternatively, the enterprise may need to grow the number of distribution channels while holding the number of new products and services steady (or the opposite). The process of choosing which aspects of the business are slated for growth and what strategy will be most effective for meeting these objectives is a critical part of the overall growth planning process.

There are many categories of business operations that could be targeted by the board members for growth, as demonstrated by Box 34-A (below).

Defining The Company's Growth Objectives

Box 34-A Understanding Categories of Growth

Often, growth strategies are developed to solve a specific problem or to help clear a hurdle in the evolution of business growth. Many of the problems a company faces—the need to stay competitive, foster creativity and innovation, and foster career advancement among top management; the need to build your brand, meet the challenge of overseas expansion, and strengthen the balance sheet; and the need to better leverage a portfolio of intellectual property—may be solved with the right growth strategy, if that strategy is formulated and implemented properly.

AVOIDING SOME OF THE CLASSIC
BUSINESS GROWTH PROBLEMS

Growth spurts can hit a company at any time, especially in a fast-moving economy and fast-paced business environment. Impetus for growth could be the development of new technology, a competitor's demise (or even signs of an area of weakness, short of a total demise), hiring of new personnel, infusion of fresh capital, new discoveries of opportunities or marketing breakthroughs, or a favorable shift in economic conditions. These developments can happen over an extended period of time or virtually overnight. Boards of directors need to be the gatekeepers, monitoring and directing the right pace for the company, even if that pace is inconsistent with the speed or slowness of the larger market conditions. When conditions leading to growth materialize quickly, some of the more common areas to break down include cash flow, mismanagement, customer service responsiveness, overhead costs (which spiral out of control), communications logjams, high employee turnover, rise in inexperienced senior management, and slippage in quality control. The key to managing this process is for management to anticipate the downside risks of a given growth strategy or set of market conditions providing the impetus for the plans for growth; in turn, board members must balance the company's need to be opportunistic and practical, disciplined and strategic.

These problems can quickly take a company off its growth path and will lead to a violent crash if not properly navigated. Steps that can help a company's board members keep growth on course include the following: getting high-quality advice from consultants and professional advisors, recruiting senior executives to help support growth management, and providing heavy doses of training for employees to help them understand the implications of business growth. Other steps that can help a growing company stay on course as it works on growth objectives include: developing strong financial controls and accounting/reporting systems (e.g., to manage and monitor the costs of growth); raising additional capital (e.g., to ensure that you don't run out of gunpowder halfway through the battle); and remaining disciplined enough to stay focused on the endgame (e.g., making sure that the growth phenomenon does not fuel the founders' egos, leading prematurely to lavish spending or perquisites).

Some Best Practices for Board Members to Sustain Business Growth

» Think in many directions. Business growth is not always linear, and you need to see and manage the many linkages in the networks you build. Understand the interdependency of the relationships you manage.

» Think big, act small. Big dreamers and broad visions match well with the need to be nimble and adapt quickly to changes in demand trends or market conditions.

» Avoid being penny-wise and pound-foolish. Leaders of more successful growth companies are not afraid to spend money on or devote resources to information technology, research, and design, all of which bring new products and services to the markets faster. They also are not afraid to invest in training, making sure their companies have human resources infrastructures capable of sustaining business growth.

» Understand that the management of business growth is hard work. Very few worthwhile things are accomplished easily, and the rapid growth of a business is not among them. Be prepared for buckets of stress, heavy financial pressures, and extended periods of perceived loneliness. However, stay focused on the prize, which can be quite significant if the company's growth objectives are achieved.

» Get everyone at all levels involved in the growth-planning process. Seek the input of employees of all levels in your organizations, as well as the advice of outside professionals, vendors, and customers.

» Focus on progress in bite-sized increments. While growth will often be fast-paced, that does not mean it will always be through giant leaps forward. Appreciate and reward the incremental progress that moves the company toward its growth objectives.

» Creativity is the engine of growth. Leaders of companies that successfully sustain growth are not afraid to experiment or to fail; they reward innovations by employees and strategic partners and understand both risk and the possibility of failure are part of the growth game. Growth companies may make more mistakes than others, but their leaders also learn from those mistakes more quickly and use this knowledge to identify new opportunities.

» Have fun. If you are not enjoying the ride, leave the business growth amusement park.

In the cases of rapidly growing companies, board members should guide their executives to embrace a stronger emphasis on relationship management, building valuable networks, and leveraging intangible assets to assist in leveling the playing field in order to battle against larger competitors. The ability to leverage knowledge, establish key strategic relationships (and maintain them as you would a happy marriage), be flexible in establishing new relationships as necessary, and to bring products and services to the market faster (using these strategic relationships) gives small and medium companies an edge over the larger "elephants" they compete against. Hence, the origin of the term "gazelle," used to describe rapid-growth companies in reference to an animal that navigates its way to survival in the jungle by being nimble, fast, and smart in order to compensate for the size and strength larger animals may possess. In this new economy, fast beats slow, knowledge triumphs over traditional assets, and information is king. This economy also creates opportunities for smaller companies that don't necessarily have to be bigger or wealthier than their bigger competitors; rather, they need to find their niches within that networked economy and fill that space better than anybody else can.

BEST PRACTICES IN STRATEGIC PLANNING FOR TODAY'S BOARD OF DIRECTORS

In a company or organization's early stages, the emphasis is on survival: how board members and company leaders properly launch and grow the company by attracting and sustaining customers, and what resources they will need to support the selected strategy are among the key concerns. Yet what happens later? Once an organization reaches its initial set of fundamental goals, focus shifts away from mere business planning and on to strategic planning for growth. Strategic planning is an ongoing process that seeks to articulate and clarify the future direction of the company in the following key areas:

- The targeted markets that and customers who will sustain growth plans and objectives;
- The innovations and additions to the company's products and services that will foster new growth opportunities;
- The quality and sophistication of technology the growing company uses to support its customers;
- The quality and sophistication of training and support systems;
- The value and recognition of the emerging company's brand, from a customer-awareness perspective;
- The development of operating systems, practices, and procedures based upon internal company best practices as well as overall industry-wide best practices;
- The exploration of new domestic and international markets;
- The organization of supplier councils, co-branding alliances, and other key strategic relationships;
- The development of strategies for alternative sites and related new market penetration strategies; and
- The development of advanced branding and intellectual property protection strategies.

KEY STRATEGIC PLANNING ISSUES

Some of the more critical questions that board members and executives need to be asking on a quarterly or periodic basis include:

- What are our targeted customers' common characteristics?
- What are our most successful employees' common characteristics?

- What can we do to attract more people like these in the recruitment and selection process?
- What are our company's five greatest strengths?
- What are the five greatest strengths of our system?
- What is being done to build on these strengths?
- What are our five biggest problems?
- What are we doing to resolve these problems?

The strategic planning process should be addressed in the board of directors' agenda, as well as during periodic meetings among the company's leadership and periodic strategic planning retreats, and in a written strategic plan that should be updated annually. Strategic planning meetings and retreats could be focused on specific themes, such as any of the following: brand building and leveraging, rebuilding trust and value with customers, litigation prevention and compliance, leadership succession and planning, international opportunities in the global village, leadership and productivity issues, financial management and performance issues, creativity and innovation, diversity and recruitment, technology improvement or communications systems, alternative site and non-traditional location analysis, co-branding and brand-extension licensing, or systems-building for improving internal communication. Any or all of these topics are appropriate either for one meeting or for discussion on a continuing basis. An outside facilitator, such as an industry expert, or the company's senior management team, can lead the strategic planning meeting.

A model agenda for a board- or executive-level strategic planning retreat is set forth below:

STRATEGIC PLANNING MODEL AGENDA

A. Evaluating Our Strategic Assets and Relationships
   1. Overview
      - Goals and Objectives of the Meeting
      - Key Trends in Domestic and International Business Growth
   2. Assessing the Strengths of Our Customer Relations
      - State of the Union
      - Common Critical Success Factors
   3. Evaluating Our Team
      - Management Styles and Goals: Reality and Practice
      - Motivating and Rewarding Employees
      - Protecting the Knowledge Worker
      - Providing Genuine Leadership
   4. Our Strategic Partners
      - Key Questions:
         i. What do we expect from our vendors and professional advisors?
         ii. What can we do to enhance the efficiency and productivity of these relationships?
         iii. Do all of our strategic relationships truly yield mutual rewards?
   5. Our Targeted Customers
      - Identifying and Dealing with the Competition
      - Customer Perceptions of Quality and Value
      - Growing Company-Customer Communications
      - Customer Satisfaction Surveys
      - Exploring Two-Tier Marketing Strategies

B. Asset-Building Strategies

    1. Building and Leveraging Brand Awareness
- Building Overall Brand Awareness
- Brand Leveraging Strategies
- Building an Arsenal of Intangible Assets

    2. Co-Branding and Strategic Alliances
- Identifying Goals and Objectives
- Targeting and Selecting Partners
- Structuring the Deal

    3. Shared Goals and Values
- Enhancing Intra-Company Communications
- Building Trust and Respect

    4. The Role and Value of Technology
- How Technology Is Changing the Way We Work and Consume Products/Services
- The Impact of Technology on Recruiting, Training, and Supporting Employees
- The Impact of Technology on How the Emerging Growth Company Will Market Its Products/Services to Targeted Customers

    5. Development of Branded Products and Services to Strengthen Revenue Base
- Affinity/Group Purchasing Programs

AN ALTERNATIVE, MORE GENERIC AGENDA
WOULD READ AS FOLLOWS:

I. Basic Introduction
    a. Ground rules
    b. Process
    c. Expectations
II. Define strategy and tactics, and the difference between the two
III. Define the strategic planning process
    a. Strategies
    b. Tactics to use
    c. Actions
    d. Accountabilities (who will do what)
    e. Timeline within which it will happen
IV. Select: what outcomes do we want at the end of the day (brainstorm and idea dump) and what do we choose to defer for another day (parking lot)?
V. Divisional leader updates: Strategic opportunities to address various functional areas
VI. Get alignment around imperatives (deep discussion)
VII. Define the strategic plan's "pillars"—revise, rename, or ratify
VIII. Get alignment around constituencies and stakeholders
IX. Get alignment around what our customers really need (the value proposition)
X. Get alignment around our resources and how we will allocate them
XI. Get alignment around what mode we will use to execute our plan

XII. Rank-order our strategic imperatives

XIII. Define roles and responsibilities: What role will each of the board members and executive leaders play in plan implementation?

XIV. Milestones/deliverables/concrete action items

For today's boards of directors and company leaders, the model strategic planning process looks like this:

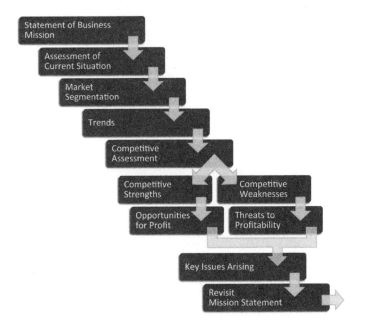

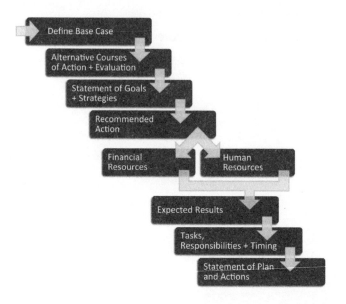

Box 34-C Summary of Steps in the Strategic Planning Process

One of the final steps in an effective strategic planning meeting is to develop a list of specific and concrete action items. Company leaders may be able to implement some action items right away, while others may take some time. The board members are responsible for evaluating, prioritizing, and communicating to the executive team both the importance of and the sequence for these action items.

The strategic planning process is a commitment to strive for the continuous improvement of company leaders' strategic objectives. The process is designed to ensure that maximum value is being delivered, day in and day out, to the growing company's executive team, employees, shareholders, vendors and suppliers, and, of course, its customers. In addition, the process ensures company leaders are not afraid to ask these questions: "Where are we? Where do we want to be? What do we need to do to get there? Finally, what is currently standing in our way of achieving these objectives?" This process means ensuring the company takes the time to develop a mission statement and define a collective vision, and then to develop a series of plans for achieving these goals. Board members must stay focused on these objectives and provide guidance to the enterprise's other leaders regarding how these objectives will be achieved. The focus must be on brand equity, customer value and loyalty, and shareholder profitability. The guidelines and protocols for internal communications must encourage honesty and openness, without fear of retaliation or politics.

Mapping Out Your Ecosystem

Ecosystem mapping is a key strategic component of the strategic planning process:

» Every company, regardless of size or industry, operates within one or more ecosystems.

» Where do we fit in?

» Who are the key players and stakeholders? What are their key issues, concerns, and needs? Who are the decision-makers? The influencers? The gatekeepers? The referral sources?

» What are the dynamics? The pecking order? The politics? The hurdles and barriers?

» Have company leaders conducted a meaningful competitive analysis?

» Where are the windows of opportunity? What relationships are penetrable or opaque?

» What are the key associations, clubs, and professional societies, etc.? What groups ought there to be?

SOME FINAL THOUGHTS ON EFFECTIVE STRATEGIC GROWTH PLANNING

Effective strategic planning at the board level is not an easy process. After years of working with hundreds of companies of all sizes and in many different industries in developing strategic plans, I have pulled together some tips, thoughts, and observations that should govern your planning best practices, which are listed below:

- Have the right mix of talent to develop and maintain your plan. The wrong planning team will yield the wrong planning decisions, leading the company down a path of disaster.

- Think long-term but act short-term. Be ready to modify the plan based on changes in market conditions but without forgetting the long-term goals. Near-term challenges must always be balanced against long-term strategic priorities. Keep the end in mind and don't stray from basic character provisions, mission, and core values.

- Effective strategic planning is a continuing process, not a standalone task.

- Don't buy in to the mantra that planning is a thing of the past. Some people believe market conditions are too dynamic and uncertain to make long-term strategic planning possible, but this is simply untrue. In fact, fast-moving business conditions make the need for strategic planning that much more critical, provided the plan does not sit on a shelf but is monitored and modified as conditions may warrant.

- Invest in systems that will gather competitive intelligence. Remember, information rules. If the executive team is not providing a brand with reliable and durable data on the trends affecting competitors and customers, the company is dead in the water. Data gathered becomes a key component of the strategic plan and a trigger point for changes to the plan or strategy selected. As people say, "Garbage in leads to garbage out."

- Protect your key assets. You can develop strategic plans until you are blue in the face, but if a strategy's success depends on the company's ability to keep and leverage key intangible assets, then company leaders must take the time to protect intellectual property and to reward and motivate employees.

- Be sure to connect the dots. A well-drafted strategic plan reveals understanding of and anticipates how all market forces and players fit together, taking into account social, environmental, political, and economic influences while figuring out how these factors come together to enable growth plans. The ability to view things from 30,000 feet— that is, with perspective—and see the dynamics of markets at different levels is key to effective growth planning. Because these market conditions are never static, and because the relationships connecting the dots constantly change, you need to keep climbing the mountain to look down on the valley.

- Build an organization that has a deeply rooted commitment to growth. The commitment to strategic planning must begin at the top, with the board members and company executives, whose mission and passion become contagious. Because of that contagion, everyone in the company focuses their efforts on meeting strategic planning objectives. To achieve this, the company's leaders must clearly communicate and reinforce growth plans, objectives, and strategies; reward those who contribute to achieving these goals; and monitor the company's progress, changing course and direction as may be necessary, based on the board members' feedback and direction. If the course does need to change, shifts in direction must be regularly shared with the company's employees, along with an explanation of why such change is required. Employees at all levels will resent a change in direction if they do not know the reasons for it or understand it, or if they are not told how or why their positions and tasks must change in order to meet these new challenges.

- Don't be afraid to measure and monitor performance. Board members must develop an objective set of metrics for each key area of the strategic plan. These metrics must be continuously monitored and periodically measured against the company's key goals and then discussed with executives via progress reports to board members. Remember, we tend to manage what we measure. Metrics may include sales, profitability, number of new customer relationships, growth market partners, number of new employees, customer satisfaction, level of employee turnover, inventory cycles, number of new offices opened, warranty returns, or number of new rounds of capital (raised at favorable valuation rates). Regardless of the specific metric(s) selected, the board members must oversee systems to track and measure these performance indicators. In addition, they must have the expertise in place to understand, analyze, and properly react to this data once it is reported.

- Develop high-quality products and services. As veteran entrepreneurs and professional advisors will always tell you, a strategic plan will be completely ineffective if the "dogs will not eat the dog food." At the end of the day, all strategic plans must revolve around a set of high-quality products and services that the customers truly want, need, and will be evangelical about sharing with others.

Navigating Through the Most Difficult Strategic Planning or Growth Questions

» What are the macro and micro trends that present the best opportunities and the most difficult challenges to the company?

» Have we embraced candor, integrity, and transparency in our most recent SWOT (strengths, weaknesses/limitations, opportunities, and threats) analysis? Do we suffer from "rose-colored glasses" syndrome? Alternatively, are we still slaves to the "elephants in the room" or to the "sacred cows"?

» Should we only grow where we are planted? And if yes, do we go deep or go wide?

» Do we grow primarily through organic strategies or through external relationships?

» What role should M&A play? Where are we on our buy versus build analyses of the most critical opportunities?

» Which growth opportunities offer durable and recurring revenue opportunities and profitable business models?

> » If this company were to be put up for sale tomorrow, why would a buyer find it attractive? What aspects of the business would serve as skunk repellant?

Organic vs. External Growth Strategies (How do you want to grow?)

Organic

- Raising capital for organic growth and expansion
- Penetrate new domestic and international markets
- Sales and marketing to attract new customers
- Deepening and widening of existing customer relationships
- Adding new product lines and services (Innovation)
- Recruiting to build/deepen teams and human capital capabilities

External

- M&A
- Technology licensing (Licensing Out vs. Licensing In)
- Brand licensing
- Business format franchising
- Joint Ventures and alliances
- Strengthening and deepening channel partner relationships

THE BOARD MEMBERS' ROLE IN M&A

In 2011, over $3 trillion in reported global mergers and acquisitions (M&A) transactions were completed (this reporting often does not include tens of thousands of middle-market and smaller deals). In 2012, and beyond, this trend does not appear to be slowing down; thus, board members need to remain up-to-speed on current M&A trends and best practices. The reasons behind this acceleration of M&A activity can be broken down into several subcomponents:

1. The low-cost, virtually unlimited access to capital for transactions and investments (for example, the cash stockpiles of the Fortune 1000, private equity funds, family business officers, and sovereign governments had reached over $7

trillion as of spring 2012; Apple® itself was sitting on cash stockpiles in excess of $100 billion);

2. Globalization and growth acceleration in emerging markets have led to an increase in both outbound and inbound cross-border transactions;

3. Technology, velocity of change, and intensity of competition have forced companies to diversify, integrate supply chains, and gobble up market share;

4. Finally, the graying of the world's population means that the Baby Boomers are preparing to sell or transfer ownership control of the enterprises they launched twenty or thirty years ago (Mass Mutual estimates that from 2010 to 2025, over $40 trillion in intergenerational wealth will be transferred across the globe).

Board members must embrace key principles of due diligence, buy versus build analysis, financial analysis, and risk assessment as primary factors in their decision-making and evaluation processes, both for M&A and other capital investment proposals. Transactions should help drive shareholder value, be aligned with both short-term and long-term strategic objectives, and be accretion-based, not dilution-based, to the market price of company shares, as well as to the brand, reputation, and consumer perception of its core products and services. Screens and filters need to be in place to ensure that risk is avoided and strategic objectives are met. The new corporate governance paradigm, and state of the law, is that board members can and will be held both accountable and responsible for misguided strategies and/or transactions that are not carefully assessed or evaluated. Risk tolerance and patience levels for post-closing integration must be clearly defined. One clear trend in 2012 has been an increase in volume in the number of deals but decrease in the size of deals as boards attempt to mitigate risk by engaging in M&A in "bite-sized" chunks. Another key concern is a trend known as the "de-merger" or attempts by many companies to engage in divestitures to shed the company of assets that are no longer a strategic fit or which may be best as spin-offs or sales to third parties. Shareholder activists in 2012 have put pressure on the boards of Heartland Financial and Marathon Petroleum to divest assets or divisions that are no longer adding shareholder value.

Board members and company leaders must embrace the notion that there is no more complicated transaction than a merger or an acquisition. The issues raised by both are broad and complex, ranging from valuation and deal structure to tax and securities laws. It seems that virtually every board member or executive in every major industry faces a buy-or-sell decision at some point during his or her tenure as company leader. In fact, people estimate that some executives spend as much as one-third of their time considering merger-and-acquisition opportunities and other structural business decisions. The strategic reasons for considering such transactions are also numerous, ranging from achieving economies of scale to mitigating cash-flow risk (via diversification) to satisfying shareholders' hunger for steady growth and dividends. The Federal Government's degree of intervention in M&A transactions varies from administration to administration, depending on the issues and concerns of the day; the Obama administration has been very active in enforcing a wide range of laws that affect M&A deals closing, from antitrust and labor laws to OSHA and CFIUS regulations to the Foreign Corrupt Practices Act (FCPA), as well as a host of environmental and tax laws that could affect a transaction's timing and feasibility.

In recent years, merger-and-acquisition activity has increased significantly within industries that are growing rapidly and evolving overall (such as healthcare, information technology, education, infrastructure, and software development), as well as traditional industries (such as manufacturing, consumer products, and food services). Many recent developments reflect an increase in strategic buyers and a decrease in the amount of leverage, implying that deals are being done because they make sense for both parties. That was far from the case in the highly leveraged, financially driven deals of the late 1980s.

Board members and leaders of companies in small- to middle-market segments need to understand the key drivers of valuation, since they are often able to focus their operating goals on maximizing the potential valuation range. Therefore, it is important to know that the multiple of earnings that a seller can obtain for its business directly correlates with the following characteristics:

1. Strong revenue growth
2. Significant market share or strong niche positions
3. A market with barriers to entry by competitors
4. A strong management team
5. Strong, stable cash flow
6. No significant concentration in customers, products, suppliers, or geographic markets
7. Low risk of technological obsolescence or product substitution

Successful mergers and acquisitions are neither arts nor sciences; they are processes. In fact, regression analysis demonstrates that the number one determinant of successful deal multiples is the business' growth rate. The higher the growth rate, the higher the multiple of cash flow the business is worth.

For example, when a deal is improperly valued, one side wins big while the other loses big. By definition, a transaction is a failure if it does not create value for shareholders. The easiest way to fail, therefore, is to pay too high a price for something. To be successful, a transaction must be fair and balanced; it must reflect the economic needs of both buyer and seller, and must convey real and durable value to shareholders of both companies. Achieving this involves review and analysis of financial statements; genuine understanding of how the proposed transaction meets each party's economic objectives; and recognition of the deal's tax, accounting, and legal implications.

A transaction with the complexity of either a merger or an acquisition is fraught with potential problems and pitfalls. Many of these problems arise in the preliminary stages, such as when the parties force a deal that shouldn't really be done (i.e., some couples were just never meant to be married). Other times, inadequate, rushed, or misleading due diligence results in mistakes, errors, or omissions: for example, risks are not properly allocated for during the negotiation of definitive documents, or it becomes a nightmare to integrate the companies after closing. These pitfalls can lead to expensive and protracted litigation unless an alternative method of dispute resolution is negotiated and included in the definitive documents.

WHY BAD DEALS HAPPEN TO GOOD PEOPLE

Nobody ever plans to enter into a bad deal. Yet many well-intentioned board members and business executives go through with mergers and acquisitions that they later regret. Classic mistakes include a lack of adequate planning, an overly aggressive timetable to closing, or a failure to look closely at possible post-closing integration problems. Worst of all, the projected synergies may turn out to be illusory. What is this "synergy" and how can you be sure to get some? The key premise to "synergy" is that the "whole will be greater than the sum of its parts." However, the quest for synergy can be deceptive, especially if there is inadequate communication between buyer and seller. This type of situation usually leads to a misunderstanding regarding what the buyer is really buying and the seller is really selling. Every company's leaders say that they want synergy when doing a deal, but few take the time to develop a transactional team, draw up a joint mission statement of the deal's objectives, or solve post-closing operating or financial problems on a timely basis.

CHAPTER 35

BUILT TO SCALE

How Emerging Growth Companies Have Created Breakthrough Growth Through Exceptional Advisory Boards

By Marissa Levine, CEO, Information Experts

Where do executives and entrepreneurs begin the process for recruiting qualified and effective members of their boards of directors and boards of advisors? As a serial entrepreneur and the member of many for-profit and non-profit boards, I have five best practices and observations that can be summarized in the following acronym: SCALE. In order to truly be in a position to "scale" your company's growth strategies, by recruiting effective board members, the process should be as follows:

S	=	SELECTION
C	=	COMPENSATE
A	=	ASSOCIATE
L	=	LEVERAGE
E	=	EVALUATE

My book, *SCALE: How to Assemble, Compensate and Leverage Your Strategic Board to Take Your Business to the Next Level* (2012), provides more detail on the SCALE™ system.

The SCALE™ model is a proven methodology used by owners of rapid-growth companies to build their boards of directors and the advisory boards they need to become exceptional, connected, knowledgeable leaders and to develop companies centered on durable and profitable business models. I created SCALE™ because I have a strong passion for helping other entrepreneurs remove the roadblocks impeding their abilities to reach their greatest personal and professional potential. Surrounding ourselves with the people who can help us get from where we are now to where we want to be is an essential part of achieving that outcome. While all entrepreneurs have dreams of building sustainable, profitable companies, they often lack the knowledge or skills required to move their visions and dreams to reality. Business leaders need to surround themselves with people who know how to build infrastructure; who can teach them about leadership; who can open doors, make connections, and drive sales; and who have already overcome challenges other leaders will eventually face at different levels of growth.

The SCALE™ system addresses many of the common challenges in establishing an effective board, including:

- "I don't know how to find good candidates."
- "I don't know what or who I need."
- "I don't know how to pay my board members."
- "I don't know what to expect from my board members."
- "I don't have time."
- "My business is too small for a board."
- "This is going to cause waves in my company."
- "I get plenty of good advice from lots of other people."
- "I'm not ready yet."

In answer to these challenges, here is an overview of the process that I have developed:

S = SELECT

Let's begin with the important task of selecting the right composition and mix of board members to SCALE a business. You should invest as much time in the selection of your board members as you do in the selection of your employees. Before asking for recommendations or conducting candidate interviews, your executive team must conduct an organizational audit to identify gaps in knowledge, experience, or skill sets, as well as to define the expectations and skill sets expected from board members. Uncover the gaps by asking such questions as:

- Where does your company need the most guidance and strategic direction?
- What skill sets is the company missing at the leadership level to help it achieve its strategic goals?
- Does the company need to focus on building its pipeline?
- Does the company need access to certain people or contracts in a specific vertical market or government agency?
- Is the company hitting another stage of growth and therefore needs to upgrade its accounting system or financial processes?
- Is the company implementing a new IT architecture or building more advanced database and data-gathering tools?
- Are you evaluating outsourcing non-core functions?
- Are you trying to launch a new organization inside your firm, such as a project management office (PMO) or harvest research and development?

- Is the company trying to achieve a specific certification (for example, ISO or CMMI)?

The board of directors is an extension of your company, of you, and of your brand. Everyone that is affiliated with your company—your customers, employees, partners, and board members—all reflect your mission, values, reputation, and future. Based on my experience, there are nine specific attributes that are essential for selecting effective board members. They are:

- *A solid track record of high integrity and strong character.* This is the single most important character trait of any board member. In board meetings, you'll be sharing highly confidential information about all aspects of your company. Public disclosure of your shared information could have potentially disastrous effects. Trust is paramount.

- *Generosity of spirit.* Look for board members who have a track record of helping others and giving back to the entrepreneurial community. The authentic desire to help others will go a long way as you integrate board members into your company.

- *Recognized, seasoned expertise.* Your board and your organization shouldn't be testing grounds for ideas that "may" work. The premise behind having a board is to receive guidance from those that know more than you and have a proven track record of success.

- *Having already accomplished what you want to accomplish.* If your company is at $5 million now and you want to get it to $10 million in the next eighteen months, you must surround yourself with people who are already where you want to be. If you want to apply for a specific certification, you will need a board member who has already gone through that process. If you want to shift your business model from one that is product-centric or service-centric to one that is customer-centric, you will want to work with a business owner who has experienced the same transition.

- *Great connections.* This is especially true for a board member who will play a key role in your company's sales or business development efforts. A well-connected board member will open new doors and bring in opportunities you might not have discovered. Every board member should greatly expand the business' network of resources.

- *Playing well with others.* A board is a team of highly experienced professionals who may or may not know each other. The last thing you want to worry about is a clash of personalities or an ego that is difficult to manage. When board members come to the table, they must understand that the meeting is not about them. It's about the organization they are serving.

- *Not being a yes-person.* A board is in place to guide as well as challenge the organization's current state of affairs. Board members must be willing to voice concerns and suggestions with as much candor and honesty as possible. They must have guts to ask tough questions, and they can't be easily intimidated.

- *Reliable availability to show up at meetings.* Avoid candidates who will be available in name only. A board member candidate may have all of the right qualifications, but if he or she travels extensively or can't be available between meetings, he or she probably isn't a good fit. All board members must attend all meetings, and, depending on the agreement in place, they may be required to attend addtional meetings throughout the year with potential customers or existing company leaders.

What to Avoid

Just as with your employment selection process, it's important to know what you do not want in a board member. Here is a list of avoid-at-all-costs traits:

- *Being a jack-of-all-trades.* Your board should be a collection of experts and specialists. While all board members will bring deep experience with them and will have valuable input on a variety of topics, ideally you want a collection of true experts. The goal should be to stack your boardroom with people who are at the level of mastery in a specific organizational function, rather than mediocrity at several levels. You want the best, and being the best requires a laser focus.

- *Having a self-focused agenda.* Service on the board should not be motivated by ego or greed. Board members must be committed to putting the best interests of the company ahead of their own. Some candidates will be interested in board participation in order to build their resumes, expand their networks, make additional money, or perhaps even solicit your company to become a customer or client. All of these things may be acceptable as secondary objectives, but the primary driver for all board participation should be to help your organization grow.

- *Inexperience.* You are implementing a board in order to gain access to expert talent. This is a time for you to surround yourself with people who have a long, proven track record of performance. The last thing you want to do with your board members is have to mentor them. They are there to mentor you.

- *Ego.* With experience often comes ego. There's no room for big egos or an "I'm always right" mindset at the board table. In your search process, look for humility, a commitment to teamwork, and modesty. Egotistical behavior negates the value of experience and can unravel or jeopardize even the strongest boards.

- ***Being in the exact place you are now.*** The primary reason you are putting an advisory board in place is to move your company from one level to the next. If you are currently at $50 million and you want to scale to $100 million over the next two to three years, you need people on your board who have accomplished this milestone or surpassed it. Your entire company will change during this growth spurt. (See Chapters 33 and 34.) These are difficult and sometimes painful transitions. You will experience changes in customers, personnel, processes, infrastructure, and culture. Your HR, IT, and legal needs will grow increasingly complex. Your board is going to be an instrumental component in your navigation of these changes, so you require members that have already gone through such a change.

Your specific criteria will drive your selection process. The goal of having specific criteria is to help you align candidates with your specific needs at this precise time. This should help you identify candidates who understand your market, customers, current level of growth, and business processes. Once you've conducted an organizational audit and identified your five to seven most important priorities (and hence, your selection criteria), you can create your targeted search criteria.

Where Can You Find Your Candidates?

Once you have conducted your organizational audit, committed to the list of essentials, and defined your search criteria, it's time to hunt for your prospects. To retain the right members, CEOs must cast a wide net to find candidates who have the skills, experience, desire, and time necessary to drive performance.

Here are nine sources of advisory board candidates:

1. **Your current advisors**: attorneys, bankers, accountants, and insurance agents. Your network of paid advisors is a great first place to look. All of these people work with other companies that are similar in size to your own. They belong to deep networks of business owners and industry experts. Personal introductions and recommendations are key to finding trusted advisors.

2. **CEO/entrepreneur networking communities.** There are many communities for business owners. Vistage, the Entrepreneurs' Organization (EO), the National Association of Women Business Owners (NAWBO), and local Chambers of Commerce are perfect places to identify business owners who may be a fit for your board or who can recommend candidates.

3. **Networking events targeted to CEOs/executives.** There are many such recognition events these days, and they are great places to meet other high-performing executives.

4. **Non-profit/philanthropic organizations.** People who serve on the boards of nonprofit organizations have already proven themselves to be generous and capable leaders.

5. **Do your research and then reach out to specific people based on a specific need.** Stay informed about industry leaders. If you learn of someone who may be a fit, connect with him or her.

6. **Industry-specific or function-specific networking groups.** If you are trying to break into or expand your presence in a specific vertical market, join networking communities specifically targeted to those industries. In the D.C. region, for example, there is an abundance of government contracting organizations. Similarly, there are specific groups organized according to job function: CFO alliances, program management communities, and so on.

7. **Online communities.** LinkedIn® is a powerful connecting tool. Users are allowed to join up to fifty groups, which connect them with like-minded professionals. These groups provide perfect platforms for inquiring about potential board members.

8. **Authors.** There are many local authors who have made themselves known and accessible through social media platforms such as Twitter®, LinkedIn®, GooglePlus®, and Facebook®. No longer are authors elusive, unconnected, or unapproachable. With the growth of the self-publishing industry, authors are now intentionally connected to and integrated with their reader base. They are often well connected to experts, because of their research, and therefore make great sources for potential board recommendations.

9. **Your own employees.** Look inside your own organization for recommendations. These people certainly know your

company. They have their own networks and can potentially identify strong board candidates.

The differences in these mindsets will absolutely affect how you come across to your candidates and who ends up serving on your board. If you are at the point of recruiting board members, it's because you have built something great, and you're committed to making it even greater. Serving on your board is a privilege and an opportunity that you will extend only to those who have demonstrated their integrity, value, and commitment. Board formation and recruitment is a strategic imperative, not a reactive act of desperation. Recruit from a position of strength rather than from a position of need. By adopting this mindset, you rightfully remain in the driver's seat for selection because you will have more eager candidates than you will need.

C = COMPENSATE

Busy people who are protective of their time will, nevertheless, consider serving on your board if doing so provides them with networking, visibility, valuable communication, a collaborative learning environment, an opportunity to connect on a deep level with other industry leaders, the chance to provide mentorship and coaching, opportunities for personal and professional growth, or resume development.

Lois Juliber is a former Vice Chairman and Chief Operating Officer of Colgate-Palmolive. Since retiring in 2005, she has focused her energy on serving on corporate boards (DuPont, Goldman Sachs, and Kraft) and supporting not-for-profit organizations in education and microfinance (Wellesley College, The MasterCard Foundation [as Chairman], and Women's World Banking). Regarding her board experience, Juliber says, "For a potential CEO and existing divisional business manager, it is a great developmental experience to join a board. It gives the person a totally new orientation and experience. It is a real expansion of personal capacity."

A well-thought-out compensation plan demonstrates to board members that:

- You value their time and respect the commitment they bring to your organization;
- You are willing to invest in the board, which makes it more likely that you will implement suggestions;
- You are committed to growing your company;
- You will reinforce good will among the participants.

That being said, you want to avoid—at all costs—board members who serve on boards strictly for the money. The best board members are those people who genuinely love helping other businesses succeed and do not view board compensation as a stream of income.

There are many different options for board compensation, and these fall into monetary and non-monetary categories.

Cash Consideration

- Per-meeting fee. This fee really depends on the size of your company and what you can afford. Fees can range from $500 to $5,000 per meeting for each board member. The benefit of the per-meeting fee is that it encourages participation at meetings from all parties. For a meeting to be as effective as possible, it's important to ensure complete participation of all members for the entire event.
- Annual retainer. Some companies pay annual retainers either in addition to the per-meeting fee or in place of it, depending on specific arrangements. The annual retainer

allows for additional availability between meetings, which is especially important if a board member is serving as a mentor to other people in the organization, or if a board member is involved in business development efforts and thus may be required to attend potential customer meetings. The range of retainer fees varies widely, ranging from $5,000 to $50,000 per year.

- Commission structure for business development efforts. If you are bringing people onto your board to assist with business development and they are essentially an extension of your sales team, you may want to create a separate commission-based compensation structure for them.
- Expenses. If a board member requires travel, lodging, and meals, typically you will also have to pay for these expenses.

Non-Cash Consideration

There are also several non-monetary compensation options:

- Equity, stock options, non-voting shares, and other tools are available to facilitate part-ownership in the company. Think through this option carefully. Be sure to have a way of redeeming or retrieving shares from non-performing board members, and to avoid conflicts of interest or "dead" equity.
- Reciprocal board service. Many owners of growing businesses offer to serve on the boards of their advisors.
- Provision of products or services in exchange for board service. If your organization can provide value to your board members, they may be open to this exchange. For example, if your company provides web design or IT

services, your board member may have a need for these services and may be open to a trade.

- Donation to a charity, participation in a charity event, or commitment to a board position for a nonprofit or philanthropy organization. If your board member is involved in a specific cause, he or she may prefer that you support that organization with your time, money, or talent.

You can make the compensation package as simple or as complex as needed, depending on what works for your company. If performance targets are prerequisites for certain levels of financial or equity participation, then be sure that those metrics are clearly communicated and understood.

A = ASSOCIATE

Okay, so you've done a thorough job of identifying, screening, and selecting your candidates. You've narrowed your pool to those you believe are the right people to get you from where you are now to where you want to be. Once offers have been made and accepted, the key challenge is to integrate the board members into the fabric of the company on an expedited basis.

During the interview process, you had an opportunity to connect one-on-one with each board member and educate him or her on the current state of your business. Now that these members are on board, you need to integrate them into the company at a deeper level. Prior to the first meeting, there are several things you can do:

- Provide each member with a thorough, in-person orientation to your business. Invite members to visit or tour your office and meet key figures on your team.

- Schedule a one-on-one lunch with each board member to get to know all of them on a more personal level, and to address any additional questions.
- Solicit input from each board member about best practices for holding board meetings or kicking off a new board of advisors. Welcome contributions from the members.
- Distribute the agenda or presentation well before the meeting, so that you can get right to work when everyone arrives.
- Have the schedule and the ground rules for the meeting distributed in advance.

The Day of the Meeting

There are several ground rules to follow for your board meetings:

- Each meeting requires a schedule and an agenda. To be respectful of everyone's time, it is essential that the meeting stay on track.
- All parties must have the opportunity to weigh in on an issue if they have something to contribute.
- Establish a "parking lot" for tangential issues that arise throughout the day. It's disrespectful to ignore or minimize them altogether.
- If certain discussions don't lead to resolution in the allotted time, vote to determine if the discussion should be tabled or if it should continue, even though it will roll into the next segment of the meeting. Consider the option of continuing discussion of a specific topic over a conference call, video call, email, or separate meeting.
- Record the meeting's minutes (obtain consent prior). If possible, video the meeting or use a technology such as

WebEx so that you can access the recorded version at a later date.

Here are the goals of the first meeting:

- Establish connections and facilitate chemistry and open dialogue among the board members.
- Demonstrate your willingness to accept new ideas, constructive criticism, and feedback without being defensive.
- Share necessary information and get everyone on the same page.
- Review your strategic plan.
- Introduce your organization and team to the board.
- Begin the process of integrating your board members into your company.

One of the most common questions about board meetings is, "How often should a board meet?" The answer depends on the company. While many experts suggest a quarterly meeting, experience has taught me that this may be too frequent. It really depends on what initiatives you are carrying out. If an organization is working on initiatives that may take a long time to implement, meeting every three months may not make sense. In addition, some companies have specific time periods over the year during which it is simply impossible to focus on strategic planning.

Don't hold a meeting just for the sake of holding a meeting. Too many meetings will force the board to find issues to solve, rather than focusing on strategic imperatives. However, you still want to keep your board engaged and connected. Engaging the board between meetings through conference calls, one-on-one meetings, and consulting for specific initiatives is very important. My company, Information Experts, relies on its individual board members for very specific requirements. One of our board members (along with someone else in his organization) attends our weekly sales calls in order to review our pipeline and current opportunities. Another board member spends a great deal of one-on-one time with our VP of Operations. Still another board member heads up a large contract we won, and he provides mentorship through this program. The important thing is to make the board members' availability work for you, in the manner that makes sense to your organization.

Length of meetings

A board meeting should not be any shorter than three hours. Anything shorter will not allow members to dig deep into issues, and won't allow all members to participate fully. Conversely, aside from the first kickoff meeting, these meetings shouldn't last longer than six hours. If you can't fit your agenda into six hours, you have too many issues to address—and you probably need more frequent meetings. Some organizations' leaders like to plan retreats or daylong, off-site meetings to conduct annual reviews, but this amount of time should not be standard practice for every meeting.

It's essential that employees feel some connection to the board members, know who they are and why they were selected, and have the opportunity to meet them from time to time, especially in small and mid-sized companies. The value of your board can cascade throughout your entire organization. Thus, in your interviewing and screening process, it's important to communicate that part of the board members' responsibility is to integrate fully into the organization by providing mentorship, coaching, and representation at industry events. In addition, you can ask your board members to attend company events, such as holiday parties, team-building events, and all-hands meetings. While 100 percent participation may be excessive, it's great to have board members see the company in action and connect on a personal level with its employees.

L = LEVERAGE

Most business executives and founders who finally take the time to put a proper board in place still don't know how to leverage their board members fully. An organization can leverage its board by doing the following:

- Providing mentorship to employees;
- Expanding the business development/sales team;
- Accessing people and customers who are otherwise unfamiliar;
- Using their names (where appropriate) as a competitive advantage in proposals;
- Establishing new offices, functions, or practice areas in the organization;
- Pursuing certifications, grants, and set-asides;
- Overhauling or implementing key processes;
- Connecting with other strategic partners in key accounts or creating new business support relationships (accounting, banking, or legal);
- Evaluating whether to outsource core functions or keep them in-house, making recommendations for service providers, and evaluating proposals;
- Providing direct mentorship to employees, subject to time availability;
- Finally, remembering the board isn't in place just to improve the CEO's performance, but is also in place to

improve the organization's overall performance and that of the entire leadership team.

Establishing a board is a perfect way to provide mentorship to your leadership team and to give them access to the skills, knowledge, and resources they need to do their jobs well. If you've assigned accountability for and ownership of specific outcomes and performance to your leadership team, then you must be the bridge between what they have and what they need. This is one of the CEO's most important jobs: to provide access to the knowledge, skills, tools, and resources employees need to succeed. Mentorship and coaching may occur through the development of one-on-one relationships, or may be group-based.

At Information Experts, one of our board members has become a close confidante of and mentor to one of our vice presidents. Not only has the board member been a source of knowledge and experience, he has also acted as a confidential sounding board. Employees often need someone to confide in, outside of the organization, to discuss strategy, performance, or other organizational issues. Your board members have deep connections. Perhaps you have made some board selections specifically to ramp up your business development. Retired corporate and government executives are great board candidates. They have time on their hands and enjoy helping hard-working, small businesses grow. If you want to leverage your board members' business development capacity fully, the relationship has to extend outside of the boardroom.

At Information Experts, some of our advisory board members attend weekly sales calls. They are heavily involved in our opportunity decisions and closely mentor the program managers responsible for specific accounts. They attend customer visits along with our team and proactively make introductions. Especially as regards business development, your board members can't be passive, with their engagement limited to quarterly meetings. In some circumstances, companies may set up additional compensation measures for board members that are heavily involved in business development.

As companies grow, they may need to pursue certifications to remain competitive. These include International Standards Organization (ISO) certification, Capabilities Maturity Model Integration (CMMI) certification, Project Management Institute (PMI) certification, American National Standards Institute (ANSI) certification, 8a certification, Women's Business Enterprise National Council (WBENC) certification, Service Disabled Veteran-Owned Business (SDVOB) certification, HUB zone certification, and others. Many certifications programs require process overhaul or standards manuals development. One of the most lucrative federal programs is the Small Business Innovation Research (SBIR) program for companies that are developing unique technologies. An SBIR expert would be a very valuable board member for any company looking to submit a proposal for this program.

At Information Experts, we knew we were maxing out the functionality of our existing accounting system and would need to migrate to a system that could handle higher accounting volume. One of our advisory board members had significant experience with setting up financial and accounting systems in growing government contracting firms (which is why we brought him in). He worked closely with our COO and VP of Operations to evaluate our system, made recommendations, and made introductions to companies we could use to outsource the entire function. Then, he evaluated proposals from each of these firms, made recommendations, and negotiated on our behalf. When a board member is able to recognize where the organization needs support, and, more importantly, able to bring that support into the organization, such actions reassure everyone in the company that we have a clear line of sight on where we are going, and that it's okay to not have all of the answers internally. Most small businesses don't have all of the answers internally. It's those firms that are open to direction from others that are able to grow. Your board members are one of your greatest competitive advantages . . . if you leverage them well. They will help you retain top talent, recruit top talent, and fulfill your potential. With the right support team and the right guidance, the sky is the limit for your company.

E = EVALUATE

As your company evolves and grows, so will your board. This is why it is essential to be looking for potential board members continuously and have a succession plan in place. Even once you have established your board, you must always be thinking about the next evolutionary phase and terms of services to allow for the exit of certain board members and the entrance of fresh ones who have fresh ideas and perspectives. You should always be interviewing and meeting prospects for the board, just as you should interview and meet prospects for your employee base. The time to recruit and interview new employees or board members is not when you are in a desperate state of immediate need. This should be an ongoing process.

So, how will your organization change as a result of your board and its composition? There are many things that can shift. I've identi-fied a few of them here:

1. Your personal role. As your company grows from, perhaps, a "solopreneur" structure to a company with board members or employees (or from under $1 million to perhaps $5

million or $10 million), your role will shift from practitioner to manager to leader, and, perhaps ultimately, to adviser or bridge-builder. It's unavoidable. You can't stay in the trenches when you need to be at the 50,000-foot level to set your strategy and growth path.

2. Your employees. For a variety of reasons, employees that help you reach one growth stage may not be the employees you need to reach another growth stage. This is absolutely the hardest part of business ownership . . . weighing your loyalty to one employee against your loyalty to the rest of the company. Of course, each employee is different, and sometimes a long-time employee does evolve and grow along with the company, either in his or her original role or a different role. However, often, as a company grows, it will require new experiences, ideas, and leadership.

3. Your company's mission. An effective board will evolve the company's focus. One aspect of business I am finally accepting is attrition and change is not such a bad thing. Organizational shifts won't sit well with everyone and, as the culture shifts, some will leave. However, you will also be able to attract talent who previously may have skipped over your company. Somehow, it all balances out . . . it's the yin and yang of business growth. We're only as strong as our weakest links, and embarking on aggressive shifts or goals inevitably reveal an organization's weakest links.

4. Your company's customers. As you grow, you will outgrow some of your customers. Customers who were ideally suited to your company five years ago and seemed like the right size may eventually seem too small or not strategic enough as you continue along your path of growth. Fur-

thermore, going deep into customer organization takes a great deal of time, money, and resources. Often, when a company grows, its leaders need to narrow focus to a handful of key accounts, rather than spreading the organization too thin. Customers who are good sources of revenue but have limited depth may not be a good fit for your growth. Finally, markets invariably shift, so what they will need and buy will shift as well. You will need to ensure your solutions are aligned with your customers'.

5. Your company's marketing and business development strategy. As you shift your company's customer base and continue to move it in a more strategic direction, the message and outreach strategy will shift as well. The opportunities the company pursues will shift dramatically. You will need to close larger contracts to keep pace with your company's growth. When your company has a target of $10 million, a $1 million contract is significant. When you have a target of $50 million, a $10,000 contract is not worth the investment of your time or allocation of your resources. Unmanaged growth is one of the biggest threats to a growing business.

6. Your company's IT and financial infrastructure. As your company grows, its IT infrastructure will need to keep pace with its growth, not only in terms of bandwidth, but in terms of hardware, software, applications, mobile connectivity, and security. Growing companies have increasingly complex finance and accounting requirements. Your system requirements and your personnel requirements in this space will continue to evolve.

7. Your company's recruiting strategy, culture, and HR infrastructure. As an organization grows, it must invest in its recruitment strategy, as well as in HR infrastructure, to ensure legal compliance and also to provide competitive benefits packages. The evolution of culture is sometimes a bitter pill to swallow. As a company moves from the entrepreneurial start-up phase to a more mature phase, the culture can't help but shift. The organization has to stop revolving around a core group of people and must shift to being process-centric. Hero mentalities, in which the company survives on the backs of a small group of employees, are dangerous and unhealthy. Processes alleviate the burden of dependency, enable the company to function like a well-oiled machine, and strongly position the company for growth.

8. Your company's external advisors. Finally, your company's advisors will likely change. As your company travels its path and reaches its milestones, it's important to re-evaluate those people who are guiding you. A board is a fluid dynamic of a business, and will continue to evolve alongside of that business.

Evaluating Your Board

The most effective way to establish evaluation criteria for your board members is to create a baseline for performance matched up against your specific requirements at the time you engage your board. Just as you hold your executive team accountable for specific goals, you can ask your board for the same accountability. Most companies evaluate their board members annually against specific tasks or milestones. Especially if it has a board in place, a company should experience a lot of change in twelve months. At the board's one-year anniversary, your executive team can evaluate who on your advisory board can still add value, and who has fulfilled his or her objectives. Keeping in mind that you should always be actively looking for potential board members, it's a great idea to plant the idea of board service in the mind of anyone you think may be a fit. If you have acted as an honorable executive, finding new board members should never be a challenge.

When it's time to exit existing board members, it's wise to approach the situation as you would an exit interview with an employee who is departing your company. The exit is a great opportunity for you to gain insight into the departing party's experiences. You may have questions for the departing board member about your leadership, your organization, the effectiveness of the board, how you managed the board, and if the board met its objectives while the member was active. The goal at the conclusion of such a relationship is to have delivered a mutually rewarding experience to both the board member and the organization.

About the Author

Marissa Levin is the Founder and CEO of Information Experts, a company which helps companies and agencies align their business and human capital strategies through compelling, integrated communications and educational programs. Levin leads the effort to define and shape the organization's values, mission, vision, growth strategy, brand, and corporate culture. Information Experts, which started as a one-woman operation in Levin's spare bedroom in 1995, has evolved into a high-profile, multi-million dollar enterprise. Through her leadership, the firm has grown into an award-winning, full-service, SBA 8(a) certified small business. She is the author of *Built to SCALE: How Top Companies Have Created Breakthrough Growth Through Exceptional Advisory Boards*, which will be published in the summer of 2012.

CHAPTER 36

Looking Toward the Future

The Business Case for Corporate Governance

By John D. Sullivan, Ph.D., Executive Director, Center for International Private Enterprise (CIPE), and Anna Nadgrodkiewicz, Program Officer, CIPE

Historically, in the developed economies, key drivers for the adoption of good corporate governance have been the following: the search for investment capital, the desire to be listed on major global stock exchanges, the need to gain access to technology, and the desire to build solid supply chains. In today's global economy, corporate governance is becoming increasingly recognized as a key factor affecting businesses' success in emerging markets as well.

Opportunities and competitive threats created by the global economy make instituting good corporate governance practices key to developing a strategy for the company to prosper. Improving corporate governance allows companies to attract greater investment at lower cost, strengthens corporate strategy and its implementation, clarifies accountability, enhances shareholder protection, and helps to attract and retain quality employees.[1] This is true not only for large, publicly listed multinationals but for other types of companies as well. For controlling shareholders, corporate governance clarifies roles and improves accountability, enhances senior executives' professionalization, and increases company value.[2] Crucially, for society as a whole, corporate governance minimizes the occurrence of corruption, reduces the risk of devastating systemic crises, and improves productivity.

UNDERSTANDING CORPORATE GOVERNANCE

Corporate governance is at the core of a modern company's strategy and operations because it addresses issues vital to that company's performance and to its very survival. From board selection and strategic decision-making to day-to-day operations and legal compliance, corporate governance is a way for companies to create a framework for sound business practices, sustained growth, and risk management.

The basic concept of corporate governance is a principal-agent model used to ensure the profitable performance of corporations and the efficient use of resources, and to solve problems related to the separation of ownership and control.[3] The principals are owners of company assets; the agents are managers responsible for company operations. The idea behind corporate governance is to ensure that

---

1   John D. Sullivan and Philip Armstrong, *Introduction to Advancing Corporate Governance in the Middle East and North Africa: Stories and Solutions* (Center for International Private Enterprise and the International Finance Corporation [Global Corporate Governance Forum], Feb. 2011).

2   See the publication cited above for recent case studies featuring interviews with companies in the Middle East and North Africa that use good corporate governance to address a range of business issues, from attracting investors to managing risk.

3   Adolph Berle and Gardiner Means, *The Modern Corporation and Private Property* (New York: Macmillan Co., 1932).

the agent—the manager—acts in the best interest of the principal. Therefore, at its core, corporate governance entails an internal control system for transparent decision-making to which company executives should be held accountable.

In this basic model, directors represent the shareholders, vote on key matters, and appoint and monitor the management, while the management carries out core company functions and reports to the board of directors. Many people think of corporate governance as limited to this internal company dynamic between the shareholders, board of directors, and management. The revised Principles of Corporate Governance published by the Organisation for Economic Co-operation and Development (OECD) in 2004 capture the essence of that dynamic:

Corporate governance involves a set of relationships between a company's management, its board, its shareholders, and other stakeholders. Corporate governance also provides the structure through which the objectives of the company are set and the means of attaining those objectives and monitoring performance are determined.

However, the OECD Principles also make it clear that corporate governance involves more than just internal company structures and requires external supporting institutions that promote transparent and efficient markets.[4]

Many people also think of corporate governance as something applicable only to large corporations in developed economies with little relevance to the broader private sector or to issues affecting the development of countries around the world. In the global economy, however, it has become increasingly obvious that the external factors that guide the behavior of companies, such as regulatory frame-

---

4   For the full text of the OECD Principles, see http://www.oecd.org/dataoecd/32/18/31557724.pdf.

works and market institutions, are equally important to making the system of corporate governance work. Moreover, in many countries, publicly listed corporations are not the most important economic actors in terms of employment and growth. Instead, other types of business—from family-owned companies to small enterprises—play a dominant role in the economy. Those companies also need good corporate governance for better sustainability and in order to become integrated into the global supply chains.

As a result, the understanding and application of corporate governance has evolved in the last few decades, as people recognize that corporate governance does not exist in a vacuum. Its successful implementation depends on a country's overall institutional environment, not just on a company's internal practices. Therefore, to strengthen private sector governance, countries and companies alike should also focus on broader reforms of the judicial systems, property rights, freedom of information, and other institutions key to market economies and democratic governance.[5] These institutional dimensions of corporate governance must be understood in order to appreciate corporate governance's importance for business growth, especially in emerging markets.

INSTITUTIONAL DIMENSIONS OF CORPORATE GOVERNANCE

The external factors that affect corporate behavior include various stakeholders who need to be considered in decision-making,

---

5   See "The Linkages Between Corporate Governance and Development" in E. Hontz and A. Shkolnikov, eds., *Corporate Governance: The Intersection of Public and Private Reform* (CIPE and USAID, 2009), p. 8; also available at http://www.cipe.org/programs/corp_gov/pdf/CG_USAID.pdf.

such as employees, customers, suppliers, lenders, and communities in which the company operates. Reputational agents, such as accountants and independent auditors, lawyers, credit rating agencies, investment bankers and advisors, financial media, and corporate governance analysts, are also crucial in shaping company decisions. So are shareholder rights organizations, corporate governance institutes, and directors' associations, given their roles in corporate governance-related advocacy, professional standards, and self-regulation.

Another key external factor is the regulatory environment. It involves various standards (accounting and auditing, for instance); laws and regulations applied to companies; stock exchange and securities market regulations; debt and financial sector equity requirements; rules governing market competition; investment; and corporate control.

The growing recognition that corporate governance requires functioning of both internal controls and external supporting institutions is illustrated by the evolution of the OECD Principles of Corporate Governance. The OECD Principles, created in 1999, initially focused on five core areas of corporate governance: the rights of shareholders and key ownership structures; equitable treatment of shareholders; the role of stakeholders; disclosure and transparency; and the responsibilities of the board members. However, it soon became apparent that this scope did not sufficiently reflect the external, institutional factors that drive corporate governance.

When the authors drafted the original Principles, they primarily looked at OECD countries with developed capital markets and well-established corporate structures. The Principles assumed that all the other institutions of a market economy were in place. Furthermore, they did not touch upon forms of business common in many countries, such as family firms or state-owned enterprises (SOEs), nor did they address the differences between dispersed and concentrated ownership structures. Those shortcomings highlighted a discrepancy between the traditional definition of corporate governance and its actual practice.

That is why, in 2004, a revision of the OECD Principles added another key tenet to the existing five: ensuring the basis for an effective corporate governance framework. This tenet states that "the corporate governance framework should promote transparent and efficient markets, be consistent with the rule of law, and clearly articulate the division of responsibilities among different supervisory, regulatory, and enforcement authorities." This principle now makes explicit that the existence of good public governance and market institutions cannot be assumed and should be enhanced through reforms where needed.

The Principles' revision process, in which the Center for International Private Enterprise (CIPE) and its partners from around the world participated, also captured the fact that the value of corporate governance goes beyond the performance of individual companies. The private sector, as a whole, plays a vital role in market economies and countries' development prospects. Therefore, institutions of good corporate governance—in order to operate effectively—must exist in the context of broader institutions that guarantee transparent governance and competitive markets.

BUSINESS CASE FOR CORPORATE GOVERNANCE

Given that corporate governance is relevant to individual companies and countries alike, building a business case for implementing good corporate governance practices has two equally crucial aspects: it needs to demonstrate benefits both at a company level and at a systemic, country-wide level.[6]

Business Case for Companies

As mentioned earlier, traditionally, corporate governance has been associated with large companies in developed markets for which the key benefit of good governance is being listed on a stock exchange and able to raise outside capital. However, corporate governance can deliver benefits to other types of companies because it provides a framework for efficient, transparent, and accountable decision-making. That framework is needed in every enterprise, regardless of the size or form of ownership. All companies must have a way of reconciling divergent interests, planning for strategy and succession, accessing capital, cultivating company image in the community, and ensuring legal compliance. Corporate governance is a key tool for achieving those business goals.

Family firms are one such example. Given that their owners and managers are the same, the conventional model of corporate governance has generally not been deemed applicable to them. Yet, those firms—prevalent in many developing countries—face serious governance challenges that require clear rules and decision-making frameworks. Common problems in family-owned firms include nepotism, personal conflicts between different family members, lack of clear separation of interests and assets between the company and family, and succession issues that threaten the company's survival beyond that of the founder.

---

6   This section draws upon Aleksandr Shkolnikov and Andrew Wilson's "From Sustainable Companies to Sustainable Economies" in E. Hontz and A. Shkolnikov, eds., *Corporate Governance: The Intersection of Public and Private Reform* (CIPE and USAID, 2009), pp. 6-30; also available at http://www.cipe.org/programs/corp_gov/pdf/CG_USAID.pdf.

In those companies, good corporate governance can, among other qualities, help ensure sustainability in the second and third generations, improve professionalism of management, enhance access to capital, and increase the price and volume of traded shares. Better corporate governance practices also help family firms achieve clearer distinctions between representatives of ownership (directors) and management (CEO and other executives), as well as help improve the quality of decision-making by recruiting independent board members. Those findings have been borne out by a study of corporate governance practices of the fifteen largest family-owned companies in Brazil.[7]

Improving corporate governance in the state-owned enterprise (SOE) sector is another example of benefits at a company level. By adopting good corporate governance rules, leaders of SOEs can make the state an effective and more responsible owner, improve board quality, tie management incentives to company performance, and establish clear lines of accountability that ultimately go back to the taxpayers.[8]

Small and medium-sized enterprises (SMEs), although not associated with the classic corporate governance model, can also greatly benefit from improved internal governance. Most leaders of SMEs cite access to credit as one of the biggest challenges their enterprises face, especially in economies in which capital markets are underdeveloped and small companies primarily rely on banks for financing. Without proper accounting procedures and disclosure of financial information, bank loans are not forthcoming.

---

7   The Brazilian Institute of Corporate Governance (IBGC), *Corporate Governance in Family-Owned Companies: Outstanding Cases in Brazil* (Sao Paulo: Saint Paul Editora Ltda., 2007).

8   *OECD Guidelines on Corporate Governance of State-Owned Enterprises* ([2005]; see http://www.oecd.org/document/33/0,3746,en_2649_34847_34046561_1_1_1_1,00.html).

Many SME leaders are recognizing the need to improve their companies' accounting procedures and internal control systems in order to enhance credit worthiness. They also see the economic value of crafting internal codes of corporate governance for greater sustainability and competitiveness. By adopting such codes, SME leaders can improve the decision-making process between partners and shareholders, the transparency and accuracy of financial information, the role of executive staff, and the relationships with stakeholders.[9]

By requiring better financial information from companies to which they lend, banks can encourage the adoption of improved accounting systems and regular reporting in various types of companies. In doing so, the banking sector can promote good governance in countries where most companies rely on banks rather than stock exchanges to meet their capital needs. To do this effectively, however, leaders of the banks themselves must appreciate the benefits of good corporate governance practices.

Financial crises plaguing countries around the world have frequently been linked to insider lending or improper risk management in financial institutions. Those risks are particularly compounded in state-owned banks in which, without proper safeguards, political considerations often trump sound economic decision-making and risk assessment in lending. That is where corporate governance— through more transparency and accountability in the boardroom and through better disclosure—can make a big difference, not just for responsible bank lending but also for macroeconomic stability.

In fact, systemic failure of risk management tied to poor corporate governance practices has been at the core of the recent

---

9 See *Framework Code of Good Corporate Governance for Small and Medium-Size Enterprises* (CIPE and the Colombian Federation of Chambers of Commerce [Confecamaras]: http://www.cipe. org/regional/lac/pdf/SME_CG_Code.pdf).

global financial crisis. As the OECD report on the causes of the crisis observed, "In many cases risk was not managed on an enterprise basis and not adjusted to corporate strategy [. . .] Most important of all, boards were in a number of cases ignorant of the risk facing the company."[10] The lesson is that risk management was typically not covered, or insufficiently covered, by corporate governance practices. Many companies, including banks, have since improved board performance in this regard by developing policies for identification of the best skill composition of a board or establishing remuneration committees to better monitor the relationship between executive compensation and company performance and anticipate potential conflicts of interest.

Business Case for Economies

The institutional underpinnings of corporate governance, especially the private sector institutions and regulatory frameworks that shape business behavior, make it an essential component of public governance and of countries' economic development. Many efforts toward strengthening corporate governance in emerging markets have been focused on improving internal company practices. However, improving the broader institutional environment in which those practices are implemented is of equal importance because of the intertwined nature of the internal and external factors that influence business conduct.

Addressing institutional deficiencies that hamper effective corporate governance is one of the core benefits of corporate governance reforms, particularly for developing economies. At the most basic level, a sound corporate governance system helps to ensure that

---

10 *Corporate Governance and the Financial Crisis: Key Findings and Main Messages* (OECD [June 2009]), p. 8; available at http://www.oecd.org/dataoecd/3/10/43056196.pdf.

companies operate on a level playing field, and that the rights of shareholders and stakeholders are well defined and protected. More broadly, corporate governance requires institutions, such as healthy justice systems, to enforce the rules and vibrant civil societies and independent media to monitor company conduct and expose abuses. Building these supporting institutions of corporate governance facilitates the creation of value systems based on transparency, accountability, responsibility, and fairness. Those values are not only important for ethical and sustainable business growth but are also indispensable for democratic governance.

One key area in which countries can greatly benefit from improved corporate governance is in privatization of state-owned enterprises. Introducing good corporate governance in companies scheduled to undergo privatization is particularly crucial in transition economies, in which privatizing state assets is a key part of building a market economy and in which governments depend on income from privatization to deliver services to the public.

The legacy of flawed privatization after the fall of communism in Eastern Europe shows how the lack of proper internal controls, reporting mechanisms, and shareholder protections in privatized firms led to corruption and abuse that was detrimental not just to those enterprises but to the entire transition process.

The lack of such controls prior to privatization has also contributed to other severe economic crises, such as that of Chile in the 1970s, in which family-owned banks unsustainably invested in privatized companies, or the 1994 "tequila crisis" in Mexico, in which government-owned commercial banks were improperly privatized.

Sound corporate governance is also important in state-owned firms with no immediate plans for privatization. In many countries, SOEs account for a large share of employment but are notorious for asset wasting, mismanagement, and entering into political entanglements. Establishing internal controls and clear governance rules can greatly improve the efficiency of their operations and effective use of public resources.

Corporate governance is also crucial for transforming the relationship between businesses and the state away from cronyism and preferential treatment toward transparency and accountability. As financial crises in Asia and Russia in the late 1990s demonstrated, non-transparent relationships between government officials and companies can lead to economic collapse, not just individual companies' failures.

More recently, the aftermath of the global financial crisis shows the high cost of poor corporate governance for societies that is still felt around the world. All these examples illustrate that weak corporate governance at a company level has crucial macroeconomic implications and can lead to the inability of countries to attract investment, resulting in public asset stripping, state capture, and, in extreme cases, financial disaster.

Corporate governance can also be a key anti-corruption tool with many economic benefits. Certainly, legal reforms, such as better procurement codes or simplification of tax codes, are needed to create stronger anti-corruption environments in countries, but robust corporate governance at a company level can greatly supplement such reform efforts. Internal controls limit opportunities for corruption by making bribery harder to conceal, integrating the values of transparency and accountability into a company's operations, and implementing strict policies of zero tolerance for corruption among employees and directors.

In sum, corporate governance clearly delivers palpable economic benefits to countries that put in place better internal and external drivers of company conduct. Studies show that those benefits include higher investment levels, lower costs of capital, and lower costs of doing business, all of which lead to stronger economic growth and more employment opportunities.[11] Improved company performance, through better management and allocation of resources, helps to create wealth and better relationships with stakeholders, which in turn helps to improve social and labor relations. Finally, at the systemic level, better corporate governance can help reduce the risk of devastating financial crises.

DRIVERS OF BETTER CORPORATE GOVERNANCE: IN SEARCH OF BENEFITS

Corporate governance reforms can be driven by two distinct factors: crises or searches for benefits. Responses to crises are often rushed, tend to focus on new regulations and stricter penalties, and do not take many issues affecting corporate behavior into account. A better approach to corporate governance reforms is the one driven by a search for benefits: for example, the business case for companies and economies to embrace better corporate governance and be proactive about it, rather than simply reacting to crises. That, in turn, makes them better prepared to deal with a crisis when it does occur.

When considering the significance of corporate governance for business growth, it is therefore important to recognize that drivers of corporate governance are not limited to the rules and competitive pressures that discipline companies into compliance. There are also many positive drivers that incentivize companies to implement good

---

11 Stijn Claessens, "Corporate Governance and Development," in *Global Corporate Governance Forum Focus I Publication* (see www.gcgf.org).

corporate governance in search of benefits, such as attracting invest-ment and lower cost of capital.

A well-governed company, even one in a poor investment envi-ronment, can do better than its competitors, and that is the premium an investor will pay for. According to the Global Investor Opinion Survey conducted by McKinsey and the Global Corporate Gover-nance Forum, (the survey canvassed more than 200 professional investors in thirty-one countries in Asia, Europe, Latin America, the Middle East, Africa, and North America), a significant majority of investors say they are willing to pay a premium for a well-governed company.[12] Corporate governance also helps strengthen competitive-ness. Studies show links between stronger shareholder protection and larger stock markets,[13] stronger corporate governance and lower cost of capital,[14] and greater equity rates and higher returns on investment relative to the cost of capital.[15]

That said, there is no silver bullet or a single model of effective global corporate governance that would automatically translate into business growth. Corporate governance systems and their effective-ness in different countries vary depending on the following: whether ownership and control of firms is dispersed (as in the United States and United Kingdom) or concentrated (as in continental Europe,

---

12 McKinsey & Company and the Global Corporate Governance Forum, "Global Investor Opinion Survey: Key Findings" (McKinsey & Company, Jul. 2002), http://ww1.mckinsey.com/client-service/organizationleadership/service/corpgovernance/PDF/GlobalInvestorOpinionSurvey2002.pdf.

13 Rafael La Porta, Florencio Lopez-de-Silanes, Andrei Shleifer, and Robert Vishny, "Legal Determinants of External Finance" (*Journal of Finance* 52.3 [1997]) pp. 1131–50.

14 Alexander Dyck and Luigi Zingales, "Private Benefits of Control: An International Com-parison" (*Journal of Finance* 60): pp. 537-600; Tatiana Nenova, "The Value of Corporate Votes and Control Benefits: Cross-Country Analysis" (*Journal of Financial Economics* 68.3 [2003]), pp. 325–51.

15 Data on returns came from Dennis Mueller, Klaus Peter Gugler, and Burcin Yurtoglu, "Corporate Governance and the Returns on Investment" (Working Paper, Jun. 2003) and the European Corporate Governance Institute, Brussels (which in turn uses data from Worldscope). The data on equity rights comes from Rafael La Porta, Florencio Lopez-de-Silanes, Andrei Shleifer, and Robert Vishny, "Law and Finance" (*Journal of Political Economy* 106.6 [1998]), pp. 1113-55.

Japan, and many of the emerging markets); what legal and regulatory frameworks, as well as historical and cultural legacies, are in place; and which industry sectors are considered.[16] Various models used by companies have their own strengths and weaknesses and the search for best practices and benefits should be considered in that context.

Universally, though, the key benefit that corporate governance can deliver to companies around the world comes down to building a board that performs, since it is the board members who ultimately contribute to generating sustainable business growth. Implementing good corporate governance is, therefore, not a matter of simply ticking a box; rather, it is a process in which the core values of transparency, fairness, accountability, and responsibility are integrated both into a company's strategic direction and its day-to-day operations.

Those values can become institutionalized only if a company adopts a robust code of corporate governance, and the board members fulfill their fundamental duties of care and loyalty to place the company's interests always above board members' personal interests. As demonstrated by the failures of corporate governance that contributed to the recent global financial crisis, it is also crucial for the board members to understand the business judgment rule properly and make informed decisions that responsibly take into account the level of associated risk. Good corporate governance is, therefore, a key tool for ensuring ethical business conduct and managing risks.

Skeptics may say that if a company follows good corporate governance and ethics principles it may, in the short run, lose a business deal to a company that is less scrupulous. In an interconnected and modern market economy, however, that works only once. Well-run

---

16 Maria Maher and Thomas Andersson, "Corporate Governance: Effects on Firm Performance and Economic Growth" (OECD, 1999), p. 44; also available at http://www.oecd.org/dataoecd/10/34/2090569.pdf.

companies that are consistently profitable have to be able to do business repeatedly with the same customers. Thus, ethical business practices translate into the ability to retain existing customers and gain new ones. They also have a positive impact on attracting and retaining top talent and improve relationships between employees and management. Finally, ethical business practices matter for a company's reputation and long-term prospects. Managing today's global supply chains and serving increasingly value-conscious consumers requires being able to demonstrate proper and fair conduct all the way down that supply chain, including to sub-contractors and vendors.

People should also keep in mind that business ethics comprise a set of evolving guidelines—and the standards in most societies keep going up. Conduct that was acceptable fifty or even twenty years ago in the area of equal employment opportunities or environmental protection, for instance, is no longer acceptable today. Similarly, the current standards keep evolving, especially because of the rising pressure on board members to become more sophisticated in risk management, in light of the global financial meltdown. As standards change, companies need to revisit their corporate governance guidelines and ethics codes to update and refresh them as needed.

CONCLUSION

The essence of inclusive market economies is the institutional framework in which private entrepreneurs have opportunities to create and build wealth, maximize their value to society, and grow their countries' economies. Corporate governance is a key element of that framework because it helps create a fair, level playing field among companies. Corporate governance can also become a focal point for reform of broader institutions or ideas needed for a well-functioning market economy, such as property rights, judicial system and enforcement mechanisms, securities markets, free press, rating agencies, and other checks and balances.

The importance of corporate governance in today's global economy is magnified by the fact that the principles of good corporate governance are applicable to a wide variety of firms, not just large companies listed on major stock exchanges. From SOEs to family-owned firms and SMEs, corporate governance offers a valuable toolkit for introducing transparency, accountability, responsibility, and fairness into decision-making, helping to ensure greater competitiveness and sustainability.

By improving company procedures and by building responsible boards, corporate governance contributes to business growth. Yet, its significance goes beyond improving company performance and maximizing shareholder value. The external drivers of corporate behavior, from the regulatory framework to independent media, are equally important as internal controls, and reforming them helps to transform the institutional framework in which companies operate. That transformation is of great significance for organizations conducting business in emerging markets and for the overall development prospects of those countries in which they exist.

Efforts to reform corporate governance around the world must therefore focus on both the internal and external factors that drive corporate behavior. Attempting to transfer international best practices in corporate governance into a country where market and public governance institutions are weak will not succeed unless people pay attention to reforming those broader institutions too. Moreover, reformers should seek to integrate local business communities in the process of developing corporate governance codes in their countries in order to create a sense of ownership and opportunities for feedback.

The ultimate goal of corporate governance reforms is to create value systems that guide ethical company behavior and strengthen the institutions and rights that allow businesses to compete fairly and generate economic growth. There are two paths toward improving corporate governance in companies and countries. One is reactive, associated with failures and collapses; the other is proactive and has to do with the search for benefits. Both have been responsible for bringing attention to corporate governance issues in recent years. Yet, it is the latter that shows the business case for corporate governance and provides positive incentives. By helping companies and countries attract investment, reduce corruption, and facilitate institutional reform, an effective corporate governance framework supports a foundation for sustained growth and a stable and vibrant global economy in the future.

About the Authors

John D. Sullivan, Ph.D. is the executive director of the Center for International Private Enterprise (CIPE), an affiliate of the U.S. Chamber of Commerce. As associate director of the Democracy Program, Sullivan helped to establish both CIPE and the National Endowment for Democracy in 1983. After serving as CIPE program director, he became executive director in 1991. Under his leadership, CIPE developed a number of innovative approaches that link democratic development to market reforms: combating corruption, promoting corporate governance, building business associations, supporting the informal sector, and creating programs to assist women and youth entrepreneurs. Today, CIPE has more than ninety full-time staff members and offices in Afghanistan, Egypt, Iraq, Pakistan, Romania, Russia, and the Ukraine.

Sullivan began his career in Los Angeles' inner-city neighborhoods, helping to develop minority business programs with the Institute for Economic Research and the Office of Minority Business Enterprise. In 1976, he joined the President Ford Election Committee in its research department on campaign strategy, polling, and market research. In 1977, Sullivan joined the Public Affairs Department of the U.S. Chamber of Commerce as a specialist in business and economic education.

Sullivan is a member of the Advisory Board of the Millstein Center for Corporate Governance and Performance at the Yale School of Management, the Council on Foreign Relations, the Russian Institute of Directors' Advisory Board, the Bretton Woods Association, and the American Political Science Association. He is also a member of the U.N. Global Compact Working Group on the Tenth Principle and the OECD MENA Investment Task Force.

Born in Bisbee, Arizona, in 1948, Sullivan was raised in Pittsburgh, Pennsylvania. He received a doctorate in political science from the University of Pittsburgh and is the author of numerous publications on the transition to democracy, corporate governance, and market-oriented democratic development. Sullivan, an adjunct faculty member at the George Mason University Graduate School of Public Affairs, now resides in Alexandria, Virginia, with his wife Patricia.

ANNA NADGRODKIEWICZ is a Program Officer for Global Programs at CIPE, where she works on projects involving democratic and market-oriented reform around the world. Prior to joining CIPE, she worked as a business consultant in her native Poland on the issues of competitiveness and market entry in Central and Eastern Europe. She holds a master's degree in German and European Studies from Georgetown University in Washington, D.C.

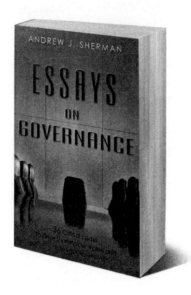

How can you use this book?

MOTIVATE

EDUCATE

THANK

INSPIRE

PROMOTE

CONNECT

Why have a custom version of *Essays on Governance?*

- Build personal bonds with customers, prospects, employees, donors, and key constituencies
- Develop a long-lasting reminder of your event, milestone, or celebration
- Provide a keepsake that inspires change in behavior and change in lives
- Deliver the ultimate "thank you" gift that remains on coffee tables and bookshelves
- Generate the "wow" factor

Books are thoughtful gifts that provide a genuine sentiment that other promotional items cannot express. They promote employee discussions and interaction, reinforce an event's meaning or location, and they make a lasting impression. Use your book to say "Thank You" and show people that you care.

Essays on Governance is available in bulk quantities and in customized versions at special discounts for corporate, institutional, and educational purposes. To learn more please contact our Special Sales team at:

1.866.775.1696 • sales@advantageww.com • www.AdvantageSpecialSales.com